Diasporic Inquiries into
South Asian Women's Narratives

Diasporic Inquiries into South Asian Women's Narratives

Alien Domiciles

Edited by Shilpa Daithota Bhat

LEXINGTON BOOKS
Lanham • Boulder • New York • London

Published by Lexington Books
An imprint of The Rowman & Littlefield Publishing Group, Inc.
4501 Forbes Boulevard, Suite 200, Lanham, Maryland 20706
www.rowman.com

6 Tinworth Street, London SE11 5AL, United Kingdom

British Library Cataloguing in Publication Information Available

Library of Congress Cataloging-in-Publication Data Available

ISBN 9781498591768 (cloth)
ISBN 9781498591775 (electronic)

Contents

Acknowledgments   vii

Introduction   1
    Shilpa Daithota Bhat

Part I: Domicile Tropes

1   "You are here, says the arrow": The Body as Home in the Poetry
   of Moniza Alvi   21
   Setara Pracha

2   India, Heat, Dust, and Tea?: Alienness and Marketability in
   Ruth Prawer Jhabvala and Nicole C. Vosseler   39
   Alejandra Moreno-Álvarez

3   "[A] girl from the village: totally unspoilt": Nazneen's
   "Unhomeliness" in Monica Ali's *Brick Lane*   53
   Sam Naidu

Part II: Shifting Domiciles

4   Ethnography of a Hyphen? The Gendering of Gen-X Diasporic
   Agency   73
   Gurbir Singh Jolly

5   Migration and Sexuality in S. J. Sindu's *Marriage of a
   Thousand Lies*   95
   Maryse Jayasuriya

6   Reimagining Reluctance: The South Asian Diaspora and Global
   "Homing" in Mira Nair's *The Reluctant Fundamentalist*   107
   Shuhita Bhattacharjee

Part III: Domicile Significations

7   Negotiating the "Postcolonial Exotic" through Subversive
    Third-Person Narration in Jhumpa Lahiri's *The Namesake*   131
    Lara Virginia Kattekola

8   Singing the Subaltern Woman: Film, Feminism, and Qawwali in
    the South Asian Diaspora   153
    Lauren Bettridge

9   Song, Narrative, Belonging: The Place of Song in the Oral
    Histories of Sri Lankan Tamil Women in London   179
    Jasmine Hornabrook

10 Domesticating the Alien: Culinary References and Food Rituals
    in *Song of the Sun God*   201
    Shashikala Assella

Index   215

About the Editor   217

About the Contributors   219

Acknowledgments

I am thankful to all the contributors for their studies to this anthology that focuses on the notion of domicile in the world of women hailing from the South Asian diaspora. The scholars have brought their acumen and experience into their work and have chosen narratives that represent multiplicities of belonging and mobility patterns that characterize wide-ranging texts. This book wouldn't have been possible without their scholarly work. I am thankful for their patience and professionalism during the review process.

Many thanks to the extremely cooperative and professional Lexington Books (Rowman and Littlefield) team who have helped me throughout the editing and production process. Working with them has been an amazing experience.

I am deeply grateful for my husband's companionship and my daughters' love that nourish my work.

Introduction

Shilpa Daithota Bhat

The migration of South Asian women to other countries has resulted in the making of a culturally alien hostland, their homeland, generating a host of critical ontological questions, rethinking of homing paradigms and provoking cross disciplinary readings of wide ranging narratives, spanning written texts, media representations, music, cuisine, and films thereby producing alternative imaginaries of the domicile in a culturally alien geographical space. This anthology is an exploration of the notions of alienness and domiciles from the vantage point of South Asian diasporic women with analytical and theoretical implications of transnational migration, taking into account historical as well as contemporary dynamics. By prioritizing the concept of the domicile as the primary analytic, the cultural space of transnational migrants can be viewed as multi-paradigmatic, inconsistent and contested. Circumscribed within transnational migration is the ideological representation of identities in multifarious discursive contexts with reference to home. Psychologically, owing to push-pull factors, cross-border travel is the domain of historic spaces—of trauma, nostalgia, memory, a distinctive sense of permanent cultural loss, manifesting expressions of painful emotions but nevertheless the immigrants explore new lands, having to move forward since this turns out to be the only alternative for all practical purposes, in the construction of a unique domicile overwhelmed by the challenge of alienness.

"Home" in diasporic narratives has always been a slippery construction—the dialectics of which are layered, diverse, and heterogeneous. The notion of the domicile is spatial as well as psychological. Suvadip Sinha (2012) states "The mother-as-nation and nation-as-mother axes of substitution, as reproduced in the diaspora narratives, not only operate within the oedipal narrative of trauma, they also aim to transform the homeland into an organic, a *priori*

1

being" (188). The notion of the "mother" land or the umbilical cord connection transforms a diasporic migrant's relation with the homeland to a resilient physical connection but as Brah (1996) underlines, homing doesn't imply, the desire of the members of the diaspora to actually return and settle in the ancestral homeland. It is purely a "desire" that exists in nostalgic expressions and memories; and is specifically articulated in narratives through wide ranging linguistic devices, forms, metaphors, emotive plots, and historical and political contingencies. Collaboratively, these elements interweave to produce diasporic subjectivities, conceptions and epistemes, individual and collective experiences in narratives. The diasporic orientations, nevertheless, differ for people hailing from different regions of the world in terms of individual lived, day-to-day experiences. In several cases, historical and political turbulence acted as primary causes of impelled migration resulting in large-scale people movements. In South Asia, the indentured labor system (*grimit/girmit* system) and the *kangani* system in the nineteenth and early twentieth centuries, introduced by the colonizers led to Indians travelling and settling in plantation farms in far-flung European colonies. The partition of India and Pakistan in 1947, the movement of Gujarati people to Africa to construct railway lines or for purposes of trade and commerce triggered regular migration. Similarly, there was movement of Punjabis from the Punjab state in India to Canada. Anita Rau Badami's *Can you Hear the Nightbird Call?* (2005), captures this history comprehensively in the fictional representation. Push-pull factors of various kinds impelled demographic movements that led to the formation of diasporas whose subjectivities hinged on personal encounters with new cultures in hostlands.

The displacement of Indians hasn't always been forced and this layer in diaspora formation is critically significant in examining how homing or establishing a domicile in a hostland can mean different things to different people, underlining the highly subjective experience. Gujarati migration to Africa, for instance, was voluntarily undertaken to further trade and business interests. Gunvant Rai Acharya's *Dariyalal* (2000 [1932]) is a pioneering fictional depiction of sea-faring merchants from Gujarat who migrated to Africa during the seventeeth century. Manubhai Madhvani's *Tide of Fortune: A Family Tale* and Mehta's Dreams *Half-Expressed*—both nonfictional narratives expatiate elaborately, the migratory propensities of the Gujarati businessmen to East Africa, and how, due to the ethnic cleansing policy pursued by Ugandan dictator Idi Amin, the South Asians first migrated to Britain (as Africans or Asians in Africa, were seen as British subjects); and later dispersed to different parts of the world. Gijsbert Oonk, in his seminal research study, *Settled Strangers: Asian Business Elites in East Africa (1800–2000)*, refers to the *dhow* stories that capture the discourse of aspiring Gujarati traders in Africa. Cynthia Salvadori's *We Came in Dhows* (2015), is a compilation of the several *dhow* stories of Indians, traversing the oceans to try their luck in trade and business in Africa. Oonk's study highlights the trade and business aspects of Gujarati migration and he terms the migrants of this region as "global citizens" due to the characteristic of Gujaratis to travel, settle, and adapt in multifarious contexts and cultures. The migrants who traveled from Africa constituted the twice-displaced; and later those who migrated from the UK, thrice-displaced generations, producing further complexities in the conceptualization of homing and loss of home. It is this complexity that allows for the study of displacement, homing, and sense of alienness in hostlands and what it means to define home in the diasporic subjective experience. What is notable is that women accompanied the migrating men but their narrative is largely missing from diasporic discourses.

In contemporary times, migration for acquiring education and employment has caused the production of "new diasporas" (Mishra 2007). Even in this case, where the migration is not forced, the notion of an "imagined community" (Anderson 1983) strongly persists, imparting the process of diaspora formation certain common characteristics and experiences of the "old diasporas." Nostalgia, memory, loss of home, sense of unbelongingness, and cultural alienness are experienced even by the members of the new diaspora, particularly where there are challenges of acquiring citizenship and so the immigrant feels neither "here nor there." The lack of belongingness aggravates the sense of alienness and lessens the feeling of a stable home in the adopted homeland. Concomitant to this is the necessary feeling of "missing home." Again, the "missing" part gestures at the transient experience and doesn't actually imply that the diaspora community wishes to return home in reality. Therefore the dilemma of homing and lived experiences continues to be inscribed variously in narratives, offering scope for in-depth examination to unearth the possibilities of unravelling the implications of "home."

"The term 'domicile,'" Alison Blunt (2005) suggests, "invokes geographies of home, settlement, and residence" (5). Blunt clarifies, "As a space of belonging and alienation, intimacy and violence, desire and fear, the home is charged with meanings, emotions, experiences and relationships that lie at the heart of human life. Studies of home as a space of lived experience and imagination range from a focus on everyday life and social relations to domestic form and design, and material, visual and literary cultures of home" (5). The conceptualization of home through the use of the term 'domicile' is emphasised not only through "the spatial politics of home" (5) but also "apolitical celebrations of home" (6). Interestingly, Dwyer (2000) suggests "Diaspora discourses celebrate migrancy and multiple homes" and "metaphors of home are also particularly gendered" (483). Equally intriguing are the ideas of Zhang (2004), who suggests:

> the poignant expression of worldly homelessness, however, is not a denial of the hope for home, but rather an assertion of re-homing desire in the age of

global diaspora. Modern diaspora disrupts the apparent closure of home and generates transnational, translocal communications and communities. Under such circumstances, the earlier conceptualizations of home based on a singular location are no longer adequate to describe the new dimensions and transformations of home, which has been re-versed in diaspora not as a "felicitous space" of living, but rather as "a process of (be-)coming." (103–104)

Both the material as well as the psychological dimensions of homing is critical in symbolizing the tension that characterize the conceptualization of the domicile. Anh Hua (2011) highlights that the members of the diaspora "rewrite their citizenship status" (46) and "stake claims to their multiple identities, multiple homes and affiliations" (46). These views reassert the evolving idea of homing that is complicated by practical aspects like citizenship that is absolutely essential in defining the identity of the immigrants. In other words, the notion of homing for the diaspora can be situated in varying contexts and homeland perception is not the same as it used to be in the past (Safran 1991, Cohen 2008). Drawing from these perceptions of homing and domicile, this anthology, through existing diasporic theorization and conceptualization seeks to critique relevant narratives to examine the discursive practices and processes of diaspora making. Some questions that this edited anthology raises are: How do South Asian women's narratives negotiate home in terms of identity-production and culture? How do migration and hostland cultures intervene in South Asian women's narratives in the process of subjective and individual perceptions of belonging and homing? What are the roles of the sense of alienness and domiciling in this matrix? And finally, how do South Asian women navigate the dichotomies that emerge from hostland complexities? These angularities will be looked at through the prism of diasporic, feminist, and postcolonial theories, applied to different narratives to critique the various facets of homing and diaspora.

The diaspora community is impelled to go beyond the idea of being in-between the hostland and homeland; and acculturate in the adopted land for purposes of dignified existence. Therefore, they define themselves through the framework of cultural adaptation, ethnicity, race, their original homeland, and the political and familial circumstances that compelled cross-border international migration. These issues are further intensified when exploring the narratives of women since "gender as a dynamic within the diaspora" (George 1996, 187) is a paradigm that helps unravel certain pressing themes in terms of negotiating the homeland-hostland quandary and the notion of alienness. The idea of homing in the adopted hostland has been one of the most mystifying and ambiguous for diasporic migrants. Concretizing the concept has been an Olympian feat for scholars in the domain, since the term has varied meanings and implications for those who happened to experience migratory movements at different points in history. For the indentured laborers of the nineteenth and twentieth centuries, homing or creating a domicile in a foreign land had a different connotation in comparison to those who migrated in other contexts such as the Gujarati traders who migrated to East Africa for purposes of established businesses. Returning "home" was a challenge for the indentured migrant laborers but the Gujarati traders visited their homeland regularly. Similarly, the notion of a permanent domicile and homing existed/exists on rather shifting grounds for the twice or thrice migrants or women, since identity production and definition connote complex subjectivities. Crucially, this ambivalent relationship between home and abroad and gender has been pondered over, perceived, and expressed in myriad forms by creative writers, musicians, or film directors. It is this ambivalence that makes long-term transnational migration and settlement quintessentially diasporic—the fact that conceptually, diasporic domiciling persists on an ever-shifting, ever-moving territory, defined predominantly by the very nature of international movement.

The variegated formats which individuals have experimented with, to explore and define identity, contour one's conception of "home." The sense of disjuncture is palpable among the South Asian diasporic narratives and this is heightened in gendered discourses because of the differences in experiences. It is this interstice that is of interest to the volume—since it offers a space to examine narrative practices that challenge the dynamics of interdisciplinarity and women's perceptions of hostlands. To achieve the goal of unraveling the fine threads of the area, the contributors to this anthology look at the microhistories as well as the big picture, in terms of historical implications that characterize "home making" and "place making" through diasporic lens. The difference in subjective experiences, as the contributors highlight, layer the discourse of narration and therefore gesture at the South Asian woman's subjecthood to allow close analysis of the subtleties of othering, domicile and diaspora formations.

CULTURAL IMPERATIVES AND ALIENNESS

While answering the question "Is Sisterhood Global?," Avtar Brah (1996) asserted "Our gender is constituted and represented differently according to our differential location within the global relations of power [. . .] realised through a myriad of economic, political and ideological processes" (102). Brah's perception was in the light of a conference she attended in Nairobi in 1985 which was attended by "over 10,000 women from more than 150 countries" (102), yet the experiences shared were different and "heterogeneous." The suggestion of complexity and range of experience hinging on region, country, and cultural setting is critical in recognizing and interpreting the differences that define the existence of women in various locations. Borrowing this idea to look at the various cultural formats that document the experiences of the South Asian diasporic woman would yield productive conceptions that characterize the cultural imperatives in a wide variety of narratives, because even if the diasporic woman comes from different countries in the South Asian region, the differences in culture, language, religion, and other factors, exert tremendous impact in the manner in which the South Asian woman negotiates within the diaspora. To capture and interrogate "differences" or "heterogeniety" in the experiences of women, there is a need to attempt to look at an array of themes as well as formats in pursuit of new interpretations of what it means to exist in diasporic discursive contexts.

When referring to globalizing tendencies and women, Avtar Brah invites emphasis on "whether working in electronics factories, textile sweatshops, performing outwork from their homes, or [. . .] holding jobs in the commanding heights of the economy—women have become emblematic figures of contemporary regimes of accumulation" (1996, 176). The diasporic movements of the South Asian woman are characterized by questions of the quality of life she leads in the adopted hostland where depending on circumstances she chooses to work in specific sectors and occupations. Of course, this is contingent on the opportunities available to her and the best choice she can make in the wake of dealing with alienness and maintenance of the domicile. Here, it is necessary to note that the experiences of the women coming from various South Asian counties have different shades. The lived perceptions and involvements in the host society are not homogeneous; rather, they are marked by tremendous differences and discernments. A closer analysis reveals the stark heterogeneity that scripts the lives of the South Asian women hailing from different regions.

Feeling alienated in the hostland implies cultural distantiation, necessitating the production of new relationalities while at the same time underlining multiplicities of belonging. Conceptually, this has been intertwined with nostalgia, a sense of unbelonging, culture shock—yet the members of the diaspora as Brah suggests have a homing desire but which doesn't necessarily mean going back to the original homeland. Bhabha (1992, 1994) highlighted ideas of interstitial space, cultural hybridization, sense of unbelonging, and mimicry that allowed migrating people to deal with their day-to-day realities. This is the complexity and dilemma that characterizes migratory processes and to negotiate this, culture becomes a rescuing element. Homing, while being a physical need and challenge in the host land, is also a concern in the psychological realm because they tend to evoke fresh multiple realities. Mythology, language, cuisine, art forms, film, literature, music, and other narratives occupy the domain of multi-sensory spatial interactions. Writers like Anita Desai, Shankari Chandran, Uma Parameswaran, Bharati Mukherjee, Chitra Banerjee Divakaruni, Shauna Singh Baldwin, Anita Rau Badami, Moniza Alvi, S. J. Sindu, Kiran Desai, Monika Ali, and several others have depicted the South Asian diasporic woman's experiences that draw from cultural experiences. Interestingly, today the intervention of digitized spaces has led to new thematic discussions on the bridging of relational gaps between the homeland and hostland cultures due to virtual networking. This is reminiscent of the notions of old and new diasporas (Mishra 2007). In his recent study, Mishra (2015), in referring to the indentured labor system, highlighted that the old diaspora that stemmed out of political push factors like the indentured labor/*girmit*/contractual system were primarily associated with tremendous pain and trauma:

> Diaspora theory is predicated on some statement about the "homing" principle, the wish to return which remains unfilled. In the plantation diaspora, the right to return home was built into the agreement with the qualification that a free passage would be available only if one had completed two five-year indentures. But crossing the Kala-Pani meant that an unproblematic return into a world left behind was not easy. (557)

To add to the psychic alienation was the feeling of having lost religion—a factor that was too close to the people involved. The emotional disruption was immense because migrating individuals felt lost, broken, and traumatized since the belief was they had lost a significant aspect of their personalities and identities that were constituted by religion. However, in the contemporary digital world characterized by virtual social networking and cosmopolitanism, the notion of returning home and the cultural amalgamations and adjustments has a completely different contextual implication.

It is intriguing to examine wide-ranging narratives and cultural productions that suggest the intractable sense of homelessness inscribed within them. Uma Parameswaran, an Indo-Canadian diasporic writer, deployed the story of the Indian mythical Trishanku to conceptualize the subjectivity of diasporic migrants. Trishanku who belonged to Lord Rama's[1] lineage, wanted to visit the heavens with his corporal body. For this, he seeks the help of the powerful sage Vishwamitra, who with his supernatural abilities propels the king toward the heavens. The mighty *Indra*—lord of the heavenly dominions summarily kicks out the king for his unwelcome intrusion. Vishwamitra cannot accept to see his mystical powers failing, and Indra is not ready to allow a mortal into his kingdom. This tension results in the suspension of Trishanku in mid-air—that is neither here nor there—in the middle of nowhere, much like the dilemmas of the members of the diasporic community. This lack of belonging or being neither here nor there constitutes the feeling of homelessness. In the Trishanku myth, eventually, a separate special heaven is created for Trishanku and conceptually, this "separate heaven" becomes the domain of homing for the diaspora migrants. It is from this vantage point of homelessness feeling that diasporic migrants consider their "third space" (Bhabha 1994) as the constricting and confining experience of unbelongingness. Theoretically, this establishes inherent contradictoriness but is simultaneously potentially emancipatory. Parameswaran deploys this myth-metaphor to describe the experiences of the members of the diaspora. The sense of unbelongingness has been ingeniously described by diasporic writer Tahmima Anam, whose work *The Bones of Grace* (2016), depicts the searching of the bones of the primordial *Ambulocetus*—the ancient species of whale (in Dera Bugti, Pakistan) believed to have walked before learning to swim in the oceans, can be a metaphor for framing the discourse of the in-between space—a situation akin to third space (Bhabha 1994), or a sense of unbelongingness—much like the theoretical implications of the *Trishanku* metaphor suggested by Uma Parameswaran (1988). The central protagonist Zubeida in *The Bones of Grace* tours Pakistan in her quest to assemble the bones of the ancient whale and during this scientific touring, suggests that she feels like she is occupying an interstitial space (Bhabha 1993). Such metaphorical and mythological comparisons gesture at the efforts at locating and precisely carving a stable home.

Nostalgia and longing for the original home, due to a sense of being in a foreign space, is a common theme in diaporic narratives. M. G. Vassanji who was born in Africa travels to India, his ancestral homeland and records his touristic adventures, in his travel narrative *A Place Within: Rediscovering India* (2008). He compares the dualistic lived experience in the two continents: "I grew up in Dar es Salaam, on the coast of East Africa; the memory and sight of that city, of that continent, evoke in me a deep nostalgia and love of place. India, on the other hand, seemed to do something to the soul; give it a certain ease, a sense of homecoming, quite another kind of nostalgia. During each visit I sought it more, as intensely as ever. There was no satisfaction" (x). Vassanji's travel in India as a nostalgic visitor remembering his ancestral associations is with reference to history and politics; at the same time, he traces the cultural and religious poetics of the Khoja community, establishing the connection between "routes and roots."

Popular diasporic filmmakers like Gurinder Chadha and Mira Nair illustrate the notion of homing through their films and documentaries. Chadha's first documentary *I'm British But . . .* (1989), produced in collaboration with the British Film Institute, London, delineated the travails and psychological experiences of the South Asians settled in the UK. These fourth-generation South Asians frequently tour their ancestral homelands, meet their kith and kin, maintain connections with them but are determined to continue in their chosen hostlands. Their sense of homing in the hostland implies a negotiation and adaptation of their cultural roots in the host society. It is more about engaging in dynamic cultural integrative practices. For instance, the fusion of Punjabi folk music or Bangla music with British pop culture and the resulting musical production, embodies a sense of adapting and establishing certain markers of home culture in the host society. So, it is not complete giving up of one's roots yet there is a flavor of alienness.

Mira Nair's documentary *So Far from India* (1983) presents the lives of Gujarati Indians—specifically the distance that plagues the existence of Ashok Seth and Hansa. Seth works in New York in a newspaper stand and feels that life is better in the United States. He has left back his pregnant wife Hansa at home and she is a village girl, engaging herself in household chores. To capture the homing experience of Seth, Nair—as one with connections with India shows shifting images from New York to Ahmedabad, and these visuals generate the discourse of homing for Seth in New York, for whom "home" in Gujarat is ambivalent, as he has already accepted the United States as being more comfortable. Nair extensively tours India to capture Indian experiences of migration for this documentary and in the process explores and happens to represent the formation of diaspora communities abroad.

In these various examples (and there are so many others) of diasporic narratives, we find recurring patterns of nostalgia and sense of alienness while at the same time there is the palpable exhibition of the notion of domiciling. This expression is vented at various intensities depending on subjective experiences vis-à-vis gender, education, employment status, family, nationality, and so on. The economic or occupational aspect is a notable one. Anita *et al*, observed that among Pakistani and Bangladeshi women in the UK, there is less economic activity and "explanatory factors relates to the characteristics and preferences of women themselves, including lower levels of educational qualifications and fluency in English, particularly amongst women born overseas" (760). The relation between the skills and "preferences" of South Asian women and the kind of occupation they might get are closely intertwined. In her study of "bharatanatyam as a cultural occupation and its role in identity formation" (44), Kumar gives the example of the performance of the South Indian classical dance form, the Bharatanatyam,[2] in Los Angeles and states "A performative theory of culture reconfigures culture as a highly creative, action-oriented process. Thus, culture emerges through occupation" (44). Adding another layer to this complicated course is the idea of intergenerational influence (Rajiva 2012). Rajiva poses intriguing questions in this regard: "If diasporic daughters struggle with feelings of ambivalence towards their families' pre and post migration class identities, how does this ambivalence reveal itself in subjects' narratives of class? Are these stories inflected by parents' own negotiations with migration, class status and work opportunities?" (2012, 19). The influence of parents and homeland narratives about one's ancestral connections, economic conditions and culture affect the occupational and educational choices of the 'diasporic daughters' (Rajiva 2012). This interconnectedness between culture and occupation in the diasporic context is essential to understand how culture intervenes and persists in hostland acculturation mechanisms. It also highlights that diaspora cannot be understood fully only through a single method of narration due to several factors like skills, occupation, culture, ethnicity, identity, and nationality. The process of identity construction for South Asian women, therefore, is protracted. Discussing identity and nationalism in the context of Tibetan diaspora, Anand (2000) suggests "Identification should be seen, not as an artefact or an outcome, but as a construction, a process never completed. Identities are increasingly fragmented and fractured; never singular but multiply constructed across different, often intersecting and antagonistic, discourses, practices and positions" (273). The implication of this statement is further intensified in the context of global migration and in particular women's migration since identity construction hinges on a host of factors including family networks and migration.

Exploring several types of narratives has the potential to provide a wholesome view of how the South Asian woman defines her identity in the hostland. Gesturing at the "identity of unbelongingness" in his article, Seddon (2010) notes:

> The historical process of othering through the discourse of Orientalism has previously helped Europeans define themselves in terms of what they are *not* as well as providing a monolithic construct by which the other is both comprehended and imagined. But this faulted process of othering presents itself as little more than an inverted form of self-definition and identity reification because, in its final analysis, the self simply becomes everything the other is not. (564)

This perception is critically significant because Seddon underlines how the foreign "other" is defined automatically while the Europeans see themselves "in terms of what they are *not.*" In the context of diaspora discourses, this idea generates fresh possibilities of revisiting and redefining existing conceptualizations of foreignness, sense of unbelongingness, and othering in hostlands. Hogarth (2015) endorses "The notion of belonging is also predicated on that of unbelonging and brings into sharp focus the dichotomy of the 'us' and the 'other'" (784). The etching of binaries is what scholars consider as producing tensions in the sense of alienness and belongingness and therefore, negotiating the interstitial space of cultural and racial differences becomes a challenging phenomenon for South Asian diasporic women. Interestingly, the process of defining alienness simultaneously evokes personal ethnic community and culture, as Campbell-Hall (2009) observes: "The idea of renegotiating the definition of a domestic community is not, however, simply influenced by the binary tensions between East and West, but by the very notion of what is considered normative within contemporary society" (173). The cultural tension therefore, is between the self and the other and the complex considerations of acculturation in the host society because what is "normative within contemporary society" is subjective, personal, and flexible—it fluidly shifts from the rigidness of pure and pristine homeland cultural orientations. In their "documentary involving seven women" (15, 2009), Chapra and Chatterjee note "For women, it is not only about navigating the Diaspora but also the borders and negotiating these international spaces with local realities" and "Home as well, is a complex notion for women as some of us leave home to make and maintain another home" (16). Chapra and Chatterjee's study endorses how stories within diaspora discursive practices help in reconsidering patterns of migration of women in general, in the context of international mobility, constituting a revelatory approach through variety in narratives and "story telling." The suggestion through various scholarly perceptions is that of the several layers operating within the matrix of homing poetics and the sense of alienness. Therefore, an analysis of multiple forms of narratives can be enriching and productive.

The authors of the essays in this anthology explore a wide variety of dimensions from varying perspectives but with the primary focus on the challenge of domiciling in an alien geographical terrain. This notion while obviously suggesting the physical dwelling space, is also psychological and emotional in narrative representations. Therefore, we find that an exploration of different modes of narrative patterns help in studying the complex strands that characterize the South Asian woman's diasporic narratives and this is precisely what scholars in this volume have attempted to accomplish.

STRUCTURE OF THIS ANTHOLOGY

The contributors to this anthology have taken up diverse themes and narratives that articulate the notion of foreignness when examining the idea of the domicile. The essays have been categorized as "Domicile Tropes" (Pracha, Moreno-Álvarez and Naidu), "Shifting Domiciles" (Singh Jolly, Jayasuriya and Bhattacharjee), and "Domicile Significations" (Kattekola, Hornabrook, Bettridge and Assella), highlighting in their chosen narratives, the comparative approaches, movements, and implications of the South Asian women's diaspora.

In her examination of Moniza Alvi's poetry, Setara Pracha frames her argument through the central analytic of the body as home. The construction of diaspora and identity happens via historical, political, and literary lenses, bringing to the fore critical episodes of partition and colonial histories of South Asia that intersect cultural productions. Pracha critiques the various tropes of language, costume, cuisine, and geography that contour Alvi's poetry and how these underline the negotiation of alienness in a foreign land that must be translated into an adoptive homeland. For instance, the specific choice of wearing a sari as suggested in Alvi's poetry, becomes a modality for the perception of the "other," an instance of the "exotic mundane" that permeates the literary art of hybridized authors. Historical episodes like the partition of India and Pakistan loom large in diasporic creative work, since it propelled a mass displacement that resulted in intense psychological pain and a sense of permanent disjunction and irretrievable loss. Pracha suggests that Alvi's work engages with this trauma yet significantly signposts more hopeful future scenarios.

Alejandra Moreno-Álvarez focuses on notions of alienness and marketability in the narratives of Ruth Prawer Jhabvala and Nicole C. Vosseler. She interrogates the themes of otherness, European and Indian connections, exoticization, interracial relationships, while at the same time exploring the influence of the mixed origins of the authors on their narration. Through the prism of the term postcolonial literature and contrastive analysis, Moreno-Álvarez critiques *Heat and Dust*, considered "canonical" and *The Sky Above Darjeeling*, a mere "romance." This becomes the vantage point from which the definition of alienness and lived experience in the works are suggested as explicated in subtle ways, contributing to viewing of the East as the "other." A significant critical dimension is the marketability aspect of *Heat and Dust* due to its Man-Booker Prize status. In a contradictory situation, *The Sky Above Darjeeling* does not have the advantage of such commercial presentation in the market.

Sam Naidu, in her close analysis of the character of Nazneen from Monica Ali's *Brick Lane* (2003), outlines a literary lineage of women's novels in order to contextualize this novel as South Asian diasporic women's writing, and examines the disruptions to the realist mode found therein. In interrogating this topic, Naidu emphasizes that such an alternative narrative mode which utilizes the epistolary tradition and the use of fantasy and phantasmagoria, is critical to the representation of the "unhomed" state of the female migrant in transnational literature. In describing this literary lineage that spans nineteenth-century novels by women and African-American women's writing, Naidu avers that a transnational feminist aesthetic is evident in writing by women of the South Asian diaspora (Compare this with the discussion earlier in this introduction, on Avtar Brah's question "Is Sisterhood Global?"). Nazneen, Naidu argues, confronts her multi-locationality (in terms of temporal and spatial dislocation), and in so doing, reconceptualizes traditional gender roles, while at the same time adapting to the exigencies of being affiliated to both homeland and diasporic home. This chapter offers a close reading of Nazneen's journey from a small village in Bangladesh to her being authentically and syncretically domiciled in Brick Lane, London.

Gurbir Singh Jolly's in-depth examination of the troubled dynamics of the politics of hyphen, hinges on scholarly anthropological observations, the sense of self, the girlhood narrative in South Asian women's narratives, otherness, and identity of an individual in an alien environment. He looks at a wide range of research studies and narratives that are informed by historical exigencies, colonial, and gendered perceptions. To these viewpoints, Gurbir brings his own personal experience and suggests he felt like a foreigner and not quite like an immigrant. This deep personal recollection intertwined with his parents' experiences in a comparative frame is critical in inscribing the sense of alienness that migration happens to generate in the lives of diasporic communities. The contending frame of the East and the West and whether there is a possibility of the twain meeting, proposes a dynamics of integration in an "in-between" tentative dwelling space—a potential site for the unfamiliar and strange.

Maryse Jayasuriya takes up the study of the challenges of the LGBTQ community through her critical discussion of S. J. Sindu's novel *Marriage of a Thousand Lies* (2017). While situating her analysis within the context of sexuality, identity and the Sri Lankan Tamil diaspora in the United States, Jayasuriya interrogates the complexities that characterize the nature of the domicile for immigrants. The dimensions of gender identity and the construction of hostland "reality" for the diasporic community is a perennial difficulty which they grapple with through negotiating their cultural expectations and their personal experiences. Jayasuriya locates Sindu's work within the genre of Sri Lankan Anglophone fiction, comparatively referring to novels by Shyam Selvadurai, Punyakante Wijenaike, V. V. Ganeshananthan, and Mary Anne Mohanraj. The opposition between the realities of personal and sexual identities and the idealized perceptions of the Sri Lankan diasporic community is a major theme that has been employed to investigate the notion of the domicile in this chapter.

Shuhita Bhattacharjee examines Mira Nair's creative rendering of *The Reluctant Fundamentalist,* a film based on Hamid Mohsin's novel by the same title. The intriguing aspect as suggested in this study is the notion of othering, the experience of Islamophobia, and the locating of the diasporic "home" in a transnational global space. That the film is produced by Nair who is from the South Asian diaspora, that the writer, Hamid, is of Pakistani origin, and that the plot is set in America and Lahore—all contribute to layered complexities underlying the idea of alienness. Bhattacharjee looks at the challenge of adapting the novel into a film, and examines how the latter takes a crucial new direction. By taking into consideration Nair's and Hamid's own perceptions about their divided origins, and by paying attention to the way diasporic subjectivity builds on notions of homeland-hostland, Bhattacharjee is able to show us the commentary the film offers when read against the backdrop of profoundly transformative geopolitical conflicts in a post-9/11 and post-Osama world.

Positioning and prioritizing writing and consumption practices of literature in contemporary "postcolonial industry," Lara Kattekola configures notions of postcolonial exoticization in the context of authorship and materiality with reference to Jhumpa Lahiri's *The Namesake*. She calls attention to Lahiri's strategic textual interventions, namely her subversive employment of a reliable, omniscient, third-person narrator. Kattekola illustrates how the narration avoids projecting notions of stable textual truths and momentarily evokes rhetorically-charged scenarios, juxtapositions cultural differences, or promotes textual ambiguities, inviting metropolitan audiences to assume transactional reading modes that require readers' active engagement in the interpretive task of meaning making. She examines the discourse of postcoloniality and the binary of "us/them" through the cultural differentiation that emanates from diasporic settlements. She highlights the evolving and shifting processes of identity creation in the hostland, especially via resistance to hegemony, represented through the behavior of the characters. Like Alejandra Moreno-Álvarez's essay in this anthology that explores the marketability dimension of narratives, Kattekola analyzes the material features that characterize the myriad negotiations and conceptual encounters of othering and exoticism. This critical standpoint affirms the significance of spatial and material dynamics that co-create the importance of literary interventions in the conceptualization of alienness and diasporic discursive practices.

Song and dance is an inextricable aspect of diasporic narrative experience. Bollywood films that articulate the expatriate experience make use of cultural productions to highlight the reconnecting-to-homeland desire and it is interesting to note that there have been a lot of research studies on diaspora and the Punjabi bhangra form. While this is a fascinating trajectory to undertake and explore diasporic subjectivities, a study of other forms of underexplored narratives can help build capacious understanding of the politics and aesthetic tensions characterizing diverse forms of South Asian diasporic subjectivities. Lauren Bettridge's "Singing the Subaltern Woman: Film, Feminism and Qawwali in the South Asian Diaspora," is centrally concerned with the notion of nostalgia, homing, and *qawwali*—musical narratives popular in South Asian Bollywood and diasporic films and the masculine diasporic rap by the Swet Shop Boys, who reinvent the original *qawwali* form and reconceptualize the traditional form. Through a uniquely female lens, Bettridge examines the genesis of the *qawwali* form, a traditionally male-dominated form, to consider notions of alienness and home. In her critical study of the musical genre, Bettridge reinserts the figure of the Subaltern woman back into the frame.

Jasmine Hornabrook looks at the genre of Carnatic music in London—a form extremely popular in South India and Sri Lanka. The author has collected information on the subject via the re-telling of personal histories by individuals; and through ethnomusicological fieldwork interviews and personal interactions with the first generation Tamil women migrants of the Sri Lankan diaspora. The forced and violent political migration that was triggered in Sri Lanka in the 1980s led to the citizens to move and settle in different parts of the world; and Hornabrook's study focuses on the migration of Sri Lankan singers and musicians specializing in Carnatic music—the language of rendition being primarily Tamil. The narratives Hornabrook examines are those that were composed by Tamil saints and encapsulate devotion to Hindu Gods; and this narrativization and practice of the musical form engenders a sense of togetherness and belonging to the original homeland.

Shashikala Assella explores the trope of cuisine in Shankari Chandran's *Song of the Sun God*, to investigate alienness and the notion of domicile; and how home transforms into a space of dynamic interactions, nostalgia, and belongingness. Assella notes how transnational travel and cosmopolitan social changes have led to shifting away from strict ethno-national memberships leading to fluid individualized diasporic identities. Nevertheless, home-cooked food becomes an element of longing since it is a cultural reminder, in addition to its contribution to strengthening of family relationships. The characters navigate the hostland via cooking experiences that form an essential part of their ethno-national identity while also establishing their unique individual selves. Gastronomy becomes a medium to reconnect with home allowing such narratives to generate a broad system of discourse that does not intervene in the integrative practices of the diaspora. The members of the diaspora community are able to position themselves in the hostland through their everyday practices that underline their uniqueness that are predominantly drawn from their ethnicity.

CONCLUSION

The narratives on the South Asian diasporic woman gesture at the mobility patterns that influenced cultural productions, building on the articulation of cultural and historical particularities. To borrow Velickovic's phrase, to a certain extent, this book is an attempt at "productive engagement with histories of loss" (67) in terms of the feeling of having lost a part of one's culture and identity due to leaving one's homeland which the diasporic members attempt to retrieve through reconnecting with ethnic cultural practices in the adopted alien domicile. While considering a range of perspectives on the relationalities of the individual (vis-à-vis domicile tropes, significations, and shifting domiciles) with the hostland and construction of the "self," there is the production of a common space for dialogue on the subject. The narratives that have been theoretically critiqued in this anthology enunciate a conceptual grid through which diaspora has been underlined as an area that offers scope for fresh interpretations and analyses, with respect to the gender aspect that undergirds migration from South Asia, signaling the centrality of women in the narratives and how they navigate intercultural challenges in alien domiciles.

NOTES

1. Lord Rama is worshipped as a Hindu God, and is a celebrated figure in the *Ramayana* epic. It is interesting to note Walcott's (1991) reference to the enactment of the *Ramayana* in the Caribbean islands, by the indentured Indian laborers. This recreation of cultural codes gestures at efforts at reconnection with home culture. For those unfamiliar with the epic, R. K. Narayan's *Gods, Demons and Others* (1964); and C. Rajagopalachari's *Ramayana* (1900), might be useful.

2. Bharatanatyam is a popular classical dance form in Southern India.

REFERENCES

Acharya, Gunvantrai P., and Kamal Sanyal (2000). *Dariyalal*. Calcutta: Dictum in association with Thema.

Ali, Monica. 2003. *Brick Lane*. London: Black Swan.

Anam, Tahmima. 2016. *Bones of Grace*. [s.l.]: Penguin Books India.

Anand, Dibyesh. "(Re)imagining Nationalism: Identity and Representation in the Tibetan Diaspora of South Asia1." *Contemporary South Asia* 9, no. 3 (2000): 271–87.

Anderson, Benedict. 1983. *Imagined communities: Reflections on the origin and spread of nationalism*. London: Verso.

Anitha, Sundari, Ruth Pearson, and Linda Mcdowell. "Striking Lives: Multiple Narratives of South Asian Women's Employment, Identity and Protest in the UK." *Ethnicities* 12, no. 6 (2012): 754–75.

Badami, Anita Rau. 2005. *Can you hear the nightbird call?* Toronto: A. A. Knopf.

Bhabha, Homi, K. 1992. "The World and the Home," *Social Text*, 31.32: 141–53.

———. 1994. *The Location of Culture*. London: Routledge.

Blunt, Alison. 2005. *Domicile and diaspora: Anglo-Indian women and the spatial politics of home*. Oxford: Blackwell.

Brah, Avtar. 1996. *Cartographies of diaspora: contesting identities*. London: Routledge

Campbell-Hall, Devon. "Renegotiating the Asian-British Domestic Community in Recent Fiction." *Journal of Postcolonial Writing* 45, no. 2 (2009): 171–79.

Chadha, Gurinder, and Eliza Mellor. 2013. *I'm British but—*. Bucksport, ME: Northeast Historic Film.

Chapra, Aisha, and Soma Chatterjee. "Talking Race, Talking Colour: Racialized Women, Their Home and Belongingness in Multicultural Canada." *Canadian Woman Studies* 27, no. 2/3 (2009): 14–20.

Cohen, Robin. 2008. *Global Diasporas: An Introduction*. Seattle: University of Washington Press.

Dwyer, Claire. "Negotiating Diasporic Identities: Young British South Asian Muslim Women." *Women's Studies International Forum* 23, no. 4 (2000): 475–86.

Hogarth, Kathy. "Home Without Security and Security Without Home." *Journal of International Migration and Integration* 16, no. 3 (2015): 783–98.

Hua, Anh. 2011. "Homing Desire, Cultural Citizenship, and Diasporic Imaginings." *Journal of International Women's Studies* 12(4): 45–56.

Kumar, Anita. "Bharatanatyam and Identity Making in the South Asian Diaspora: Culture through the Lens of Occupation." *Journal of Occupational Science* 18, no. 1 (2011): 36–47.

Madhvani, Manubhai, and Giles Foden (2009). *Tide of fortune: A family tale*. Noida: Random House, India.

Mishra, Vijay. 2015. "Plantation Diaspora Testimonios and the Enigma of the Black Waters." *Interventions* 17(4): 548–67.

———. 2007. *The literature of the indian diaspora: theorizing the diasporic imaginary*. Abingdon: Routledge.

Nair, Mira. 2004. *So far from India*. New York: Filmakers Library.

Oonk, Gijsbert 2009. *Settled strangers: Asian business elites in East Africa (1800–2000)*. New Delhi: SAGE Publications.

Parameswaran, Uma. 1998. *Trishanku and other writings*. New Delhi: Prestige.

Rajiva, Mythili. "'Better Lives': The Transgenerational Positioning of Social Mobility in the South Asian Canadian Diaspora." *Womens Studies International Forum* 36 (2013): 16–26.

Safran, William. 1991. "Diasporas in Modern Societies: Myths of Homeland and Return." *Diaspora* 1(1): 83–99.

Salvadori, Cynthia. 1996. *We came in dhows*. Nairobi, Kenya: Paperchase Kenya Ltd.

Seddon, Mohammad Siddique. "Constructing Identities of 'difference' and 'resistance': The Politics of Being Muslim and British." *Social Semiotics* 20, no. 5 (2010): 557–71.

Sinha, Suvadip. 2012. "Return of the native: Swades and the re-thinking of diaspora." *South Asian Popular Culture* 10(2): 185–96.

Rajagopalachari, C. 2015 [1900]. *Ramayan*. Bombay: Bharatiya Vidya Bhavan.

Vassanji, Moyez G. 2008. *A place within: Rediscovering India*. Toronto: *Anchor Canada*.

Velickovic, Vedrana. "Melancholic Travellers and the Idea of (un)belonging in Bernardine Evaristo's Lara and Soul Tourists." *Journal of Postcolonial Writing* 48, no. 1 (2012): 65–78.

Zhang, B. 2004. "The Politics of Re-homing: Asian Diaspora Poetry in Canada." *College Literature* 31: 103–25.

Part I

Domicile Tropes

Chapter One

"You are here, says the arrow"

The Body as Home in the Poetry of Moniza Alvi

Setara Pracha

Poems critiqued in this chapter:

Skin and Blood: "The Country at My Shoulder"	*The Country at My Shoulder* (1993)
Costumes and Disguises: "The Sari"	*The Country at My Shoulder* (1993)
Roots and Water: "England"	*How the Stone Found It's Voice* (2005)
Corporeal Locations II: "And If"	*A Bowl of Warm Air* (1996)
Locating the Self: "Half-and-Half"	*How the Stone Found Its Voice* (2005)
Lexis: "Throwing Out My Father's Dictionary"	*The Country at My Shoulder* (1993)
Future Dialogue: "Hindi Urdu Bol Chaal"	*A Bowl of Warm Air* (1996)

SKIN AND BLOOD: "THE COUNTRY AT MY SHOULDER"

Moniza Alvi's poems are trying to find their way home. The need for stable markers, guidance regarding direction, and a sense of human transience is communicated in the phrase, "You are here, says the arrow" ("The Double City," lines 39, 66). The search for a stable security of place and personhood

21

permeates Alvi's poems and yet the maps, disguises, masks, and trails in her work ultimately suggest the ephemeral and mutable nature of identity. This study examines the ways in which this South Asian poet portrays the multiple and complex effects of migration, on the individual, from the place of birth to an adopted homeland.

Alvi's work frames feelings of alienation and foreignness, employing the mixed-race body as the nexus of expression for her discussion of belonging and geographical location. These tropes mapped out on the human form convey a variety of attitudes to difference that range from negative, through ambivalent, to celebratory. In this analysis I will demonstrate how Alvi employs the corporeal to articulate perceptions of otherness from the perspective of a female Pakistani poet living in contemporary Britain. Muneeza Shamsie cites Alvi as part of a key movement in fiction and poetry by South Asian Muslim writers, positioning her as a bridge between Islam and Christianity, her father's and mother's faiths. Shamsie comments that "her lyrical poetry celebrates her dual inheritance" while modifying the "symbiotic Euro–Muslim past" into a "equitable, multicultural future" (Shamsie 2011, 154). However, as this critical commentary demonstrates, in Alvi's poetry, "your body is your country but your country is not necessarily your home."

The issues of who has the authority to write, whose story is written, which audience is the focus, and in what language texts are composed, are central to any discussion of postcolonial poetry, and are identified by Dennis Walder as key areas of complexity (Walder 1998, 89). The work of South Asian women poets writing from within Britain continually teases at these subjects as they constantly return to themes of belonging, language and home. Walder notes the absence of women and migrant authors in early theoretical models of postcolonial literature and the recent emphasis on hybridity as part of a move toward a more "liberatory mode" of writing (Walder 1998, 81). Alvi uses the corporeality of the individual human hybrid as a symbol for the broader diasporic experience on a global scale. The themes under examination include gender, speech, and place; these range across her work and are collected in *Split Country: Poems 1990–2005*.

Each poem under review is considered with respect to its historical and cultural context and, where appropriate, the theoretical and political background is offered for additional depth of understanding. Theorists such as Avtar Brah, Dennis Walder, and Louis Althusser provide an affirmative position from which to observe and critique the practice of South Asian diasporic writers. Through the close reading of postcolonial verse and critiquing the literary art of one diasporic author, this study contributes to the ongoing development of critical understanding of Partition by those most affected. Avtar Brah's definition of culture is used to signpost Alvi's work as engaging in "the symbolic construction of the vast array of a social group's life experience," from this perspective her verse bears witness to the unfolding stories of the diaspora and forms part of a general record, both an "embodi-ment," and a "chronicle of a group's history" (Brah 1996, 18).

These literary additions to the discourse of otherness resist outmoded but persistent notions of the one-way British colonial influence on India (exam-ples include language, the railways, the Civil Service) substituting chronicles and celebrations of Asian culture, a culture that is itself an intricate matrix of "class, caste, region, religion, gender" (Brah 1998, 41). Alvi is the child of an Indian father migrating to the UK and an English mother returning to her birthplace and, as a result, she occupies a unique position with regard to foreignness and the body as the site of a contested home: her ethnic and multicultural origins are inscribed in her work. Alvi's poems represent the experience of transplanted individuals, enacting cultural transformation as an ongoing act in which cross-fertilization is shown to enrich indigenous Eng-lish culture.

Alvi was born in Lahore, Pakistan in 1954 to a white, British mother and a Pakistani father, and came with her family to the UK as a newborn. She did not return to Pakistan until after the publication of her first collection of poems *The Country At My Shoulder* (Alvi 1993). Alvi uses her art to convey a wistful and ambiguous perspective on both her adopted country (England) and the country of her birth (Pakistan) that arises—at least in part—from her mixed descent. Alvi explores the domicile tropes of home and abroad from her privileged position as a dweller in postimperial Britain, illuminating the position of those caught up in the diaspora, unwilling and unable to abandon their history. Her Janus-like verses simultaneously interrogate the past and the present, exploring lingering nostalgia for the precolonial era and assess-ing the trappings of belonging.

"The Country at My Shoulder" is positioned midway through a section entitled "Presents from Pakistan" that contains eleven poems separated from the others by a page break in the original collection and an asterisk in her selected works *Split World*. This text initiates the use of the corporeal by immediately posing a nation just behind the voice of the text as though it has a fleshly existence. The country appears to be following the speaker, a con-stant haunting witness. This is a resonant image for those who lived through the diaspora, as it is for those responsible for Partition, whose deeds have a half-life years after the deaths of individual participants.

The text is imbued with unease, and tension builds through a series of interleaved images of everyday life, and trauma, leaving the audience certain that the country will "burst" but with no sense of when this will occur (line 2). The word *"burst"* first appears in line two prefixed by "soon," is repeated in line 28 prefixed by "when," and finally repeated with "soon" in the last line (line 42). The country is a geographical location but exists more vitally as an idea in the minds of its citizens, and is shown to have corporeal exis-

tence—and as such cannot be dismembered without risking the existence of
the entire self.

> The country has become my body—/
> I can't break bits off. (lines 33–34)

The speaker resists the fragmentation of their body despite its apparently
composite nature, either by themselves or others. One cannot "break bits off"
a person without damaging the whole self, and this portrays the division of
the Indian nation by the process of Partition. This moment in stanza 14
comes toward the end of the poem and it typifies the way Alvi shows the
female body as a site of resistance as well as a mere symbol. The prevailing
picture of the immigrant woman as engaged in a hopeless search for security,
doomed to be the victim of alterity as an alien in a foreign land is modified to
that of a symbol of unity demonstrating repudiation of the dominant (male)
culture. The use of "can't" implies a defiant "won't," tying the facts of
postcolonial nationhood to the individual body in a manner that serves as a
critique of imperial geographical division (of East from West Pakistan).

It has taken time for individual experiences of Partition to seep out of an
aging generation born during the Raj, to be transposed into art by the inheri-
tors of their migrant stories. Alvi's verse offers forms of resistance to the
dominant narrative of hopeless and helpless human transplants by tying together the personal and the global. Her verse resonates with new ideas and
new connections, centralising the mixed race figure as a metaphor for the
division of "mother India" and pointing the way forward through division
toward a more hopeful future. Alvi demonstrates how identity politics is
most effective when expressed through actual rather than imagined symbols,
the personal rather than the general: the self, not the othered.

In this poem the central event is an execution "in the square" (line 9) and
the speaker stands "to attention" in the "white-hot afternoon"; a soldier might
be about to shoot the condemned person or simply a spectator watching
women crying. The imminent bloodshed is foregrounded in the choice of
action verbs in the first tercet, "burst," "spill, "run," all intimate violence and
the line "rivers will spill out" heralds blood as much as masses of people
fleeing their homes (line 3). Details of the heat and clothing suggest that this
country is India or Pakistan, a country the voice of the poem regards as
crumpled and neglected like an old map: "I try to shake the dust from the
country/smooth it with my hands" (line 6).

The melancholy speaker weeps over the nameless country in the final
stanza as their nationality gradually becomes clear. From the migrant's vantage point there is great need for tenderness and understanding in postcolonial relations, and the unnamed countries of Partition haunt the text, the poem
operates as a broader comment on the situation in multiple ex-British colonies (examples include Ireland, Israel, Cyprus). In contrast to the earlier text

"Presents From My Aunts in Pakistan" in which the speaker is alienated by the Indian garments, here the tone is assured and the voice of the poem is comfortable enough to "water the country with English rain/cover it with English words" (lines 40–41). Next, the English lexicon comfortingly blankets the violent events, perhaps truthfully communicating the explosive situation while also intimating the colonial language as a potential cover-up.

The tiger, national symbol of India and a recurrent motif in Alvi's work, has been shot in the tenth stanza but its dead mouth remains "fixed in a roar" (line 31). The reader learns that the animal has been killed by an Indian relative, not shot by a great white hunter in the tradition of Rider Haggard's character Allan Quartermain. The skin is now a lifeless ornament and the speaker wants to hide its "head in a towel," unable to look at the mortifying relic of beauty destroyed through human aggression (lines 31–32). Alvi's play with the national symbols evokes Tipu Sultan's well-known automaton of a tiger mauling a British figure (created c. 1780) and the silenced tiger's impotent roar is a warning that violence will burst out. Alvi's choice of the tiger has further resonance in that tiger skins are illegal unless killed prior to 1947, a significant date for the South Asian diaspora, and Tipu Sultan's automaton is not displayed in its home country of India but is itself a migrant to the Victoria and Albert Museum. Items that celebrate the Raj abound in contemporary Britain, but there remains no museum to Partition.

The sobering images of people begging for mercy and the dead tiger are immediately juxtaposed with imagery from Bollywood films with their joyous celebration of dramatic emotion. Alvi offers the cinematic representation of ethnicity in the popular tropes of flowers, dancing, and clothes and contrasts this with the English rain, English words, and the poet Christina Rossetti. Each nation is represented with stereotypical images (rain, tigers) as the quintessence of the country "at my shoulder." The poem hovers between past, present, and future transmitting an increasing sense of anxiety before ending with the final image of a "meteor," falling to earth to create unknown havoc (line 42).

COSTUMES AND DISGUISES: "THE SARI"

The sari is used as a symbol of how we wrap ourselves in identity in this poem. Touching the skin, clothing can be changed to suit the context, just as ethnicity is a choice for those whose skin color allows them to "pass" as indigenous. The poem takes the form of a birth myth for a mixed-descent girl child and starts with the unborn fetus staring out at the world from the watery womb through a "porthole." This window on the world also serves as a conceit for the act of poetic creation. Alvi's verse encourages her audience to take another view of things, one provided by the poetic window she crafts.

The window, or "eyehole" in Anglo-Saxon, also enables the reader to look in on Alvi's thoughts and feelings beyond the ventriloquism through voices in the text.

The gentle humor of the device is reminiscent of Sylvia Plath's childhood poems ("Riddle," "Morning Song") and the final image is of the sari being tenderly "wrapped" around the speaker's body as swaddling comfort then, as the wrapping motif is repeated, more sinisterly as a shroud. In Alvi's poetic stance, the sari is an emblem of ideology that cannot be escaped. Louis Althusser's theoretical stance can be applied here as he opines that "ideology is eternal," it predates birth, and exists post-death, from which perspective we are all wrapped up in its folds. Applying Althusser's ideas to Alvi's material shows that the person of mixed-decent must try not to "misrecognise himself" as a part of society rather than the product of it (Althusser 1972, 175).

The elegant beauty of the sari, a feminine and authentic South Asian garment, is employed here as a motif to warn against the dangers of nationalism (Grayling 2002, 1). The sari cloth is presented as powerful and as public as any flag of communal belonging for a nation, the same flag that drapes the coffins of those who die for the rhetoric of nationalism. The reader is confronted with the idea that total allegiance to a tribe or nation implies a darker set of potential allegiances at the extreme end of which lies totalitarianism. Between the lines of this poem is the warning that twentieth-century history is littered with instances of uncurbed nationalism, a pertinent point from a poet deeply engaged with issues of identification and alienation.

> Eventually
> They wrapped and wrapped me in it
> Whispering *Your body is your country.* (lines 20–22)

The text foregrounds the sari, deploying it as an emblem of visible South Asian culture and tribal inclusion, to highlight the problematic nature of exclusive groups: for every person allowed entry it is necessary that others are denied access. To wear the sari is a public statement, a sartorial announcement of Asianness that Alvi highlights elsewhere as a potential shield, or armor, against racism. These garments are "so stunning they ward off insults,/silks that could brush against years/of criss–cross graffiti" ("The Asian Fashion Show," lines 9–11). However, clothing that identifies the wearer as foreign is also treated with ambivalence, for example few pupils attend the Asian Fashion show and those who do are "Asian girls" (line 3). The speaker in this verse is less than enthusiastic about shopping for "such outfits" in Wembley and Moorgate, preferring the denim and corduroy markers of Western fashion (line 17). For dual heritage children the cultural freight of clothing is heightened, yet garments can also be casually shed for convenience when crossing thresholds into new groups, a factor exploited to comic effect in the fiction of mixed-descent author Meera Syal (Syal 1996, 110).

The female fetus in "The Sari" is the voice of the poem and her porthole allows others from the "hot and brown" world to gaze into the private space of the womb. Family, servants, animals, and even politicians are interested in the birth of this child, the latter detail underlines the political consequences for mixed race children "of no fixed nationality" ("Presents From My Aunts In Pakistan," line 67) eager to find their place in a world riven with conflict along cultural and racial lines. Being of mixed descent is problematic in a resource-stretched world where developed nations constantly alter the demarcations and categories of belonging (salient examples include residential status, passports, and visas).

Alvi was born seven years after the Partition of India into East and West Pakistan, her poetry considers matters of internal and external identity and often focuses on the sites where the greatest disjunction occurs: body, clothing, language, food. The text is located in a section entitled "Presents from Pakistan" and distance is a key aspect of the word choices in the poem as the sari fabric stretches fantastically across seas and continents, from Lahore in Pakistan to Hyderabad in India and across the Arabian Sea. The UK is not mentioned as the final destination, although in stanza three, the English grandmother uses a telescope to discern her faraway granddaughter as if she is herself an explorer of other continents. The sari fabric is described in images of movement, it is patterned with English birds—nonmigratory quails and sparrows—it flutters as if in flight and is "threaded" with roads. The choice of birds is significant in a text concerned with migration and the "undulations" of land beneath the draped sari suggest feminine curves on a human form as much as actual terrain. The latter point evokes novels by colonial authors such as Rider Haggard who employed the device of female-gendered landscapes to emphasize masculine authority (McClintock 1995, 241). The historically masculine activity of exploring, founding and dividing nations is a clear subtext in a poem that uses the ultra-feminine sari to explore how migration impacts on identity.

Though beautiful and feminine the sari reads as an ambivalent motif for Alvi: "Eventually they wrapped and wrapped me in it" lends a sinister edge in the repetition of "wrapped" (lines 21–2) and the final line is an italicized whisper *"Your body is your country"* as if the comment cannot be confidently stated aloud. Alvi offers hope in her exploration of cultural signals (here clothes and places) in the way she connects them to the self, yet, for those born with the "whisper of another continent in [their] bones" the corporeal is the contested site of struggle between contrasting cultures and ideologies ("For My Daughter," lines 5–6). *"Your body is your country"* reads as a promise and a threat. For an audience caught between east and west her poetry is a means of not becoming "strangers to ourselves" or indeed, each other ("For My Daughter," line 10).

Alvi presents female clothing as disguise, as inauthentic to the self but also as armor in a repeated series of images that run through her work. The garment colors evoke the natural world of the Indian subcontinent's birds and animals: "peacock-blue," "an orange split open," "an apple-green sari," and worryingly they are "radiant," with being even when hidden in a wardrobe ("Presents From My Aunts In Pakistan," lines 2–13). The female voice of the poem desires Western fashionable clothes, she looks and feels "alien" wearing Pakistani clothes in the Western sitting room, and fails to be reborn, aflame yet un-Phoenix-like and only "half-English" (line 25). The clothes epitomize the power of a comfortably-worn identity but like a character in a Greek tragedy the speaker is rendered immobile by them: "I couldn't rise up out of its fire" (line 24). The lifeless garments have animation and the living (when garbed in foreign clothes) become uncomfortably static, alien to themselves like objects that are out of place. In this reading, Alvi signifies location as all-pervasive, even her synonym choice for the fabric pattern is one of places: "Sari borders broad like silver cities" ("Luckbir," line 2). The garment is at once a lifeless object and the representation of exotic urban space and a magical "costume" of foreignness with the power to include or exclude (line 7). In articulating these ideas and experiences Alvi frames the disjunctions central to the transplantation of peoples and the act of sharing is a positive one presenting a series of views from the other(ed) side.

ROOTS AND WATER: "ENGLAND, I AM GAZING AT YOUR BODY"

This is a text that directly uses bodily processes as a metaphor to foreground British imperial decline and the ensuing complexity of postcolonial relations. The poem title is longer than the simple "England" found on the contents page and it directs the reader toward a particular interpretation of the text. This time Alvi morphs nations into human figures rather than dressing the female human body as a metaphor for a country ("The Sari"). The lower case of the first word of the text, "stretched," and enjambment runs the title into the first line and a stanza that is redolent of the language of metaphysical love poetry as the voice of the poem gazes at the body of the beloved "stretched" and "buoyed up" by the waves (lines 1–2). Like an Elizabethan sonneteer addressing a lover the speaker describes watching the body of England "brighten and darken/go warm and cold," affectionately listing the alterations resulting from physical intimacy with the object of desire (line 3). These processes mimic the physical changes of human coitus, yet, each phrase ends on a negative note as relations alter and more than bodies seems to "darken" and go "cold."

The tone becomes more ominous as the second stanza moves toward the act of physical dominance in stanza three that reads more like rape than consensual union. By naming one of the subjects "England" Alvi distinctly associates violent sexual congress with imperial dominance and subverts the historical narrative by (re)positioning the colonizer as the victim. This predates by some way the similar pattern of recent fiction whereby power relations are inverted to dramatic effect, best demonstrated in the novels *Blonde Roots* and *The Power*, respectively focussing on race and gender. Alvi's poem draws together physical and emotional abuse on a human scale against the backdrop of the shared history of two nations; the unnamed but thematically implicit Indian subcontinent and England, the heart of empire. Seen in this light, the text offers an alternative scenario to the rapacious acts of imperialism, in which vulnerable England is the pillaged victim and the unidentified speaker/nation is the oppressor compelling the poem's audience to identify with England in the unfamiliar role of the despoiled.

Here, the speaker of the poem's body is enlarged to the scale of England's topography and, now gargantuan, they are able to "rest an elbow on a grass roundabout" (line 11) while England is "weakened" and "shrunk" and at the speaker's mercy (line 5). The anthropomorphized England begs for understanding but the speaker merely sniffs parts of the landscape with sexual animalism and presses the weight of their body against the "bulk" of the nation. Even the inclusion of England's "industrial belt" and "crags and reservoirs" has carnal suggestiveness and any hint of the initial tenderness has disappeared, replaced by a sordid act of violation.

The lines build to an act of aggressive sexual dominance in stanza three as the "wind blows across our contours" and the two nations join to become one in the collective pronoun "our" (line 13). The speaker's relation culminates in the final dismissive, postcoital, lines: "I pull myself off you./Hard to prise my stickiness from yours" (lines 18–19). In the commingling of fluids and difficult separation both sides are marked by the experience. This curious poem presenting the coupling of England and another nation is a comment on Britain's forced retreat from imperial dominance and loss of economic preeminence. The era of British imperial dominance is still regarded nostalgically by many and here it leads England to a subordinate and unfamiliar subjugation where the nation does not give orders but rather takes them. Alvi shows that colonization has unpredictable and far-reaching consequences as the forced consummation creates living issue. The following line is placed separately from the stanzas on the page to add emphasis, both syntax and graphology signal a command from the speaker to the country pinned down and helpless.

England, it's time
to call the children in. (Lines 16–17)

This raises the question of exactly where the children of colonialism, caught as they are in the fallout of historical events, are called "in" to—the colonized nation, the colonizing nation, or some other place? Two nations (England and India) are historically joined, conjoined, and messily separated. The children (nationals, migrants, immigrants) are the produce of an act that is presented without affection or tenderness. Alvi uses human sexual behavior as a metaphor for the historical relations between nation-states and in this reading the children of that union are miscegenated offspring with an equally creolized heritage of nationality and culture. The "grain of understanding" mentioned in line seven clearly indicates that it is time to be inclusive with all the children of the nation(s) and call them home to the mother country. Alvi's poetry equates colonialism and the diaspora to human processes of union, procreation, parenting, fostering, and adoption but this poem does not signpost the way home for the postcolonial hybrid.

Other poems continue the theme of female bodily processes as a means of developing a means of expressing alienation. In the poem entitled "Blood," menstruation and miscegenation are directly connected as the girl-child speaker considers "Was I more Indian or more English?," a question that seems to lie in the composition of the plasma itself (line 14). The juvenile female body is poised on the threshold of womanhood and becomes suddenly indistinct and less clearly seen as if caught in motion as a photograph is taken (line 15). "I blurred" is an odd usage for a verb more commonly used for objects than people and perfectly communicates the sense of detachment and smeared experience common to women during their menses. "Blood" and "blurred" occur in adjacent lines as para-rhyme and the association between the images hinges on the mixed race of the speaker. Her blood is itself "blurred': impure and indistinct. This is clear as she raises the question of which genetic heritage predominates, recognizing that this feeling will return monthly when her "blood seeped regularly/into the outer world" (lines 16–17). This parallels the genetic mixing of Indians and the English colonizers during the time of the Raj, when mixed-race children were designated as Anglo-Indians, a group rejected by both sides. A sense of helplessness against the power of blood as a necessary physical expulsion and biological ancestry is communicated in the final lines where sports day games involve having "hands secured behind my back" (line 22). The unwritten but implicit missing word is "tied." Most of us are powerless regarding our ethnicity and our nationality and the speakers of the poems are doing their best to navigate the complexity of the signs and signifiers of belonging.

Attitudes toward birth and host countries are not straightforwardly portrayed here or elsewhere in the corpus and in much of Alvi's verse the metaphor of maternity retains an ambiguous aspect. The child speaker in "The Laughing Moon" is embraced by the birth country only to be carelessly allowed to fall from its arms: "Pakistan held me and dropped me in the night" (line 3) and subsequently the adopting nation reveals uncertainty and a forbiddingly chill aspect: "Shakily England picked me up/with her grey fingers" ("The Laughing Moon," lines 17–18). It is midnight and despite the age of the continents the child is "new and breathing" in what reads as a hopeful reference to August 15, 1947, Partition.

CORPOREAL LOCATIONS: "AND IF"

This poem is from the collection *A Bowl of Warm Air* (Alvi 1996) and signals a return to the interrogation of places and personal choice by introducing the conceit of being able to determine one's country of birth. There is no opportunity to choose one's own birthplace, although parents may make strategic decisions as Alvi's did when they moved their daughter to England with their new baby in 1954. From the privileged position of dual nationality, perhaps better expressed in identity politics as "both/neither," the poet poses the conundrum: "which is the best place to be from?" We are living in a world where basic measures of happiness and security differ greatly between nations, there is vast disparity between economies and differences concerning life expectancy. Here the person belongs to the country and not the other way around, the "legend" of the "Eastern track" is replaced by a "gusty English lane" (lines 22–23) and the subtext is that of the path not taken, a wistful and habitual stance for the voices in Alvi's poems.

Having taken the reader to a place that is not England, a place that is hot and peopled by cattle-driving Yadavs, the speaker describes peeling back the skin from a face to find another face beneath, and so on through layers until a final face "so clear/so complex, hinting at nations/castes and sub-castes" is exposed (lines 18–20). The reference to the Yadavs concerns Indian peasant farmers who have made efforts to raise their caste by claiming royal ancestry from King Yadu. The "quality" of their blood signifies their status and the mention reifies Alvi's insistent return to skin and blood as the tropes of domicile.

The expected verb choice is "reveal" but Alvi uses "retrieve" instead to indicate that this is a recognizable countenance, once hidden but with the potential to be reclaimed, and touched. There is to be only one touch of this precious aspect of the self (line 21) before the brutal reminder in the final lines that "you'd be untouchable" (line 28). The poem starts with the tentativeness of the word "if" but ends with the blunt fact that it is others who decide who is accepted as belonging in which place, and who is excluded. Despite the increasingly liberal agenda currently, and publicly, adopted by

Western nations, for those of mixed descent the dangers of social "leprosy" are a familiar legacy.

"Untouchable" is the commonly used word for the Dalits in India, a group composed of those performing menial tasks, including burning corpses in Hindu cremations. They are as reviled as vermin, like the lifeless rat mentioned in stanza four and cannot be touched by those of higher caste as an impure touch is considered to defile the spiritually pure. Alvi's text indirectly refers to the reality that a child of mixed blood is considered impure, intrinsically wrong biologically, genetically miscegenated, and thus, untouchable by the homogenous and genetically "pure" dominant group. The authentic face lurking "down" beneath other faces and deep within this poem is that of a racial and cultural hybrid and the force of postcolonial texts (such as this one) is that they indicate real bodies as easy to misread. This retrieval feels as though the second and third faces are being fished out of a well, and the motif of something precious that has been lost is an image that recurs in Alvi's verse on languages where each new word tends to "settle like a stone/ at the bottom of a well" ("Hindi Urdu Bol Chaal," lines 45–46). Reclaiming the words of a language that is not yours from birth is as challenging an act as if they were lost objects deep in a well, and in this poem faces are like masks that can be worn or removed at will. This is a fantasy for those whose faces do not fit neatly into a visually, identifiably, racial taxonomy.

The image of the body as a map of the past and of actual places is a revenant in Alvi's work. If a map is inaccurate or misread it leads to confusion and error, displacement and disorientation. Wearing the wrong face can be wearing a mask in order to deceive but it can also be wearing the face that does not accurately correspond to ethnicity and the corresponding phenotype. As a British-Pakistani woman Alvi is well aware of the interior/exterior paradox whereby inherited genetics are seen to be at odds with a heritage of white British culture. For those of mixed descent the unwritten question at the heart of the text is "And where are you *really* from?"

The first word of the poem is "If" and the last word is "dead." On one level the text is a sardonic response to Rudyard Kipling's ever–popular poem "If," a celebration of British heroic virtues aimed at public schoolboys destined for colonial administration in the British Indian Civil Service. In "What If" the fantasy of choosing your birthplace is balanced against the actual consequences of being ethnically mixed and/or diasporic, Alvi leaves the reader wise to the dangers of indulging in "what if."

LOCATING THE SELF: "HALF-AND-HALF"

Partition is relatively recent history (seventy years) and as with other historical traumas many of those who lived through the mass migration, the refugee camps, the bloodshed, are reluctant and take time to articulate their experience. The children of South Asian migrants are able to frame the events and consequences in literature and, by so doing, they resurrect the erased and retrieve some of that which was lost. The compulsion to revisit trauma and frame it in literary art is itself presented by Alvi in corporeal metaphors: "A road winds back inside me/like the Karakoram Highway/through mountains, gorges" ("The Draught," I, lines 13–15). Her poetic tone is varied and not discouraging though the journey is challenging and the poems are scattered with images of beauty. In "Domain," at the speaker's core is a mango-like stone that contains "the essence/of another continent" (lines 4–5), they wisely "fear its removal" as even if that were possible such a major operation would kill the patient. This parallels the way the other continent is retained at the core of the collection, the individual verses and the characters within them. The conclusion of this text is a euphoric urge to embrace the heavy but indispensable stone and "run away with it" (line 10). What these lines express is that the complexities of identity retain challenging and weighty issues but these cannot be dismissed or discarded, they are integral to the person and as vital an organ as their heart.

As the daughter of parents from different nations and races it is unsurprising that Alvi's poetry is permeated with the condition of feeling "other." What is more significant is how she writes out the story of those whose bodies in themselves represent a mixture, or masala. In "Half–and–Half" she satirizes the nonsensical aspects of a human form considered to be bodily "*half*-English" ("Presents From My Aunts In Pakistan," line 25). The child voice of the poem identifies the dark line of skin running down from their naval as the literal division of the physical self into two parts, a psychological rupture encouraged by the clumsy language of otherness. In this text disunity is emphasized rather than a model of blending, or the "mosaic" encouraged by developed nations.

This focus on particular and personal demarcations in Alvi's poetry mirrors the geographical dissection of India that haunts these texts, a division that resulted in fourteen million displaced refugees and two million dead. The partition of India in 1947 is aligned directly with the somatic as if a human body is broken and dying: "there was conflict, a *fractured* land/ *throbbing* through newsprint." ("Presents From My Aunts In Pakistan," lines 58–59, emphasis mine). In this poem the "thin line" on the child's skin is a scar that physically echoes the Radcliffe Line, the British-drawn boundary line dividing India and Pakistan. This child is also half-Pakistani and, like the child, that country is not "whole" (line 6) but divided into East and West Pakistan, with "pendulous" India uncomfortably situated between them (line 8). Alvi's text spits out plosives, "Pakistan belonged to the politicians, the priests" (line 10), conveying meaning in an abrupt style matching the sardonic and critical tone. The chosen perspective depicts those in authority (politicians and priests) as people who "carved up the world"; they include the child's geography teacher, the determined transmitter of a white, Anglocentric world view. The child is "enlightened [. . .] briskly" (line 10) regarding their birthplace and the final penetrative act of colonialism is when the child is made to publicly identify the location by putting a pin in a map on the classroom wall. Like the Indian subjects eternally divided by the Radcliffe Line, the child uncomfortably performs the violation but the adult poet resists and reframes this apparently minor incident as an abuse of power with an anger that is palpable.

Alvi does not use the identifier "British" in any of her poems. She is herself British-Pakistani in the official terminology of identity categories but this inclusive indicator of nationality is ignored in favor of the culturally elite and exclusive term "English." In "Presents From My Aunts in Pakistan" the sense that ethnic and national identity can be outwardly worn and changed like a garment at will is counterposed by the corporeal quality of objects that communicate place. So, in another poem a map of India pre-Partition is treated as if it is a malleable part of human anatomy, the speaker can "lift it like a flap of skin" ("Map of India," line 3). A comment on the condition of having "no fixed nationality" ("Presents From My Aunts In Pakistan," line 67) comes just before a description of looking through fretwork, used here as an analogy for imprisoning bars, at the iconic Shalimar Gardens. The speaker is unable to break through the high walls to the utopian space beyond, a paradisial site originally designed for resting, now symbolizing freedom from the uncertainties of in-between-ness.

LEXIS: "THROWING OUT MY FATHER'S DICTIONARY"

It is notable that Bruce King's review of *The Redbeck Anthology of British South Asian Poetry* (Chatterjee 2000) singles out Alvi's three poems as among the "good" offerings of poetry about being an immigrant, citing the rest as not "about living in the present, about real events and real experiences" (King 2001, 340). This damning indictment correlates with editor Debjani Chatterjee's inaccurate statement that English is "an indifferent language of an alien shore," a position Alvi's verse certainly opposes in its subtle attention to the cross-fertilization of languages in a postcolonial context (Chatterjee quoted in King 2001, 340).

Language is a key area of interest for Alvi as she explores means of expressing the complementary and contrasting aspects of those caught between the shared history of Britain and India. This section focusses on just a few of the texts that follow the theme of communication. In "The Laughing Moon" the speaker describes an important message spinning through "a hole to the other side of the world" and this parallels Alvi's work as a poet telling her readers something important if only in the spaces between the words she uses. In her verse the taste and sound, feel and scent of words engenders a bridge between the sensory experience of knowing a language without actually speaking it, something common to the children of first generation immigrants whose perfect comprehension of parental languages often masks a lack of fluency.

> I tasted the language, customs
> of my father's country—
> its fever on biting a chilli.
> ("Indian Cooking," lines 10–12)

The limits of communication are also known to their parents and grandparents who may never successfully acquire the language of the adopted homeland. Or, they may speak the formal English of colonial education that is at variance with the everyday idioms of English as it is spoken in Britain today. The voice of the poem observes the father mentally searching for the right word to use as if he is using the book itself: "I see him/rifling through his second language" ("Throwing Out My Father's Dictionary," lines 8–9).

The subject matter underscores the pressure for migrants to acquire the speech and customs of their new homeland in order to succeed economically and socially. It also intimates why they may not have time or inclination to use that language to communicate the horrors they have tried to leave behind in the old country. Survival is the key imperative for migrants for whom the luxury of recording their experience and tracing what was lost, and found, can wait.

Alamgir Hashmi's review of the collection includes the comment that this text "asserts generation difference, and a latter-day language identity, toward which the speaker has a rather dubious and hesitant attitude" (Hashmi 1995, 44). Some of the verse conveys the nervousness of the mixed-race person learning the alien-yet-familiar parental language: "New words perch on my tongue" ("The Draught," line 45). The words are about to find utterance but like fledglings on the verge of flight they pause, momentarily wary of the chance to find freedom. This echoes the trials of second language speakers painfully aware of the dangers of trying their new skills in public conversation and highlights migrants' desire to tell their own stories in their own words. The challenging question is clear: "Can a bird sing only the song it knows or can it learn a new song?" (Carter 1979, 108). Alvi's poems form part of the answer.

Alvi's second generation speaker throws her father's dictionary away with its confidently signed and underlined flyleaf: "My father's signature is centre page" (line 7). The second generation speaker has need of a broader vocabulary to communicate their experience and the more detailed lexicon of the new dictionary is confirmed by the extensive entries and broader pages.

Unable to sign the flyleaf of the new volume, they retrieve the disintegrating book from the rubbish realizing that the recent addition of numerous imported words in their volume, such as "chador," may not be as important as they think (line 15). Alvi's choice to use English for crafting poetry may be related to her fluency in her father's languages. Many immigrants restricted their children's exposure to Urdu, Hindi, Punjabi, and so on, in the belief that skill in the tongue of the new country would serve them better. Literature about, or from, diasporic authors and poets shows that those languages are revenants in the texts, hovering on the margins of comprehension for those unable to access them.

FUTURE DIALOGUE: "HINDI URDU BOL CHAAL"

For a transplanted poet, the language of the adopted homeland offers freedom of expression yet it is also a palimpsest of the birth language, perhaps only spoken within family groups, understood but not spoken or written, deliberately erased, or simply forgotten. Being heard, the spoken and the written word serve as a combined theme that threads its way throughout Alvi's corpus but it is especially prominent in specific texts and commonly articulated through corporeal imagery.

> These are languages I try to touch
> As if my tongue is a fingertip gently
> Matching its whorls to echoing of sound.
> ("Hindu Urdu Bol Chaal," lines 1–3)

There is a tentative delicacy in the speaker's attempt to feel the languages and to taste their vocabulary, they act as a metonomic device for Partition as Hindi and Urdu actively resist being divided into separate languages. The words are "like hands banging on the table" (line 10). They also sound like materials and practices from the subcontinent; "the whisper of silk on silk" and chapattis being made in the traditional way (lines 18–19). Language is made up of a series of "meetings and greetings" between words from the various lexicons of Urdu and Sanskrit, Persian and Arabic, it is found in the whorls of a fingerprint but only if one looks closely, searching for word music and hearing the rustle of long-dead relatives quarrelling. This evocation delivers the hybrid experience of being on the edges of comprehension regarding "languages that could have been mine" (line 17) but conveys a positive message as the speaker is also "enlarged" by what they cannot hear (lines 37–38).

Like the speaker in the text, language is a series of borrowings from other places and peoples. In constant motion like the lexicon itself the speaker is following the route of a "sound system" on a journey across the globe, carrying vocabulary and meeting countries through the words borrowed from them. "Pakistan [. . .]/It is not you I am meeting" (lines 24–26). Alvi's focus on the exchange of words is an affirmation of the creative possibilities of a mixed race and diasporic inheritance. The directive to "try looping lines/ between the hemispheres" ("Fighter planes," lines 10–11) is a deft summation of her mode of poetic commentary on Partition and the diaspora. The positivity of this image captures the poet as a cosmic artist, a writer in clouds on a broad sky canvas, encouraging global change through connections between continents on a human scale.

This study explores how one poet engages with Partition and diaspora. I have argued that Alvi's contribution to poetry must not be overlooked as she explores areas of vital concern in twenty-first century society using the corporeal to illuminate issues of belonging and foreignness. The locus of the texts considered in this paper is "[h]er bodily engagement with her art, as well as her marginal predicament" (Hashmi 2001, 145). If the texts do at times present a confused picture of duality that is because we are all caught up in the "long, decolonising moment" (Walder 1998, 202), giving weight to Alvi's troubled image of "England mixed with India./A knotted carpet" ("O Maharani," lines 30–31). As Sue Dymoke observes, "The poems are all tightly constructed and have a surreal, elusive quality which rewards rereading" (Dymoke 2006, 112). It is easy to miss Alvi's deft touch and considering her work in total allows for connections that would otherwise not be missed.

As Walder argues in his summation of the work of V. S. Naipaul, we need texts such as these in order "to know where and who we are," by covering this ground Alvi's poetry successfully addresses the "instability of the colonial subject and the desire for an identity" (Walder 1998, 203). With recurrent images of "imprints like maps on our hands," Alvi suggests a map to the future, a positive image of hope indicating the possibilities of finding the way forward out of confusion to the stability of personhood and home ("The Wedding," line 34). For those implicated in the colonial and postcolonial story these verses exemplify a resistance to "the mapping of themselves by the knowledges of the past" and a marker toward the possibilities of harmonious union (Walder 1998, 208).

REFERENCES

Alderman, Naomi. 2016. *The Power*. New York: Viking.

Althusser, Louis. 1972. *Lenin and Philosophy, and Other Essays*. New York: Monthly Review Press.

Alvi, Moniza. 2008. *Split Country: Poems 1990–2005*. Tarset, Northumberland: Bloodaxe Books.

———. 1993. *The Country at my Shoulder*. Oxford: Oxford University Press.

———. 2013. *At The Time of Partition*. Tarset, Northumberland: Bloodaxe Books.

Brah, Avtar. 1996. *Cartographies of Diaspora: Contesting Identities*. London: Routledge.

Carter, Angela. 1979. *The Bloody Chamber*. London: Virago.

Chatterjee, Debjani. 2000. *The Redbeck Anthology of British South Asian Poetry*. Bradford, England: Redbeck.

Dymoke, Sue. 2006. "Review of *How the Stone Found it's Voice* by Moniza Alvi." *Critical Survey* 18, no. 3: 112–17.

Everisto, Bernadine. 2008. *Blonde Roots*. London: Penguin.

Grayling, A. C. 2002. *The Meaning of Things: Applying Philosophy to Life*. London: Orion.

Gupta, Dipanka. 2000. *Caste in Question: Identity or Heirarchy? Contributions to Indian Sociology*. London: Penguin.

Haggard, Rider. 1885. *King Solomon's Mines*. London: Cassell.

King, Bruce. 2001. "Review of *The Redbeck Anthology of British South Asian Poetry* by Debjani Chatterjee." *World Literature Today*, 75, no. 2 (spring): 340. http://www.jstor.org/stable/40156602.

Hashmi, Alamgir. 1995. "Review of *The Country at My Shoulder* by Moniza Alvi." *World Literature Today*, 69, no. 1 (winter): 144–45.

McClintock, Anne. 1995. *Imperial Leather: Race, Gender and Sexuality in the Colonial Context*. London: Routledge.

Shamsie, Muneeza. 2011. "South Asian Muslims: Fiction and poetry in English." *Religion and Literature* 43, no. 1 (spring): 149–157. http://www.jstor.org/stable/23049363.

Syal, Meera. 1996. *Anita and Me*. London: Flamingo.

Walder, Dennis. 1998. *Post-colonial Literatures in English*. Oxford: Blackwell.

Chapter Two

India, Heat, Dust, and Tea?

*Alienness and Marketability in Ruth Prawer Jhabvala
and Nicole C. Vosseler*

Alejandra Moreno-Álvarez

Heat and Dust by Ruth Prawer Jhabvala, published in 1975, and *Der Himmel über Darjeeling* (*The Sky Above Darjeeling*) by Nicole C. Vosseler, published in 2006, are romances that take place in India. Vosseler's novel belongs to the romance genre while Jhabvala's is considered "high literature," where words are used with refinement, and its style offers novelty. The plots, despite the lowbrow and highbrow classifications, are very similar in both novels, as seen in most narratives that belong to the romance genre. That is, the story focuses on a love relationship and this love is what ties together the tale that concludes with a HEA (happily ever after) ending.

In Jhabvala's and Vosseler's works, there is a European woman who falls madly in love with a "manly and strong" Indian male character. *Heat and Dust* does not provide a perfect HEA but a less optimistic ending, plus the language used is more elaborated than the simplistic one employed in *The Sky Above Darjeeling*. These two facts, the ending, plus the language used, make these novels' classification differ, where one is considered canonical, due particularly to the Man Booker Prize award, and the other is labeled, merely, as a romance. Nonetheless, there are various reasons that make possible a feasible comparison of these two literary works, such as the authoresses' European descent, the marketability, alienness, romance, and Otherness.

The romance and the spatial narration in both works are fictionalized by two European authors: Jhabvala, German-born British and American, and Vosseler, German. Jhabvala was of Polish-Jewish origin, born in Cologne, Germany, in 1927, who emigrated to Great Britain with her family at the beginning of World War II. She graduated in English Literature at Queen Mary College, London University, married Cyrus Jhabvala, an Indian architect, and moved to New Delhi, where she spent more than two decades before settling permanently in the United States, as she never felt quite settled in India. They raised three daughters, who married an Indian, an American, and an Englishman, respectively. Jhabvala, as so did her family, lived an international life, moving constantly between the East and the West. It was in 1979, in one of her lectures, when she admitted, highlighting her alienness, that she felt rootless: "I stand before you as a writer without any ground of being out of which to write: really blown about from country to country, culture to culture, till I feel—till I am—nothing" (in Rothman 2013). The concept of not belonging is one of Jhabvala's strengths, although her work, due to her origins and her British upbringing, seems tinted with preferences toward the West, as we can see in the stereotypes displayed in her literary work, which at times encapsulates the East as the Other. Jhabvala was a fruitful novelist, short-story author, and screenwriter. Much of her work is about inner travel, where characters, due to the feeling of not belonging, find new ways to feel at home in the spaces they end up inhabiting, as we can see in the short-story collection *East Into Upper East* (1998), written when she was split between New York and New Delhi. She wrote more than two dozen screenplays, most of them for Merchant Ivory productions, having been awarded with two Oscars for her adaptations of E. M. Foster's *A Room with a View* (1908) and *Howards End* (1910). She is also considered to be among the world's best authors of short stories written in the English language. In her several collections of stories, which were mainly published in *The New Yorker*, she primarily explored the complex relationship between the East and the West, especially, as Djoric Francuski underlines, "the cross-cultural experiences of Indians aspiring to a modernized way of life, on the one hand, and Westerners striving to grasp an exotic insight into some higher form of existence which they seem not to be able to endure if and when they find one, on the other" (2018, 6).

Nicole C. Vosseler, on the other hand, was born and raised in Germany, studied English, American, and German Literature as well as psychology. She is a prize-winning poet, short fiction, and novel writer. She gained critical acclaim with her debut novel *South Winds*; was awarded in 2007 with the Konstanz Young Artist's Advancement Award in Literary Arts; in 2013 won the third place at the DELIA Literature Award; and many of her works have been on the German Bestseller List (Vosseler 2006). She is also a highly regarded author of young adult fiction. In 2014, *This Very Special Night* was also shortlisted for the DELIA Literature Award.

COLDPLAY OF LITERATURE

In the case of the novels to be discussed in this article, both have been highly acclaimed: *Heat and Dust*, as I have already stated, was awarded with the Man Booker Prize in 1975, and, with it, great success—it was also made into a film in 1983 (Dir. J. Ivory)—while *The Sky Above Darjeeling* is a best seller which, due to its commercial profit, has been translated into seven languages to date. This means that both novels reach a wide readership, particularly after having been awarded and marketed.

Despite Jhabvala's literary reputation after receiving the Man Booker Prize award, Sam Jordison, on March 8, 2008, did not hesitate to publish, in *The Guardian*, the article entitled "Looking Back at the Booker: Ruth Prawer Jhabvala," where he defines *Heat and Dust* as the "Coldplay of literature": "[f]ar too dull to loathe, in short." Jordison draws a parallelism between Jhabvala's novel and E. M. Foster's set (*A Passage to India* 1924), which he describes as a "decorative version of India with brief interludes in a vaguely bohemian, cozily grubby England." Aamer Hussein, on the other hand, defines Jhabvala as the chronicler of the cultural divide, being one of the only novelists, in her opinion, who wrote, during the first stages of her literary career, about a middle- and lower-class India for foreigners to see, avoiding exoticism (2013). But for Jordison, even though *Heat and Dust* ridicules English colonials, it does still exoticize India, twenty years after its independence, with its picturesquely primitive natives, who "will never learn. Whatever they do, they will still cling to their barbaric customs" (Jhabvala 1975, 56). Jordison defines *Heat and Dust* as "securely pedestrian, slightly patronising, tinged with the exotic, [. . .] ultimately dull and pointless. It is, in short, literature for people who hate literature" (2008). It is this last argument that took me to link both *Heat and Dust* and *The Sky Above Darjeeling*. The fact that the former is defined by Jordison as literature for people who loathe literature goes hand-in-hand with the aversion at times within the academia to study in depth the romance genre. If *Heat and Dust* is about a love story, with a very similar outline as the one used in the romance genre, tinted with a very much alike story frame as *The Sky Above Darjeeling*, we might wonder why one is considered canonical while the other is mainly relegated to airports' bookshops or supermarket aisles. Why are we still split by binary thinking where one work is considered more literary than the other? Plus, if both novels deal with romances taking place in India, where the main characters are of European origin, alien to India, the same as both authors, but enchanted by India, why is India still portrayed as the Other, even more if we take into consideration the scope of thirty years since the novels' publications, as *Heat and Dust* was published in 1975 and *The Sky Above Darjeeling* in 2006? These questions, together with the need to study whether in these novels there is a decrease in the usage of binary thinking, which perpetuates India as the Other, took me to study both works together.

The first point of departure will be the highbrow and lowbrow literary criteria, where *Heat and Dust* is considered canonical and *The Sky Above Darjeeling* a mere romance. But, as we have seen, Jhabvala's novel was defined as the "Coldplay of Literature," despite the Man Booker. *The Sky Above Darjeeling*, on the other hand, has not been awarded with any literary prize, losing the possibility of a highbrow status, but, it has been highly acclaimed and its rights sold to MOBA (Czech Republic), TEA (Italy), Sonia Draga (Poland), Eksmo (Russia), and Ediciones B (Spain). Nevertheless, the novel, due to its belonging to the romance genre, and taking into account the view of Jordison, is another "Coldplay of literature." Thus, the classification criteria of highbrow and lowbrow, in the case of these novels, is erased, being both considered the "coldplay of literature."

Regarding the plot, there are similitudes. Bastei Lübbe, the largest independent book publisher in Germany, presented *The Sky Above Darjeeling* as:

> Entwining two epic love stories, decades apart, *The Sky Above Darjeeling* takes the reader from the stormy coast of Cornwall to the deserts of Rajputana and their magnificent forts and to the green foothills and valleys of the Himalaya. A sumptuous tale of forbidden love, shifting identities and colonialism, of revenge and retribution, set against the backdrop of the Indian mutiny of 1857 and British India in the second half of the nineteenth century. (Vosseler 2006)

On the other hand, Goodreads, a social cataloging website that allows individuals to freely search its database of books, annotations, and reviews, and where mostly romance novels are advertised, describes *Heat and Dust* as set in colonial India during the 1920s, which tells the story of Olivia, the wife of an English civil servant, who, longing for passion and independence, is drawn into the spell of the Nawab, an Indian prince. Being intrigued by the Nawab's charm she begins to spend most of her lonely days in his company. She becomes pregnant and unsure of the child's paternity she has to face a dilemma. Her decision, an abortion, outrages the British community, causing a scandal that will live in collective memory after her death. In *Heat and Dust*, Jhabvala explores a forbidden sexual attraction between the colonizer and the native. As we can see, *Heat and Dust* and *The Sky Above Darjeeling* deal with forbidden love, set during colonial times, where the English woman, alien to India, falls in love with the Indian man, causing scandal to the British community.

THEORETICAL AND LITERARY PARALLELISM

When *Heat and Dust* was published in 1975, postcolonial literature, theorized then as Third World literature, was emerging within the academia, and when *The Sky Above Darjeeling* came out in 2006, the umbrella term, postcolonial literature, was being, and still is, in need of a recategorization as global literatures, or transnational literatures. As we know, and as I have already underlined in "Postcolonial Studies in the Twenty-First Century" (2016), much has been written since the turn of the century about the effects of colonization within the field of humanities and social sciences which has helped to consolidate the field of Postcolonial Studies, along with the emergence of globalization theory (Krishnaswamy 2008) and cosmopolitan criticism (Spencer 2011). Some critics believe that postcolonial studies is being eclipsed by globalization studies and others advocate for interdiscursive approaches so as to go "beyond a certain kind of postcolonial studies" (Loomba, *Postcolonial Studies* 7). Revathi Krishnaswamy concludes that "to be global is first and foremost to be postcolonial and to be postcolonial is always already to be global" (*The Postcolonial and the Global* 3). It is true that postcolonial studies has moved away from areas of regional studies and its respective literatures, to fields such as social sciences or media studies, among others, all of them in the pursuit of inquiry and search for new configurations and reroutings of knowledge where dynamism, critical theory, and relevance must be always present (in Moreno-Álvarez 2016).

Theoretically speaking, there is a shift in the span of the three decades when *Heat and Dust* and *The Sky Above Darjeeling* were published. Otherness in the former one is more latent than in the latter. The Other, once displayed and consciously heard and seen, moves toward the aforementioned concept of globality, which is a way of deconstructing binary thinking that entraps the Other as passive and exotic. Literarily speaking, there is a parallelism in both works between literature and critical thinking in the path taken by postcolonial theory. *Heat and Dust* is tinted, as I have already stated, with stereotypical images where the Other—the Nawab—is described as an exotic, childish, bigoted Indian prince who gets everything he wants and who likes to entertain Europeans, from whom he completely differs. On the other hand, in *The Sky Above Darjeeling*, we are presented with Rajiv Chand, alias the chameleon, and Ian Neville—both the same person—son of Winston (British) and Sitara (Indian). This persona is a hybrid character whom, despite this hybridization that mostly agrees with global literatures, is unfortunately still exoticized by Vosseler, although the author is less explicit than Jhabvala in terms of exoticizing the Other, as if she was conscious of current postcolonial theories. Not in vain, Vosseler studied English literature, being supposedly well aware of postcolonial studies. An example of the hybridization present in the work, which is, at first, rejected by the Indian natives, can be found in the following passage:

> I would really like to see how much you have of a real Rajput and know if you deserve your genealogy. It is my blood, the one that runs down your veins, a princely blood, but I will never forget that is mixed with a *feringhi*'s one, who brought so much disgrace to us, that you are the result of an impure relation-ship, not consecrated. . . . You are my grandson, but you are also a bastard. This is the heritage that your parents have left you. Do not ever forget so. (2012, 510, my translation)

The "feringhi" is a transgressive figure, nor British, nor Indian, and, thereby, he constitutes the loss of a "conservative" cultural identity, incarnated in the figure of the grandfather. Rajiv Chand is at first rejected due to his "impure" blood, to then become the heir of his grandfather's fortune, which proves the acceptance of hybridization. Vosseler, being well aware of the need to cele-brate this hybridization, not in vain the novel was published in 2006, plays not only with this concept but is also conscious of a proper marketability in order to reach a wider readership. The latter contributes to the success of both novels.

MARKETABILITY

We cannot avoid addressing in the present article the retail expansion in the publishing industry, and with it the marketing niche these two novels are trapped within. *Heat and Dust* reached a wider audience due to the Man Booker Prize, while *The Sky Above Darjeeling*, framed within the romance genre, is in need of marketability in order to enrich sales. Claire Squires highlights how "[w]inning the Booker Prize is big business for publishing companies, as the rush to extra production referred to in this account, and the ensuing extra sales, makes evident" (2007b, 85). The Man Booker leads to the book's commodification and subsequent canonization, as I have already mentioned, and with it, in the case of *Heat and Dust*, the "commerce of an 'exotic' commodity catered to the Western literary market'" (in Huggan 2001, 106). As Richard Todd suggests in *Booker Prize, Consuming Fictions: The Booker Prize and Fiction in Britain Today* (1996), there are other factors that contribute to the marketability of the book, such as promotional activ-ities and the retail chains. All contribute to the formation of a canon of contemporary literature in English language. Also, in the case of this novel, its adaption to the big screen in 1983, directed by James Ivory, screenplayed by Jhabvala herself—screenwriter of the year, London Critics Film Award, 1984—awarded with a BAFTA, and nominated for the Palme d'Or, gave rise to *Heat and Dust*'s great success. The film became also part of an early

1980s cycle of British productions set in India. It has to be highlighted how Merchant Ivory Productions started the company's new era of large-scale production of period films based on mostly historical novels. These included *Gandhi* (1982), *Heat and Dust—Oriente y Occidente—* (1983), *A Passage to India* (1984) and the TV mini-series *The Far Pavilions* (1984) and *The Jewel of the Crown* (1984). David Gritten has pointed out how Merchant Ivory, which was not just a film industry brand leader, but the only production company with recognition worldwide, entailed adaptations from literature to coherent scripts, offering, with its period films "a way of selling the British an idealized version of how they saw history" (2006) although its initial goal was to make English-language films in India aimed at international markets. The series represented the mood of the era, with, as Gritten underlines, "its Thatcherite notions of British heritage" (2006), despite Mercant Ivory Productions triumvirate: Ismael Merchant, an Indian Muslim, Jim Ivory, a protestant American, and Jhabvala, a German Jew. They produced films that recreated the complexity of colonialism and postcolonialism explored through Britons' and Indians' experiences, pre- and post-India's independence. Usually, as it happens with *Heat and Dust*, the link is a fraught, although passionate, relationship between a British woman and an Indian man. Spectators are able to follow the story at the same time as they embed an iconic India, at times exotic, recreated for the western palate. This contributes to construct India, in the West, as an exotic, and unreal, archive.

Lynne Tatlock highlights how "as long as readers can find an empathetic point of entry into the world of the novel, [. . .] if the story is reasonably convincing within the parameters it sets for itself, readers do not have to care about the historically particular social message or 'the prejudices that no longer prevail' to experience the delicious pleasure of romance" (2010, 132). And, indeed, the works we are here discussing, both the literary and the filmic, follow the Aristotelian pattern: "A whole is what has a beginning and middle and end " (*Poetics* 335 BC). In addition, as Ingo R. Stoehr suggests, romance novels provide "wish fulfilment for the socially powerless by using stereotypical variations of the Cinderella plot in which the poor girl finds out that she is really a rich princess—or at least, against all odds, she gets the rich prince for her husband" (2001, 21), as the main characters in *Heat and Dust* and *The Sky Above Darjeeling*, Olivia Rivers and Helena Lawrence, respectively, attain.

A brief overview of the plots of the novels to here discuss corroborate the statement above: *Heat and Dust* is the story of Olivia, a beautiful, spoiled, bored English colonial wife in the 1920s who is drawn inexorably into the spell of the Nawab, a minor Indian prince deeply involved in plots and intrigues. Olivia copes with the suffocating Indian town where her husband is a civil servant by eloping with the captivating Nawab. It is also the story of Olivia's step-granddaughter who, fifty years later, is drawn to India by her fascination with the letters left behind by the now deceased older woman, and by her obsession with solving the enigma of Olivia's scandal (in Murray 2017). On the other hand, *The Sky Above Darjeeling* opens with a setting in Cornwall in 1876, where Helena Lawrence, orphaned by the death of her father, finds herself financially ruined. When enigmatic Ian Neville enters her life seemingly out of the blue, he offers to provide for her livelihood if she agrees to marry him and start a new life on his tea plantation in the north of India, near Darjeeling. At first reluctant, Helena sees no alternative other than to accept his offer, first and foremost for the sake of her little brother Jason, still a boy. Helena, once in India, is mesmerized by its colors and exotic scents, and happiness seems to be within her reach. But among moments of brief closeness, Ian remains an enigmatic stranger to her. With the help of his confidante Mohan Tajid, Helena gets to know and understand Ian's past, and with it they reach happiness ever after (Vosseler 2006).

POSTCOLONIAL AND FEMINIST AGENDA

As we can see, both are romance novels written by European authoresses, with European female characters, who play the role of Cinderella, rescued by Indian princes, with whom they fall madly in love due to their exotic charm. Both novels can be classified, not only as the "Coldplay of literature," as I have already referred to, but also as *Frauenliteratur*, a term considered obsolete in the late twentieth and early twenty-first century, which has its main domain in romance novels. Harald Martenstein establishes the distinction between literature and *Frauenliteratur*, where the former includes literary works that women write especially for other women, considered literature by the experts, and the latter, books intended for a female readership and mainly bought by women, which is classified as women's literature (in Gerstenberger 2008, 224). For Evelyn Finger, *Frauenliteratur* "today denotes something along the lines of 'prosecco-tupperware-party-lovesickness-novels'" and "she argues that the same elements are at work in both the attempt to infuse *Frauenliteratur* with a feminist agenda as well as the effort to dismiss it as fluffy romance" (in Gerstenberger 2008, 224).

Not only do these novels embrace, at times, a postcolonial agenda, but also a feminist one, with an underlying romantic scent. Both Olivia and Helena do not see India as exotic as their British counterparts. For example, when discussing the sati, that the British see as barbaric, Olivia understands it "as part of their religion, isn't it? I thought one wasn't supposed to meddle with that. . . . And quite apart from religion, it *is* their culture and who are we to interfere with anyone's culture" (Jhabvala 1976, 58). Helena, on the other hand, sees the sati as a custom: "following their sati custom, they threw themselves into their husbands' pyres, so as to join them again in death, purified and sainted by fire, which protected them from a shameful life as widows, despite this custom being banned by the British fifty years before" (Vosseler 2015 [2006], 232, my translation). We could argue, then, that both works belong to the *Frauenliteratur* genre, since, as Claire Squires suggests, they hint "towards a form of writing beyond marketing" (2017, 16), with a postcolonial and feminist agenda, although a contrapuntal reading needs to take place in order to visualize such agendas. The marketing is there, both given by the Man Booker and by the romance genre, aimed mainly at a female audience. And, if we take into account the postcolonial critique, underneath, there is a conscious agenda, which attempts, although poorly achieving it so far, to the deconstruction of the I/Other.

We have to take into account, that the readership these European authoresses aimed at are Westerners, and the India they portray, seems more than heat, dust, and tea, although, unfortunately, it still fails within exotic boundaries. Om Prakash Dwivedi and Lisa Lu, editors of *Indian Writing in English and the Global Literary Market* (2014), include the following reflection to the volume, which we could apply to the former analysis: "if one carefully notices the parameters of success of Indian writers, it becomes seemingly clear that only those Indian writers have achieved remarkable success who either write from outside or who criticize India and its sensibility, thus producing eroticized versions of Indian culture" (2014, 100). This authoresses' alienness, like the one in Jhumpa Lahiri, Shauna Singh Baldwin, Michelle de Kretser, Sugu Pillay, but to name a few, takes places in *Heat and Dust*, where Jhabvala, diluting her identity within the East and the West, narrates a two-sided prism which, as Djoric Francuski underlines, distorts each other's picture of the other (2018, 8). Vosseler, as a German author and world traveler, also follows what was suggested by Om Prakash Dwivedi and Lisa Lu, making the reader love India but, at the same time, "eroticizing" it. If we link the explanation about exoticism given by these two authors and the marketability, we come to the conclusion that India is still pictured in both novels, despite a contrapuntal reading, as heat, dust, and tea. Even though, as I have already mentioned, *The Sky Above Darjeeling* avoids evident exoticism, its book cover, due to marketing purposes, fails to do so. In *Heat and Dust*'s book cover there are two British women, Olivia and her step-granddaughter, one dressed in western attire while the other one wears a shalwar kameez, and in *The Sky Above Darjeeling* there is a woman, Helena, wearing a sari. The sari explicitly displayed in a book cover contributes, as Martín-Lucas underlines, "to the eroticization of Indian culture and furthermore, to the commodification of Indian women's experiences as represented in the global(ized) narratives" (2014, 100). Jhabvala and Vosseler write outside India, criticize India, plus they create two European characters who at first seem to respect the "morals and manners" of the time to end up subsumed, due to love, to India. This love is full of passion and desire, but the fact that it is the love between a European woman and the Nawab, in one case, and a half-Indian half-British person, in the other, converts the female characters in passive, despite their renounce to everything for love, and the Indian/Others, in exotic. Thus, if we continue to explore women's roles in both novels, we cannot neglect the marketing paratexts that use their female bodies as we can see in the femininity of the visual images used, plus the key words employed in both titles: Heat, Dust, Darjeeling. All these facts allude explicitly to the oppression of the Others: women and India.

DOPPELGÄNGER

Not only are both novels written by European authoresses, highly acclaimed and awarded, who narrate a love story placed in India where the main characters are European women who fall madly in love with Indian men, where the time frame selected is the same, that is, the first half of the twentieth century, but they both portray a doppelgänger plot. The doppelgänger used by both authors ironically contrasts with the two-sided prism of the setting, East versus West and British women versus Indian men. In *Heat and Dust*, the narrator is the step-granddaughter of Douglas and Tessie Rivers. She was brought up with a forbidden topic in the family, namely to name the first wife of her grandfather, Olivia, who happens to be the main character in the novel together with the narrator. An old friend of Tessie Rivers and Douglas from India, named Harry, appears. He gives the family the old letters written by Olivia to her sister Marcia back in 1923. The narrator travels then to India to reconstruct the story of Olivia. Jhabvala differentiates the two beings, the step-grandmother and the step-granddaughter, who conform the literary doppelgänger, by separating their stories in chapters, addressing them by years in the case of Olivia's story: 1923, and by days and months, as diary entrances, in the case of the step-granddaughter. Both Olivia and the step-granddaughter go to India for different reasons: Olivia to rejoin her husband Douglas, and the step-granddaughter to discover Olivia's life. Both try to adjust to India: Olivia in 1923, before India's independence, and the step-granddaughter fifty years later. They seem to be involved in the Indian society trying not to judge and to leave aside prejudices. The reader the novel is addressed to, European, is in front of a text that although it still recreates stereotypes they seem to be diluted in the time span of the two tales. Her social engagement with the Indian society, Olivia with the Nawab, not fitting in their typical pattern of the Victorian women, and the step-granddaughter with Inder Lal's family, together with their pregnancy by Indian men, proves that they go a step beyond the I/They dichotomy. At the beginning, Olivia complies with Victorian expectations within the domestic sphere, like the fact of trying to make the home a comfortable place for her husband and acquaintances. She also spends her time playing piano, sewing, and wearing beautiful dresses not appropriated for India. She is somehow an outsider of the British-Indian families and that is the reason for her refusal to go to Shimla in the summer, where British-Indian women spent their time due to the extreme temperatures in their Indian home towns. When she gets pregnant she is in a moral dilemma because she does not know who the father is as it could be her husband or the Nawab. Consequences differ between both characters: Olivia has an abortion and is confined to ostracism by her in-mates, being taken care of by the Nawab, although she mostly spends her time in solitude except for the Nawab's visits. The step-granddaughter, on the other hand, attempts to have an abortion but when Maji massages her in order to cause it, she feels like something positive is transmitted to her and chooses to keep the baby. Both of them take a decision, although due to the time frame, the step-granddaughter's one is more freely chosen. The baby, just an embryo in the novel, could be the hybrid subject whom Vosseler, three decades later, gives life to.

In *The Sky Above Darjeeling*, the doppelgänger is represented by Ian/Rajiv, son of Sitara, Indian, and Winston, English, half Rajput and half Angrezi (448). Both his parents, due to their forbidden love, had to escape since the Raja, Dheeraj Chand, did not allow their love. He then returned home once his mother was killed during the Indian Rebellion and his father abandoned both his son and Mohan so as to revenge the death of his dear wife. Ian/Rajiv used his double identity to achieve whatever he proposed, as if the aim of Vosseler was to dilute binary thinking by offering the reader a hybrid character. We could also apply the doppelgänger to the parallel love relationship between Sitara and Winston, and years later, Helena and Ian. The former is a union made up of a native and a British, and the latter by a British, who was brought up during her childhood in Greece, and a hybrid. This way, Vosseler goes a step farther than Jhabvala, who in *Heat and Dust* offered two brave women as main characters, who, within the scope of decades, chose to remain in India. Vosseler, on the other hand, plays with the dichotomies breaking them by ending the novel with a happily ever after between a hybrid and a British. The union of the two characters will dilute hybridization, as if Vosseler was foretelling the planetary conviviality we were soon to critically discuss. Unfortunately, Vosseler, simultaneously, seems to use the Britishness of Ian/Rajiv to criticize the West, and the Indian-ness to soften Ian's power, exoticising him, still.

CONCLUSION

The exotic trope these authoresses use when dealing with India is latent. Marketability, such as that which the Man Booker involves, as Hugh Eakin suggests, despite its "'multicultural consciousness,' has arguably done less to further the development of 'non-Western' and/or postcolonial literatures" (in Huggan 2001, 106) and it still perpetuates exoticism. For Theodor Adorno "culture industry" is a structure that produces cultural commodities for mass audiences meanwhile supporting dominant political and economic interests (1996). Both *Heat and Dust* and *The Sky Above Darjeeling* place a European woman in India during the first half of the twentieth century, where history and landscape are alike. Within the scope of thirty years the exotic trope does vary but it is still used to "sell" India and, with it, to keep on inscribing India, to the European readers, as the Other. Nevertheless, literature, and film in the case of *Heat and Dust*, co-shape and interact with the cultural industry, "thereby claiming a positive and active role in the form of participatory culture" (Ponzanesi 2014, 2), but cultural difference, key to postcolonial critique, is, in the examples provided, still exotified.

ACKNOWLEDGMENT

The research for this essay was conducted in the framework of the research project "Politics, Aesthetics and Marketing of Literary Formulae in Popular Women's Fiction: History, Exoticism and Romance" (grant reference FFI2016–75130P) (MINECO/AEI/FEDER, UE), funded by the Spanish Ministry of Economy and Competitiveness.

REFERENCES

Adorno, Theodor W., and Max Horkheimer. 1996. *Dialectic of Enlightenment.* New York: Continuum.

Djoric Francuski, Biljana. 2018. "Other-languagedness in Stories by R. K. Narayan, Saadat Hassan Manto, and Ruth Prawer Jhabvala." *CLCWeb: Comparative Literature and Culture* 20.1.

Dwivedi, O., and L. Lau. 2014. *Indian Writing in English and the Global Literary Market.* New York: Palgrave Macmillan.

Gerstenberger, Katharina, and Patricia Herminghouse. 2008. *German Literature in a New Century: Trends, Traditions, Transitions, Transformations.* Oxford: Berghahn Books.

Gritten, David. 2006. "Why we should love and leave the world of Merchant Ivory." *The Telegraph.* March 25.

Huggan, Graham. 2001. *The Postcolonial Exotic. Marketing the Margins.* New York: Routledge.

Hussein, Aamer. 2013. "Ruth Prawer Jhabvala: more than *Heat and Dust.*" *The Telegraph.* April 12.

Krishnaswamy, Revathi, and J. C. Hawly (eds.). 2008. *The Postcolonial and the Global.* Minneapolis: Minnesota University Press.

Loomba, Ania, S. Kaul, M. Bunzl, A. Burton, and J. Esty (eds.). 2005. *Postcolonial Studies and Beyond.* London: Duke University Press.

Martín Lucas, Belén. 2014. "Of Saris and Spices: Marketing Paratexts of Indian Women's Fiction." In O. Dwivedi and L. Lau (eds.). *Indian Writing in English and the Global Literary Market.* New York: Palgrave Macmillan. 99–118.

Moreno-Álvarez, Alejandra. 2016. "Postcolonial Studies in the Twenty-First Century: A book review article of literature for our times & reading transcultural cities." *CLCWeb: Comparative Literature and Culture* vol. 18, no. 1.

Murray, John. 2017. *The Man Booker Prize. Heat and Dust.* http://themanbookerprize.com/books/heat-and-dust-by.html.

Ponzanesi, Sandra. 2014. *The Postcolonial Cultural Industry. Icons, Markets, Mythologies.* New York: Palgrave MacMillan.

Prawer Jhabvala, Ruth. 1975. *Heat and Dust.* London: Macdonald & Co.

———. 1998. *East Into Upper East. Plain Tales from New York and New Delhi.* Berkeley: Counterpoint.

Rothman, Joshua. 2013. "Ruth Prawer Jhabvala's Stories." *The New Yorker.* April 3.

Spencer, Robert. 2011. *Cosmopolitan Criticism and Postcolonial Literature.* London: Palgrave Macmillan.

Squires, Claire. 2007a. *Marketing Literature. The Making of Contemporary Writing in Britain.* New York: Palgrave Macmillan.

———. 2007b. "Book Marketing and the Booker Prize." In N. Matthews and N. Moody (eds.). *Judging a Book by its Cover: Fans, Publishers, Designers, and the Marketing of Fiction.* Ashgate: London, 2007b. 85–97.

Stoehr, Ingo R. 2001. *German Literature of the Twentieth Century. From Aestheticism to Postmodernism.* New York: Camden House.

Tatlock, Lynne (ed.). 2010. *Publishing Culture and the "Reading Nation." German Book History in the Nineteenth Century.* New York: Camden House.

Todd, Richard. 1996. *Booker Prize, Consuming Fictions: The Booker Prize and Fiction in Britain Today.* New York: Bloomsbury.

Vosseler, Nicole C. 2015. *El cielo sobre Darjeeling.* Translated by Jorge Seca. Barcelona: Ediciones B.

———. 2006. "The Sky Above Darjeeling." Last modified July 15, 2018. http://www.nicole-vosseler.com/buch_darjeeling.php.

Chapter Three

"[A] girl from the village: totally unspoilt"

Nazneen's "Unhomeliness" in Monica Ali's Brick Lane

Sam Naidu

In the introduction to *Home Truths: Fictions of the South Asian Diaspora in Britain*, Susheila Nasta describes "the construction of an aesthetic framework for the genesis of the South Asian literary diaspora" (2002, 6). Nasta is here referring to British-Asian authors whose literary endeavors "figure and frame a new architecture for the im/migrant imagination, an architecture built around the poetics of displacement and the poetics of home" (2002, 7). In this chapter I contend that such "an aesthetic framework" extends to South Asian diasporic locations around the globe, and includes in "the poetics of displacement and the poetics of home" the category of gender. A wide range of women writers of the South Asian diaspora utilize a shared architecture or transnational feminist aesthetic to express their preoccupation with the gendered experience of migration. Authored by Monica Ali, herself a British Asian, *Brick Lane* (2003) is selected as an exemplar that exhibits this common aesthetic. In particular, this chapter is concerned with the central character, Nazneen's "unhomeliness" in both London and her domestic space in Tower Hamlets, which, according to Homi Bhabha is the "estranging sense of the relocation of the home and the world in an unhallowed place" (1992, 141). Bhabha elaborates that "to be unhomed is not to be homeless, nor can the "unhomely" be easily accommodated in that familiar division of social life into private and the public spheres" (1992, 141). *Brick Lane*, I argue, traces both the poetics of displacement and of home in the private *and* public spheres inhabited by Nazneen.

First, however, the literary lineage of this particular form of novel writing needs to be historicized and theorized. The global increase in volume and popularity of novels by South Asian diasporic women writers necessitates placing these works within a narrative of women's literary history. Concerned with history[1] in relation to women's writing, Firdous Azim, in her text *The Colonial Rise of the Novel* (1993), weaves together feminist and postcolonial concerns about the novel genre:

> Women's writing, its connections with social realities, the novel as a form where women emerged to create a woman-to-woman discourse, or even the status of the novel as a form which questions and disrupts the narrative terrain within a fact/fantasy oscillation—are questions and issues that have been thoroughly examined within novel criticism. However, if a historical dimension is added to this examination (and by history I mean the history of the form itself, as well as the historical moment of the creation of texts, along with a history of its reception), the complexities of the genre will be highlighted, and the need for constant re-examination and perusal felt. (Azim 1993, 212–13)

Azim's suggestion is very similar to the project begun by Elaine Showalter in *A Literature of Their Own* (1977). Showalter's aim was to place women's writing within a historical and cultural framework and to examine the relationship between dominant and muted cultures within literary practice. Showalter's early focus, however, limited to white British middle-class women writers of mainly the nineteenth century, earned her much criticism from postcolonial feminist scholars. She was, as a result, deemed part of the "high" feminist norm that marginalized and universalized "Third World" women. Azim's suggestion is an attempt to counter this hegemony by introducing a "historical dimension" to feminist literary criticism. By creating a history of women's novel writing, specific moments in specific cultural contexts can be highlighted. At the same time, points of contiguity and patterns can be discerned from such a history. As far as novel writing by women of the South Asian diaspora is concerned, "connections with social realities, the novel as a form where women emerged to create a woman-to-woman discourse, or even the status of the novel as a form" is very much the focus of contemporary academic debate and discussion. The development of a significant body of literature by women writers with a similar geographical origin and cultural heritage, who are now dispersed across the globe but who share a literary aesthetic, should be recorded as part of the lineage of novel writing.

Novels by South Asian diasporic women writers are arguably most concerned with self-discovery, or self-recovery, in the diasporic home. But these forms of self-representation also involve degrees of both imitation and protest. These novels are rooted in the tradition of the canonical English novel and they bear a resemblance to novels by British women novelists of the eighteenth and nineteenth century.[2] They also share a similar "grounded aesthetic" with Indian, African-American, and Caribbean women's writing,[3] where grounded aesthetic is taken to refer to a process "where symbols and practices are selected, reselected, highlighted and recomposed to resonate further appropriated and particularised meanings" (Willis 1990, 21). The multiple influences of these antecedents and contemporaries combine with specific and new aesthetic elements to generate a distinctive diasporic, feminist novel.

The novels by women of the South Asian diaspora share many characteristics with some of the acclaimed realist novels by English women writers of the nineteenth century. Celebrated examples of women's writing from this phase would be Charlotte Brontë's *Jane Eyre* (1846), referred to as a "cult text of feminism" by Gayatri Spivak (1995, 244), or George Eliot's *Middlemarch* (1874), novels that Showalter has categorized as "feminine," by which she means concerned with imitation rather than protest or self-discovery (1977, 100). Despite significant points of departure from this novel tradition, some of the shared characteristics of the realist mode used in both historical phases are worth noting. For example, in both, a central narrating subject, or an omniscient narrator, narrates the life story of a single, central character, thereby constructing an authentic representation of that character's social reality. However, whereas *Jane Eyre* or *Middlemarch* have a definite, single heroine, Jane and Dorothea respectively, novels by South Asian diasporic women writers often include a secondary or "sister" heroine, as evidenced by the centrality of Nazneen and Hasina's relationship in *Brick Lane* (henceforth *BL*), thus widening the scope of the central consciousness. In many of the novels these sisterly, or matrilineal, bonds surpass all other loyalties and desires. Although Nazneen's is the central consciousness developed in *BL*, great care is taken to narrate the divergent lives of sisters Nazneen and Hasina, mainly through their epistolary relationship. The exploration of female relationships, matrilineal formations, and supportive sisterhoods is an important element in these texts.

A similar trend is evident in Indian, African-American, and Caribbean women's writing of the twentieth century. In the introduction to *Motherlands: Black Women's Writing from Africa, the Caribbean and South Asia* (1992), Susheila Nasta comments on the shared strategies of resistance in this women's writing working alongside its roots in older literary forms:

> The question of new languages and literary forms springing from old roots is central to the energy emanating from the development of women's writing in the regions under consideration here. (1992, xvi)

The new literary forms of the twentieth century created by these women writers acknowledge western novelistic conventions but move beyond an individual focus to encompass other female consciousnesses, intersubjective relationships between women, and female solidarity.

Common to both the nineteenth-century novels and contemporary ones is the desire to inscribe a unified female subjectivity. The significant difference in the formulation of this unified female subjectivity is that the nineteenth-century novel was strongly aligned with Western Enlightenment discourse. Azim argues that in the nineteenth-century novel, "the portrayal of the development of a rational and unified female subject" (1993, 189) was done at the expense of "others."[4] In the case of *Jane Eyre*, the "other" is the madwoman in the attic, Bertha Mason, who has to be destroyed before Jane can step into her new role as an integrated and liberated woman, this transition being symbolized by her marriage to Rochester. In the novels by South Asian diasporic women writers, a similar desire for a coherent female subjectivity is discernible, but this formulation is based on a positive rearticulation of the notion of difference. This new notion of difference was described by Gloria Anzaldúa in her celebration of the new *mestiza* as "a tolerance for contradictions, a tolerance for ambiguity" (1987, 79). In this conceptualization of difference, the "other" is incorporated rather than destroyed.[5] Azim points out how, in the late twentieth century, radical revisions in feminist literary criticism re-formulated the notion of an allegedly unified female subject: "The recognition of the impossibility of a coherent subject-position has led to an examination of the split subject, and the class and race significance of such a subject-position for feminism" (Azim 1993, 103). This split-subject is examined in *BL*, where both Nazneen and Hasina are racked with contradictory desires for freedom from family duties and cultural restraints, and for a sense of identity and belonging within their respective milieus.

In *BL* the notion of difference is utilized in two ways: by recording Nazneen's often traumatic and harsh encounters with difference resulting in her "unhomeliness"; and, then, by celebrating her creative synthesis of difference. *BL* is therefore a protest against discrimination or oppression based on difference but acknowledges the integral role played by difference in the formation of empowered female diasporic subjects. In *BL* the fateful Nazneen's "other" is the willful and seemingly self-destructive Hasina. Instead of destroying or obliterating the "other" in order for the heroine to triumph, Ali constructs a narrative that subtly delineates Nazneen's integration of the "other" until she is able to assert her will, defy her fate, and take control of her life. In this way Nazneen's multi-locationality—her affiliations to homeland and diasporic home, are reconciled. Using a "grounded aesthetic," Ali gestures to this reconciliation through the use of symbols. Nazneen is able to synthesize cultural differences she encounters in her everyday life, until she embodies this reconciliation when she dances to western popular music and ice skates in a sari. Instead of creating a unified female subject, Ali creates a hybrid subject who has incorporated aspects of the "other" rather than destroyed it, who has resisted her oppression as a "traditional" Bangladeshi wife, and who celebrates her myriad cultural influences without glossing over any of them. Unlike *Jane Eyre's* culmination in marriage,[6] symbolically a permanent state of balance and unity, *BL* ends with Nazneen repudiating both husband and an unsuitable lover, and then she enjoys a momentary transcendence on the ice. This glimpse of utopian freedom and syncretization of different selves is what gives the novel its transformative power in terms of female subjectivity.

A further and related similarity between nineteenth-century women's novels, the novels of the twentieth century, and novels by women of the South Asian diaspora, is the desire to inscribe a woman's voice in literature. In *Jane Eyre,* for example, the heroine develops from silenced, disempowered child to fulfilled, expressive, married woman. In fact, she becomes the extremely articulate narrator of this novel. Similarly, in *BL* a turning point in the narrative occurs when Nazneen speaks out against the usurer Mrs. Islam and her henchmen sons. This voice or ability to enunciate one's position or subjectivity is integral to the development of an empowered female subject. For both Jane Eyre and Nazneen their autonomy is predicated on their ability to speak authentically. It is only when their speech is in correspondence with their feelings that they begin to be liberated. Both heroines defy the rules of social behaviour, the decorum and the hierarchies of power which are part of their respective social contexts.

RESISTING REALISM IN THE SOUTH ASIAN DIASPORA

In various historical phases the use of the realist mode of novel writing recreates the social realities of women, highlights their plights as victims of patriarchal systems of oppression, inscribes a unified or empowered female subjectivity, and articulates a female voice in literature. Although there are other literary influences, the realist novels by contemporary women writers can be seen as the literary progeny of the nineteenth-century women's *bildungsroman* in English. The combination of the legacy of colonial education regimes, the globalization of western cultural forms, and the experience of common cultural constraints by these women writers separated by more than a century, has led to twentieth-century women writers and contemporary South Asian diasporic women writers adopting the realist mode of novel writing made so popular in nineteenth-century England. Although the realist mode does dominate, not all novels by women of the South Asian diaspora employ a consistently realist mode to address feminist or diasporic concerns. More generally and not as an exception, writing by women of the African diaspora employs "superstition and magic, which is another way of knowing things" (Morrison 1985, 342) in an attempt to retrieve the "discredited knowledge" (Morrison 1985, 342) of black people and to forge a new form of epistemology. Carolyn Cooper has studied this aesthetic element, particularly descriptions of spirit possession, in writing by women of the African diaspora, and has concluded that it "signifies both the dislocation and rearticulation of Afro-centric culture in the Americas" (1992, 64). In these novels, for example Morrison's *Tar Baby* (1981), the use of this narrative technique, the mingling of the metaphysical and the fantastic within a realist setting, is deployed also to express the themes of migration and cultural displacement.

Even in the generally realist *BL*, the narrative sometimes drifts into the realm of magic and fantasy. The accounts of Nazneen's dreams, memories and ghostly visions, for example, explore her unconscious and repressed desires, offering an alternative "reality" to the realism of the main narrative. Roger Bromley has noted that diasporic fiction often uses "both the dominantly constructed orders of discourse and the unsettling, undercutting and subversive orders of dream, the unconscious and the 'mad'" (Bromley 2000, 5).[7] In *BL* it is at these moments of mental flight and altered states of consciousness that the realist mode is challenged and extended. As the author attempts to represent gaps or rifts in the subject, it becomes almost impossible to maintain a homogeneous narration of linear progress. Ali, in this instance, it seems, is not driven to construct a seamless narrative with characters who exercise complete rationality and control over their emotions. Further, Ali extends and stretches the realist mode to focus on the fissures and ruptures of her subjects who "live 'border lives,' in between nation/s, past and present, inclusion and exclusion, negotiating 'liminal,' hybridised cultural identities that subvert the idea of an essentialised subject" (Bhabha 1994, 1). The literary lineage of novels by South Asian diasporic women shows its debt to its antecedents but also reveals their own aesthetic innovations and political interventions, especially with respect to creating liminal characters that subvert the notion of an essentialized subject and resist the dominance of the realist mode.

ALTERNATING BETWEEN PAST AND PRESENT, HOMELAND AND DIASPORIC HOME

BL traces the life of Nazneen from her ignominious birth in a Bangladeshi village to her maturity as an independent and assertive woman on a council estate in London. It contains a shadow protagonist in the form of Hasina, the wayward sister in Dhaka. The social detail is expansive, covering immigrant life in London and rural and urban life in Bangladesh, for various classes. Characters span three generations, and the political scope of the novel includes racism in England and the repercussions of 9/11. At the heart of the narrative is the construction of an empowered female subjectivity and the articulation of a diasporic female voice, but the novel also contains sensitive portrayals of male characters such as Chanu and Dr Azad.

Ali herself was born in Bangladesh and immigrated to the UK with her parents in 1971 when she was three years old, but Ali does not employ an autobiographical mode of narration. Instead, an omniscient narrator tells the story of Nazneen, a village girl who becomes a flat-bound, council estate wife, incorporating vivid descriptions of her memories, reminiscences, and dreams. A tone of nostalgia permeates the earlier descriptions of Nazneen's memories of childhood in the village of Gouripur. Through sketching Nazneen's relationship with her past early in the narrative, her "unhomeliness" is emphasized. She dreams and thinks of Gouripur frequently and with an intensity that is lacking in her external life in the flat at Tower Hamlets, East London. Almost every reminiscence features her sister Hasina or her unfortunate mother. As the narrator guides us through Nazneen's interior life and develops her consciousness, we see that she constantly makes comparisons between her old and new lives as she fervently tries to position herself in the present. She also displays a self-awareness about this process, sensing that her husband Chanu is unable to accept the present: "while she wanted to look neither to the past nor to the future, he lived exclusively in both" (*BL* 2003, 121).

Nazneen's relationship with the past and the home she has left behind is represented through alternative forms of consciousness—dreams, phantasmagoria, and "madness." Cooper calls these alternative forms of consciousness "zombification," and claims that it is a common technique used by African-American women writers to "define new spaces and realities for women" (1992, 64). In the initial stages of *BL* memories, dreams, fantasies, myths, and the supernatural are used to render Nazneen's bifurcated consciousness. Vertovec and Cohen have posited that diaspora may result in "fractured memories" or "a multiplicity of histories, 'communities' and selves." This "multiplicity," according to them, used to be viewed as schizophrenic or pathological but it is now being "redefined by diasporic individuals as a source of adaptive strength" (2001, xviii). Combining this fantastical or magical mode of narration—which affords the reader a peek into Nazneen's alternative forms of consciousness—with the realist framework results in a deeper understanding of Nazneen's fractured psyche and ensuing adaptive strength. Initially, her memories and daydreams reveal her loneliness and isolation in the alien, hostile environment she has traveled to as the result of a transaction between her father and her husband. The immigrant's tendency to idealize or romanticize the homeland is portrayed through Nazneen's imaginative reconstructions of an idyllic childhood spent in the company of her vivacious sister, Hasina. But that construct of home is gradually dismantled as Nazneen comes to apprehend the truth about her mother's misery and death. Thus we also see, in these episodes, Nazneen's struggle to repudiate traditional prescriptive gender roles that have been transplanted from her homeland to her diasporic home.

In the latter stages of the novel, Nazneen has another dream of her childhood in Gouripur, in which her mother is combing and braiding her hair. But during this homely, domestic scene, she becomes trapped and imprisoned by the mat she is sitting on, and the dream turns into a nightmare about being bound and suffocated, her mother being the symbol (victim and purveyor) of this oppression. A ghost scene follows the dream. Amma walks into Nazneen's kitchen wearing her Dhaka sari (her best sari that she put on to commit suicide) and tells Nazneen that she killed her baby son, Raqib, by believing that she had the power to keep him alive. Now Amma is the symbol of Nazneen's own repressed guilt and her misguided conscience, which hold her back and prevent her from asserting her will. This past has to be exorcised in order for Nazneen to transform herself from a fatalistic, obedient wife and mother, into an autonomous, assertive woman.

The tone of memory and nostalgia which is common to most novels by women of the South Asian diaspora, is amplified in *BL*, by Ali's use of dreams and phantasmagoria to explore the contradictions and paradoxes of the immigrant's relationship with the past. Nazneen's memories of her past sustain her but they also paralyze her in a state of subservience and fatalism. These journeys into her past and her unconscious mind offer a stark contrast to the realist mode of the rest of the narrative. These episodes, which afford the reader a glimpse of an inner life, threaten to disrupt the realist mode of the novel, and they split the subjectivity of Nazneen. These ruptures in the narrative and the split-subjectivity of the central character serve to represent poignantly the complex state of being "unhomed." Crucially, the reader becomes aware of how Nazneen's subjectivity is not rooted in one place or one time—she is multiply located and, alternating between diasporic home and homeland, albeit psychically, is paradoxically how she transitions from migrant to domicile.

MATRILINEAL FORMATIONS AND SISTERHOODS

For women writers of the South Asian diaspora, one way of constructing empowered female subjectivities is by anchoring their central characters in secure female bonds of empathy and solidarity, or by inscribing matrilineages. Jasbir Jain has commented on the positive use of this aesthetic element in diasporic women's writing: "Matrilineage is a strong trope in the work of several diasporic women writers, for in this condition of uprootedness, one is free to imagine the absent and allow suppressed relationships and histories to surface" (2002, 143). These constructions recuperate the strength and power of women within family structures. At the same time, many of these novels examine the complicity of women in their own oppression and the oppression of other women. For instance, in *BL*, Amma's victimhood is transferred to Nazneen in the form of an indoctrinated fatalism that proves to be a serious handicap to Nazneen for many years.

For Nazneen, her suppressed relationship with her mother surfaces as she confronts a new life in the present. Her inner life is dominated by images of her mother and her sister. In addition to these imaginings of Amma, she engages in a highly formative epistolary relationship with her much-loved sister, Hasina. At the close of *BL*, we see Nazneen participating in a women-only business venture, surrounded by her best friend, Razia, and her daughters. The significance of these female relationships to the inscription of Nazneen's subjectivity is far-reaching, impacting on both the social and personal dimensions of identity formation.

At the outset, Hasina's primary role in Nazneen's emotional life is made clear. The only indication of will in the newly-married, brand-new immigrant, Nazneen, is to be seen in her desire for a letter from Hasina (*BL* 2003, 51). Before the birth of her children Nazneen seems to have loved only one person, Hasina. Nazneen's act of writing carefully constructed and censored narratives of her "happy" new life in London is a survival strategy for her (*BL* 2003, 142). In these letters she maintains the role of a dutiful, pious wife and fortunate immigrant that she has assumed in her external life at Tower Hamlets. In contrast, Hasina's letters are candid, crude and compassionate, brimming over with realistic detail of her often tragic life in Dhaka:

> Nazneen composed and recomposed her replies until the grammar was satisfactory, all errors expunged along with any vital signs. But Hasina kicked aside all such constraints: her letters were full of mistakes and bursting with life. (*BL* 2003, 94)

Some critics have been skeptical about this stylistic device, noting that the idiom Ali has used for Hasina's letters is distracting and unconvincing, perhaps even deprecating.[8] But I would argue that the overall effect of the use of pidgin English in the novel is to highlight that the characters are in fact Bengali-speaking, and this serves to highlight Nazneen's struggle to assimilate into an alien culture. Ali has also been accused of cramming too much social detail into these letters, thus creating in Hasina a crudely-wrought political mouthpiece.[9] Admittedly, there is something jarring between the simplicity of her translated-from-Bengali idiom and the chilling perspicacity with which she reports on subjects ranging from wife mutilation and prostitution to standards of beauty in Bangladesh and the hypocrisy of the middle classes. But most significantly, the letters at first serve to highlight the glaring contrast between the characters of the sisters, and then the gap between them begins to narrow as Nazneen becomes more assertive and less fatalistic.

Crucial to her process of transformation and adaptation is Nazneen's realization that Hasina is not just a victim of fate, "a life which has been tossed and twisted like a baby rat, naked and blind, in the jaws of a dog" (*BL* 2003, 340). By the end of the narrative Nazneen apprehends Hasina's agency and she understands what drives Hasina to make defiant and seemingly rash choices. So when Chanu asks: "Why did she do it? Why does she do these things?" Nazneen answers "Because, [. . .] she isn't going to give up" (*BL* 2003, 490). Quietly celebrating Hasina's self which has been "other" to her fatalistic, obedient self since childhood, Nazneen acknowledges her own will to live her life on her own terms. This remarkable relationship between Nazneen and Hasina places them in a long line of literary daughters, such as Elinor and Marianne in Jane Austen's *Sense and Sensibility* (1811), and Ramatoulaye and Aissatou in Mariamma Bâ's *So Long a Letter* (1982), who, through their love and support of one another, celebrate the notion of a sisterhood.

Hasina is also the one who exposes Nazneen to the bald truth about their mother's suffering and suicide:

> Amma always say we are women what can we do? If she here now I know what she say I know it too well. But I am not like her. Waiting around. Suffering around. She wrong. So many ways. At the end only she act. She who think all path is closed for her. She take only one forbidden. (*BL* 2003, 434)

Whereas Hasina expresses understanding of but also resistance to her mother's life, Nazneen's relationship with her mother is characterized by meek obedience and repression, a replication of her mother's stance in the face of an entrenched system of patriarchal oppression. Thus Nazneen represses the truth about the destructiveness of her mother's self-denial in life "I don't want anything from this life [. . .] I ask for nothing. I expect nothing" (*BL* 2003, 102), and ultimately in death, perceiving it rather as "her mother's quiet courage, her tearful stoicism" (*BL* 2003, 15). It is only when Nazneen acknowledges the full extent of her mother's capitulation and the anger she feels toward her that she can begin to break free from the cycle of oppression. While in hospital watching over her sick son Raqib, Nazneen is tempted to relinquish all agency to God and fate, but then she remembers her mother's fatalism and is angered into the realization that her mother, the saint, was wrong to abandon her child and then spend the rest of her life playing the role of a martyr: "At once she was enraged. A mother who did nothing to save her own child!" (*BL* 2003, 135).

The full horror of her mother's suffering and the sentence of victimhood, which had been transferred from mother to daughter, is realized in the "zombification" (Cooper 1992, 64) scene that culminates in Nazneen's nervous breakdown. Nazneen allows her years of repressed resentment and unhappiness to surface. She is also overcome with guilt about her affair with Karim. All the disgust and discontent she has felt toward Chanu and her imprisoned state since her marriage are projected onto this grotesque image of Amma which appears to her in this moment of mental anguish. The image of the apparition is archetypal, resembling a harpy or succubus (or *jinni*), preying on its victim:

> "No, baby, come to me." She pulled harder, so hard that Nazneen gave way and slid down to the floor. "It's easy." Amma began to cackle, and she did not cover her teeth and her mouth became wider and wider and the teeth became longer and sharper and Nazneen put up her hands to cover her face. "It's easy. You just have to endure." (*BL* 2003, 323)

Amma's adherence to this belief "You just have to endure" led to her own mental breakdown when Nazneen was eight or nine years old. The story of Amma's breakdown is recounted in Ali's story-within-a-story of "the year that Amma became possessed by an evil jinni" (*BL* 2003, 398) and a *fakir* was employed to exorcise the *jinni*. Both Amma's stoicism and the *fakir*'s sham are unmasked in this reminiscence. Amma's constant chanting of her mantra of suffering and endurance is not authentic. It masks her repressed anger that is unleashed by the *jinni*. The violence that is released is in direct contrast to the passive, stoical pose of the martyr—the role usually adopted by Amma. This violence, ultimately self-directed, is echoed in Nazneen's ghostly imagining of her mother, a symbolic image that has to be exorcised before Nazneen can assert her will and adopt a self-realizing strategy of defiance and liberation. In this depiction of a mother-daughter relationship we see a power struggle between a self-defeatist mother who continues to wield power from beyond the grave, and a daughter who struggles not only against the patriarchs who controlled her life, but also against the mother who tutored her to give in to them. In her quest for autonomy, Nazneen is aided by the solidarity and camaraderie of women like herself. At Tower Hamlets, Nazneen encounters, for the first time as an adult, the company of other women in the communal space of the council estate. It is through a crucial relationship with the spirited, gossiping, observant Razia that Nazneen becomes less isolated. Razia communicates to Nazneen her knowledge about the suffering of other women on the estate (*BL* 2003, 71). Unconventional and irreverent, Razia, helps Nazneen test the boundaries of her role as traditional wife and mother. The two women discuss their ridiculous husbands and their respective marriages and through the curative power of laughter sustain each other during domestic crises and tragedies. Razia defies the norm for a Bengali wife or widow and is unconcerned when her appearance makes her a figure of ridicule in her community. She cuts her hair, smokes, wears trousers, goes to work in a factory and learns English. Nazneen's transformation in the diasporic setting is never as extreme or overt as Razia's, but the two women share a desire to adapt and be independent. At the close of the narrative, it is Razia who shows entrepreneurial zeal by starting a fashion business that employs women on the estate (*BL* 2003, 480). In the final scene of the novel Nazneen is surrounded by Razia and her two daughters, and it is Razia's words that close the novel and proclaim the achievement of women like themselves who have negotiated empowered and liberated lives in the diasporic location: "'This is England,' she said. 'You can do whatever you like'" (*BL* 2003, 492).

TRANSPLANTED TRADITIONS: NAZNEEN'S REBELLION AGAINST MARRIAGE

The prevalence of the theme of marriage in literature by women of the South Asian diaspora is indicative of the feminist commitment of the literature. In this literature, the "traditional" South Asian marriage is most often portrayed as an institution that oppresses women: an arranged marriage is a transaction between the bride's parents and her in-laws; it is based on a code of conduct that keeps the woman imprisoned within the confines of the home; it reduces the woman to the functions of her body; it erases her sexuality and enslaves her body; unmarried women and widows are burdens to their families and are often treated as outcasts. For many immigrants this code of conduct, or variations of it, is transplanted to the diasporic location. As Alistair Cormack points out, *BL* "is particularly of interest as an examination of the double bind that female migrants face, treated as alien by their host nation and as commodities by the men in their own communities" (700).

Very early in her marriage, Nazneen overhears a telephone conversation in which Chanu describes her as:

> Not tall. Not short. Around five foot two. Hips are a bit narrow but wide enough, I think, to carry children. All things considered, I am satisfied. . . . What's more she is a good worker. Cleaning and cooking and all that. The only complaint I could make is she can't put my files in order, because she has no English. I don't complain though. As I say, a girl from the village: totally unspoilt. (*BL* 2003, 23)

This description that designates for her the role of child-bearer and domestic servant, also establishes the power dynamic in the relationship between husband and wife. Chanu has bestowed on Nazneen her functional value to him; he has plucked her from an obscure village in Bangladesh and brought her, in her state of both moral and cultural purity, to London to serve his needs. He controls her destiny, shapes her subjectivity, and determines her worth, it seems. The description also strips away any romantic notions the naïve Nazneen might have had about love or sexual desire as part of the marital relationship. But although Nazneen chastises herself for expecting more from her marriage—"She realized in a stinging rush she had imagined all these things. Such a foolish girl. Such high notions. What self-regard" (*BL* 2003, 23)—she is deeply disturbed by the prison-like situation she is in. This disturbance in her psyche is represented through her fear of the wardrobe—"Sometimes she dreamed the wardrobe had fallen on her, crushing her on the mattress. Sometimes she dreamed she was locked inside it and hammered and hammered but nobody heard" (*BL* 2003, 24). This trope of spatial confinement serves to spotlight both the physical and mental restraints imposed on Nazneen by various structures of patriarchy.

In the early days of her marriage Nazneen survives this confinement through a combination of sustaining memories of home; Hasina's letters; the routine of domestic life; and the adoption of the role designated for her by Chanu. In an act of mimicry,[10] she performs the role of innocent, ignorant girl from the village in order to get her own way. For example, her desire for a new bed is skillfully handled in an exchange with Chanu (*BL* 2003, 51) that reveals her superior intelligence and ability to manipulate him. The narrative of Nazneen and Chanu's marriage can be broken down into phases that indicate the development of Nazneen as an empowered female character. At first, she is mindful of the code of conduct, which prescribes her role as wife, but she is not without insurrection against its injustices or the capacity to wield a certain degree of power within its parameters. Then, after years of Chanu's tyranny as patriarch in the home and growing incompetence outside of the home, Nazneen's resistance to the network of taboos that bind her becomes more overt. She becomes self-employed and embarks on an affair with Karim. But the disjuncture between her inner thoughts and outward behavior leads ultimately to a mental breakdown. After the breakdown, she is openly defiant to Chanu and more forceful as a mother. Finally, as Chanu's unilateral decision to return to Bangladesh becomes more and more of a reality, and Karim's presumptions about her desires begin to oppress her, she repudiates both her marriage to Chanu and Karim's offer of marriage. Marriage then is another yoke she must throw off in order to be autonomous and authentic. Ali's treatment of this theme of marriage is expansive, detailed, and complex, showing the plight of South Asian women who are trapped by the oppressive institution of traditional marriages. She also conveys strongly the notion that women can negotiate the parameters of marriage, either by shifting them or repudiating them.

One of the gravest transgressions against traditional marriage is adultery, and so it comes as something of a shock to the reader when the pious Nazneen embarks on an affair with Karim. Her insurrections until this point in the narrative have been minor ones that went unnoticed. Through this affair Nazneen explores her sexuality and experiences autonomy over her body after years of submission to and revulsion for Chanu. This transgressive sexual desire is just as potentially dangerous to Nazneen as it is liberating. It could trap her in guilt and lead her to replicate her role as submissive wife with Karim, who sees marriage as the only logical outcome of their affair. Like Jane in *Jane Eyre*, Nazneen has to curb this sexual desire. In the Victorian novel, the dangerous sexual desire, symbolized by Bertha Mason and figured as madness and passion, is destroyed. In novels such as Walker's *The Color Purple* (1982), or Arundhati Roy's *The God of Small Things* (1997), transgressive sexual acts signify a transcendence of and freedom from societal norms. For Nazneen, her sexual desire is at first suppressed, then kindled and realized in the affair with Karim, and finally it is translated into self-knowledge and autonomy that is articulated when she turns down Karim's marriage offer.

At this point Nazneen is experiencing her first taste of power and agency but her consciousness still works in the old way and she still believes that fate is stronger than the individual will. As she becomes more sexually confident, she also becomes more defiant and more desirous of abandoning the role of dutiful wife: "He held a hand across her throat and she wanted everything: to vanish inside the heat like a drop of dew, to feel his hand press down and extinguish her, to hear Chanu come in and see what she was, his wife" (*BL* 2003, 343). Ali demonstrates how this sexual pleasure and expression of the body, what the French feminists would call *jouissance*,[11] is a conduit for a new subjectivity for Nazneen, who does eventually come to realize the power of her will.

CONCLUSION

This chapter has argued that *BL* is an account of Nazneen's journey from unhomed village girl to empowered, liberated, domiciled woman, but the village girl is never entirely jettisoned. Rather, Ali has created a protagonist who reconciles her multiple selves after a series of psychic episodes—confrontations with repressed selves and fears. Showing how the novel: resists the realist mode; evokes alternative consciousnesses for the protagonist who is initially deeply fractured by migration; examines matrilineal formations and creates a sisterhood; and, critiques the patriarchal institution of marriage, the chapter has demonstrated that Nazneen is a migrant figure who moves from extreme "unhomeliness" to a sense of belonging and a state of autonomy. She incorporates and synthesizes difference by being able to make a "home" in London without ever completely letting go of the memories, lessons and bonds which tie her to Gouripur. *BL* shows that a loosening of these ties to the homeland is inevitable but not complete, and thus Nazneen's two very different homes constitute the new, domiciled Nazneen. In a series of defiant, liberating, self-affirming acts in both the private and the public spheres, Nazneen evinces an adaptive strength that is impressive: she repudiates fatalism and the burden of her mother's anger and guilt; she develops a voice, courageously standing up to the Islams; she concocts a plan to get rid of Chanu thus throwing off the yoke of marriage; and she reclaims her body by ending her relationship with Karim with quiet determination. The result is a character who is an assertive bread-winner and protector of her family.

The full extent of Nazneen's resilience is foreshadowed earlier in the novel when a fit of anger against Chanu's ineffectuality causes her to celebrate internally her achievement as a non-English speaking Bangladeshi woman lost, alone and pregnant in London:

> *Anything is possible.* She wanted to shout it. Do you know what I did today? I went inside a pub. To use the toilet. Did you think I could do that? I walked mile upon mile around the whole of London, although I did not see the edge of it. And to get home I went to a restaurant. I found a Bangladeshi restaurant and asked directions. See what I can do! (*BL* 2003, 62–63)

This ability to observe, adapt, assimilate, blend cultural influences, defy stereotypes and find fulfillment is what confers upon Nazneen the status of heroine in this novel. Similar to Anzaldúa's new *mestiza*, Nazneen's strength is her ablility to reconcile difference and thus she "learns to juggle cultures" (1987, 79). What is also significant is that Nazneen, like Hasina, arguably the other heroine of the novel, learns to exercise her will and take risks in order to fulfill her desires. The closing, incongruous image of the novel is of Nazneen, in a sari about to physically step onto an ice rink (*BL* 2003, 492). Her fantasies about ice skating were about to become a reality, but the underlying significance of the fantasy had already been realized. The girl from the village had achieved freedom, mobility, stability, form, and grace in her new home.

NOTES

1. The relationship between history and the novel has been most notably theorized by Georg Lukács who saw the central subject of the realist novel as the carrier of its ideological content, representing changing social and economic conditions (1977, 5).

2. For example, Charlotte Brontë's *Jane Eyre* or George Eliot's *Middlemarch*. Incidentally, Susan Koshy refers to Bharati Mukherjee's *Jasmine* as a "confident appropriation of the Jane Eyre story" (1994, 72).

3. For example, Alice Walker's *The Color Purple* or Toni Morrison's *Song of Solomon*.

4. Azim's broader theory is that "the birth of the novel coincided with the European colonial project; it partook of and was part of a discursive field concerned with the construction of a universal and homogenous subject. This subject was held together by the annihilation of other subject positions" (Azim 1993, 30).

5. Gloria Anzaldúa's formulation of the *mestiza* consciousness is useful here:

The new *mestiza* copes by developing a tolerance for contradictions, a tolerance for ambiguity. She learns to juggle cultures. She has a plural personality, she operates in a pluralistic mode—nothing is thrust out, the good, the bad and the ugly, nothing rejected, nothing abandoned. Not only does she sustain contradictions, she turns the ambivalence into something else. (1987, 79)

6. *Jane Eyre* ends with the following words: "Reader, I married him" (1977, 474). Marriage in this context has been read as a triumph for Jane albeit a conservative, bourgeois triumph.

7. Perhaps the most famous examples of this mode of writing in a South Asian diasporic text is Salman Rushdie's *Midnight's Children* (1995) which features his fantastical, telepathic, one thousand and one midnight's children.

8. See Mahmud Rahman's review of *Brick Lane* on the SAWNET website http://www.sawnet.org/books/reviews.php?Brick+Lane (accessed March 21, 2018); and Nicola Walker's review "The State of Bengali England" on http://www.theage.com.au/articles/2003/08/20/1061368348340.html (accessed March 21, 2018).

9. See Sukhdev Sandhu's review of *Brick Lane* in *London Review of Books*, vol. 25, no. 19, October 9, 2003.

10. See Homi Bhabha's definition of mimicry in "Of mimicry and man: The ambivalence of colonial discourse" (1994, 85–92).

11. See the introduction to Elaine Marks and de Courtivron, Isabelle (eds.) *New French Feminisms: An Anthology* (1980) for a lengthy definition of *jouissance* and the feminist significance of the term.

REFERENCES

Ali, Monica. 2003. *Brick Lane*. London: Black Swan.

Anzaldúa, Gloria 1987. *Borderlands: The New Mestiza/La Frontera*. Berkeley, CA: Third World Press.

Azim, Firdous. 1993. *The Colonial Rise of the Novel*. London: Routledge.

Bhabha, Homi, K. 1992. "The World and the Home," *Social Text*, 31.32: 141–53.

———. 1994. *The Location of Culture*. London: Routledge.

Bromley, Roger. 2000. *Narratives for a New Belonging: Diasporic Cultural Fictions*. Edinburgh: Edinburgh University Press.

Brontë, Charlotte. 1846, 1977. *Jane Eyre*. Harmondsworth: Penguin.

Cooper, Carolyn. 1992. "'Something Ancestral Recaptured': Spirit Possession as Trope in Selected Feminist Fictions of the African Diaspora." In Nasta, Susheila (ed.). *Motherlands: Black Women's Writing from Africa, the Caribbean and South Asia*. New Brunswick: Rutgers University Press. 64–87.

Cormack, Alistair. 2006. "Migration and the Politics of Narrative Form: Realism and the Postcolonial Subject in *Brick Lane*," *Contemporary Literature*, 47.4: 695–721.

Jain, Jasbir. 2002. *Writing Women Across Cultures*. Jaipur and New Delhi: Rawat Publishers.

Koshy, Susan. 1994. "The Geography of Female Subjectivity: Ethnicity, Gender, and Diaspora." *Diaspora: A Journal of Transnational Studies* 3, 1: 69–83.

Lukács, Georg. 1977. "Realism in the Balance." In F. Jameson (ed.). *Aesthetics and Politics*. London: New Left Books.

Marks, Elaine, and de Courtivron, Isabelle (eds.). 1980. *New French Feminisms: An Anthology*. Amherst: University of Massachusetts Press.

Morrison, Toni. 1985. "Rootedness: The Ancestor as Foundation." In Maria Evans (ed.). *Black Women Writers*. Pluto Press: London. 340–54.

Nasta, Susheila (ed). 1992. *Motherlands: Black Women's Writing from Africa, the Caribbean and South Asia*. New Brunswick: Rutgers University Press.

———. 2002. *Home Truths: Fictions of the South Asian Diaspora in Britain*. Houndmills/Basinstoke: Palgrave.

Sandhu, Sukhdev. 2003. "Come hungry, leave edgy." *London Review of Books*, 25, 19: 10–13.

Rahman, Mahmud. 2003. Review of *Brick Lane* by Monica Ali. On the SAWNET website. http://www.sawnet.org/books/reviews.php?Brick+Lane (accessed March 21, 2018).

Shukla, Sandhya. 2001. "Locations for South Asian Diasporas." *Annual Review of Anthropology* 30: 551–72.

Showalter, Elaine. 1977 (revised 1999). *A Literature of Their Own*. London: Virago Press.

———. (ed.). 1985. *The New Feminist Criticism: Essays on Women, Literature and Theory*. New York: Pantheon Books.

Spivak, Gayatri. 1995. "Three Women's Texts and a Critique of Imperialism." In Bill Ashcroft, Gareth Griffiths, and Helen Tiffin (eds.). *The Postcolonial Studies Reader*. London: Routledge. 269–72.

Vertovec, Steven, and Robin Cohen. "Introduction." In Steven Vertovec and Robin Cohen (eds.). *Migration, Diasporas and Transnationalism* (Cheltenham: Elgar Reference Collection, 2001), xiii–xxviii.

Walker, Nicola. 2003. "The State of Bengali England." Review of *Brick Lane* by Monica Ali. http://www.theage.com.au/articles/2003/08/20/1061368348340.html (accessed March 21, 2018).

Willis, Paul. 1990. *Common Culture: Symbolic Work at Play in the Everyday Cultures of the Young*. Milton Keynes: Open University Press.

Part II

Shifting Domiciles

Chapter Four

Ethnography of a Hyphen? The Gendering of Gen-X Diasporic Agency

Gurbir Singh Jolly

AN ASSESSMENT OF ASSUMPTIONS

Working in English literary studies, I suspect that I am not the only member of my academic clan susceptible to assuming our semblances to ethnographers are scarce. After all, ethnographers travel, live with communities that have long evoked otherness within the Western imaginary. Ethnographers analyze cultural patterns—kin relationships, rites of passage, mourning rituals, and so on. English students sit in libraries, commonly work with canonical texts within the Western imaginary, analyzing aesthetic patterns—allusions, metaphors, lexical sets, and such. The assumption of difference *seems* safe enough: ethnographers write about cultural facts; students of literature write about literary fictions. Each discipline appears to have marked its territory in the academe, and there seems little reason for the twain to meet. The two disciplines, however, have been meeting. When considering methods of interpreting gendered ethnicity in second-generation diasporic writers' narrations of their transfigured Indian heritage, this chapter attempts to illustrate some of the discursive intersections between the seemingly disparate practices privileged in anthropology and English literary studies. Although far from constituting a marriage of minds, interdisciplinary encounters between ethnographers and students of literature have kindled thoughtful perspectives on the ideological and aesthetic designs informing how texts "represent" culturally, ethnically, and nationally circumscribed communities. This chapter proposes that the disciplinary soul-searching ventured by prominent ethnographers, nearly two decades ago, remains instructive, if not cautionary, for interpreting the contours of cultural belonging narrativized by second-generation, South Asian Canadian/American, "Gen-X" women writers of *their* time and beyond. The disciplinary soul-searching troubling ethnographic study wrestled with the ethics, conventions, and presumptions mediating how cultural "otherness" could be engaged and represented. These concerns may still prove prescient when discerning how second-generation South Asian-Canadian/American autobiographical writing, particularly by women born to post-World War II immigrants, commonly confronts modernist, ethnographically-oriented conventions of identifying "otherness," conventions that evince tenacious literary sway and risk constraining narrations of second-generation selfhood.

My discussion of this confrontation opens by briefly detailing how and why certain schools of ethnography and literary studies had been flirting with each other's interests and methods. The chapter then discusses a shared foil—essentialism—that could and can frequently inform and strain ethnicity-focused, ethnographically-oriented *literary* engagements with identification. Despite being long since refuted by developments in anthropology, essentialist myths of "pure" identities—North American or South Asian— evince the resiliency of a colonial zeitgeist, one thickly laced with ethnographically-inclined, axiomatically colonial contrasts between selfhood and otherness. These dated-but-tenacious dynamics can prove deeply disorienting along several intersecting axes of second-generation girlhood, bedeviling how second-generation narratives of heritage and belonging risk vividly riddling modernist, ethnographic conventions of situating femininity. Explicit, modernist ethnographic constructs of essential "otherness" continue to command unsettling currency in nationalist, racialized, and gendered constructs of identification, recognition, and belonging. This currency bespeaks a storied history of ethnographically inscribing ethnicity, a history that complemented colonial literary renderings of the colonized, and a history that can continue to complicate diasporic South Asian women's inscriptions of girlhood within narrative reclamations of selfhood. Although my chapter focuses the dynamics of these complications as weathered by second-generation, turn-of-the-twenty-first-century, "Generation X" Indo-American and Indo-Canadian women, readers will likely recognize generationally morphed forms of these dynamics haunting more contemporary texts. Essentialist formulations of heritage and otherness could and can be particularly violating for young women who, as the children of Indian immigrants, have had their agency over cultural identifications simultaneously sexualized and policed. In tandem with the gendered racism (or racialized misogyny) that can corrode a second-generation sense of belonging, the pressures to "preserve" (or counterpressure to reject) essentialist formulations of heritage can be formidable. My discussion then considers reading approaches that strived to engage the gendered, ethnographic dynamics of second-generation diasporic narratives of self. These reading strategies attempted to disabuse us of surprisingly dogged inclinations to assess whether these writers' identifications were, impossibly, either "faithful manifestations" of their author's narrowly ideal-ized ethnic heritage or the similarly ideologically-filtered, racialized, Anglo-dominant zeitgeist of their North American milieu. Pursuing a narrow ideal of selfhood can prove as destructive as trying to look like a Photoshopped image of yourself; pursuing two narrow ideals of selfhood renders the futility of the chase painfully unredeemable.

Forefronting these concerns, my discussion critiques strictures of how ethnicity and culture have, historically, been ethnographically delimited. My discussion then proposes approaching second-generation authors' narratives as ethnographies of a hyphen, as ethnographies that do not delimit an identity as much they deconstruct assumed limits of identification: that is, as ethno-graphic narratives engaging struggles and strategies, principally by second-generation girls and young women of color, to assert agentive identifications with their heritages despite weathering racist and sexist duress expressed in discourses of nationalist cultural "purity" and "defilement."

ETHNOGRAPHY AS LITERATURE, LITERATURE AS ETHNOGRAPHY

Since the mid-1980s, references to literary works accrued increasing prece-dent in experimental and feminist ethnographic writing. James Clifford, a prominent historian of ethnography, began the introductory chapter of his book, *The Predicament of Culture*, by quoting and discussing a lengthy sec-tion of a William Carlos William poem (Clifford 1988, 2–3). In her essay "Identifying Ethnography," oft-cited feminist ethnographer Kamala Viswes-waran analyzed a poem by second-generation Indo-American writer Kalpana Vrudhula, beautifully titled, "Do Not Belong to This or That, but I Am Here" (Visweswaran 1994, 121). The concluding chapter of *Translated Woman*, the highly-recognized ethnographic work of Cuban-American anthropologist Ruth Behar, summarizes its arguments by citing a poem by Pat Mora (Behar 1993, 321). In *Writing Culture*, an anthology which Clifford coedited, Mi-chael Fischer's essay, "Ethnicity and the Post-Modem Arts of Memory" attempts an ethnographic reading of American autobiographies, liberally quoting from poets to aid Fischer's exegesis. In *Women Writing Culture,* an anthology Behar coedited, Paula Ebron's and Anna Lowenhaupt Tsing's essay, "In Dialogue?" attempts an ethnographic reading of "African American and Chinese American narratives of identity, as found in recent works of fiction" (Ebron and Tsing 1995, 391). By treating literature as an ethnographic resource, these writers were not only building interdisciplinary bridges, they were challenging fundamental disciplinary assumptions that have guided modem anthropological and literary studies. As Visweswaran notes, "To argue that ethnography is literature is to remind us of presumptions about literature, to ask again, What is literature? To argue that literature is ethnography is to cause reflection about the functions of ethnography, to ask again, What is ethnography?" (Visweswaran 1994, 1).

Though these daunting questions continue to be debated, ethnographers who include literature in their work certainly depart from the strict methods of early twentieth-century ethnographers, like Bronislaw Malinowski, who remained interested in the "physics and chemistry of history and ethnography" (Visweswaran 1994, 5). As long as ethnographers like Malinowski stuck to such positivist pursuits of ethnographic knowledge, they could not explicitly embrace the literary dimensions of their work. As Clifford explained,

> Western science has excluded certain expressive modes from its legitimate repertoire: rhetoric (in the name of "plain," transparent signification), fiction (in the name of fact), and subjectivity (in the name of objectivity). The qualities eliminated from science were localized in the category of "literature." Literary texts were deemed to be metaphoric and allegorical, composed of inventions rather than observed facts; they allowed a wide latitude to the emotions, speculations, and subjective "genius" of their authors. (Clifford 1986, 5)

Predictably, abandoning "scientific" models of culture involved acknowledging "ethnographic texts cannot avoid expressive tropes, figures, and allegories that select and impose meaning as they translate it" (Clifford 1986, 7). Or, as David Moore summarized the argument at the time: "anthropology's 'objective' rendering of other cultures is in fact largely a product of a literary genre called ethnographic realism, composed of a complex set of masking tropes (e.g., the representation of the native point of view, the marking of fieldwork)" (Moore 1994, 358). Clifford's and Moore's comments characterize a position held by certain anthropologists who are anxious to acknowledge and study the "latitude of emotions" (Moore 1994, 358) and genre conventions that richly furnish the literary underpinnings of ethnographic encounters.

As these anthropologists started taking an interest in literature, communities within English literary studies began taking increasing interest in literature written by the traditional objects of anthropological study: third-world Others and, more recently, their diasporic descendants. Deepika Bahri's still-compelling essay, "Coming to Terms With 'The Postcolonial'" details the history and growth of this literary focus. Bahri summarized why the term that most commonly identifies these other-authored texts—"postcolonial literature"—can invite much criticism. Despite Bahri's strong critique of the often vague, euphemistic, and disingenuous application of "postcolonial," the term at very least drew attention to a series of related debates in the Western academy regarding crises in the politics of literary representation. As Aijaz Ahmad noted,

> the West learned to question their own place in the world, and hence also to question the hegemonic closure of the texts upon which their epistemologies were based. One of the side-effects of that overall crisis was that literature was pressed to disclose the strategic complicities whereby it had traditionally represented races—and genders—and empires. (Ahmad 1994, 58)

Interestingly, as anthropologists increasingly explored the literary constructs of ethnographies, postcolonial literary critics, like Ahmad, posited that the ethnographic dimensions of literature (representations of race, gender, and the colonized—traditionally the most self-conscious focus of anthropological ethnographies) ought to be subjected to critical literary inquiry. An important dimension of that critical inquiry has involved questioning the search for supposedly universal, objective literary principles that structure narratives (or, for that matter, structure cultural communities). According to Moore, such questioning has allowed "culture" to gain increasing currency as a category of politicized literary analysis:

> Though literary studies too was once a largely self-described objectivist enterprise (this may surprise some anthropologists), in marked contrast to anthropology the loss of objectivism left literary studies emboldened rather than unsure, and it has expanded indeed at anthropology's expense . . . while literary studies' job market overall grew a reasonable 15 percent from 1985 to 1990, the academic subcategory of "Minority" literature (included the "sub-sub" categories of Post-Colonial, Third World, American-Marginal, and African-American)—right square on anthropology's traditional terrain—experienced a stunning 636 percent job growth during that time, the bulk of the profession's expansion overall. (Moore 1994, 347)

Moore contended that the study of "other" cultures had been shifting from anthropology to literary studies because literary approaches to cultural analysis more easily accommodated explorations of subjectivity and specificity (in contrast to modernist objectivity and universality). Moore intoned that when cultural differences are not evaluated against supposedly objective and universal scales of cultural evolution, then anxieties about otherness can start being addressed and diffused. Moore, however, was hardly suggesting that literary studies represents a promised land toward which the "other" should venture an exodus. Rather, he argued that deconstructing textual representations of otherness should be an interdisciplinary project. After all, despite an abundance of critical postcolonial theories, I suspect that when many students of literature journey into a text by a "minority" writer (or some other pigeon-holed sub-sub group), they resemble modern ethnographers journeying into the "exotic" locales of their fieldwork. Like ethnographers, many readers are drawn to, anticipate, and study the "foreignness" of the writer's world. Like ethnographers, many readers must negotiate their own foreignness in relation to the "other" they encounter. And, like ethnographers, many of these readers will produce texts (literary essays) emerging from that encounter. Students of noncanonical, postcolonial English literature, it seems, could benefit from subjecting themselves to some of the fittingly difficult questions with which turn-of-the-century ethnographers contented.

TROPES OF OTHERNESS AND SUBVERSIVE HYPHENS

My exploration of this trope begins by considering how communities had and often continue to be been identified, ethnographically speaking. Ethnographers typically begin their projects by identifying the specific cultural practices of the peoples they intend to study. Conventionally, the people studied have been identified as the ethnographic "object" (as opposed to the ethnographer, the "subject"). For example, A. R. Radcliffe-Brown, in 1922, studied the Andaman Islanders in the Bay of Bengal; Margaret Mead, in 1928, studied Samoans. What had these titles—"Andaman Islander" and "Samoan"—meant to these ethnographers? Traveling to communities in the Bay of Bengal and Samoa, Radcliffe-Brown and Mead were not simply visiting peoples who were innocently identified by the geography they inhabited. They were traveling to communities and regions that had already been inscribed with an identity within the western imagination—"clearly defined others," as Clifford put it, "defined as primitive, or tribal, or non-Western, or pre-literate, or nonhistorical" (Clifford 1986, 23). Historian and ethnographer Laurent Dubois argued that before ethnographers could present an analysis of their fieldwork, they needed to acknowledge the role politics and history played simply in identifying their field site:

> The traveler, seeking that which is outside what is known, finds that all landscapes are inscribed, or even scarred, with a previous presence that anticipates theirs. There can be no travel outside the historical and cultural relationships that arise out of colonial histories. . . .
> . . . The place toward which we travel—the supposed source of our knowledge (in anthropology, the process of fieldwork)—is constructed, theorized, limited and defined before it is ever experienced. (Dubois 1995, 317)

Though Radcliffe-Brown and Mead stretched western imaginings of these "others," they could not entirely divorce themselves from colonial identifications of peoples outside the west: Radcliffe-Brown would list *Structure and Function in Primitive Society* (1952) as one of his major publications, and Mead would list *Sex and Temperament in Three Primitive Societies* (1935) as one of hers. Mead and Radcliffe-Brown illustrate how the seemingly cursory task of identifying a community locates that community within the identifier's political psyche. "Margaret Mead," observes Rey Chow, "found the interest of certain Arapesh Indians (in Highland New Guinea) in cultural influences other than their own 'annoying'" (Chow 1993, 28). Mired in essentialist models of ethnic identification, Mead's early work not only failed to recognize the elasticity of cultural identity, it also refused to acknowledge the agency of the community she studied—as if she knew, better than they could, what an "authentic" Arapesh Indian should care about.

Cultural identifications, for second-generation diasporic writers, can similarly "annoy" ethnographically-oriented conventions for locating culture. These texts can confront readers with a range of cultural affinities and anxieties that riddle attempts to distill essentialist, narrowly idealized forumulations of "authentic" belonging. Broader complexities of nationalist identification can manifest intimately in these writers' texts, reminding readers that the terms "Canadian," "American," and "Indian" signify hotly contested national identities, not to mention cultural sensibilities. Identifying as *Indo*-Canadian/American entails subscribing to particular interpretations of the names on both halves of the hyphen. Commonly, for second-generation Gen-X Indo-Canadians/Americans, "Indo" enveloped our parents' narratives of migration from a place and a time that existed principally in our imaginations. "Canadian" and "American" were and remain terms that technically refer to ethnically diverse populations, but they still too commonly evoke narratives of Anglo-descended peoples. Although second-generation Indo-Canadian/American writers hardly share similar (let alone singular) interpretations of what it means to be a Canadian, American, or Indian, their narratives bespeak cultural identifications that resist being ethnographically scripted into canonical narratives of national cultures.

Identifying as Indo-Canadian/American, however, entailed more than negotiating narratives on both sides of the hyphen. These attempted identifications also entailed coming to terms with the mediating function of the hyphen itself. The simple dash signified more than the relationship between adjective and noun. The hyphen symbolically embodied tensions, transferences, and transitions between some of the more pronounced narratives that enmeshed our understanding of selfhood and otherness. Between my Indo and my Canadian there is a hyphen that suggests several complimentary and conflicting relationships. In moments of rare clarity, I experience that hyphen as a steady bridge or clean artery connecting my multiple heritages. Sadly, and too commonly, that same hyphen seems sharp as a syringe, infecting my sense of self with an awareness of my otherness. Or taught as a tourniquet, keeping my color from bleeding into this cutting white country. As Nasser Hussain succinctly observed: "hyphens are radically ambivalent signifiers, for they simultaneously connect and set apart; they simultaneously represent belonging and not belonging" (Hussein 1989, 8). Perhaps that ambivalence, which so clumsily sutures fragments of my identity, also encases the dynamics of my identity in a way that neither "Indo" nor "Canadian" can.

Few writers had or have explored the loaded semiotics of the hyphen more eloquently than Asian-American critical theorist Trinh Minh-ha. According to Trinh, the "challenge of the hyphenated reality lies in the hyphen itself: the becoming Asian-American; the realm in-between, where predetermined rules cannot fully apply" (Trinh 1989, 157). Far from condemning us to perpetual unbelonging, Trinh suggests that the hyphen allows us to question the "authenticity" of essential identity and, instead, explore the existential processes of identification. Appreciated through Trinh's eyes, the hyphen erodes colonial and patriarchal models of naming and evaluating identity and, in this small-but-significant step, positions identification as an incomplete and, therefore, an ever-provisional process. The incompleteness of this process muddies long-standing ethnographic conventions through which identities, firstly, can be represented as the culminated continuity of identifications belonging to a protagonist or ethnographic subject. Secondly, this incompleteness embroils ethnographic readings—that is, readings for "culture" in a text—in the political exigencies of imperialism and patriarchy. As Stuart Hall describes the kernel of this paradoxical step toward ethnographic incompleteness, the "shift is best thought of in terms of a change from a struggle over the relations of representation to a politics of representation itself" (Hall 1995, 224).

Commenting on the predicament that many second-generation South Asian children face, Himani Bannerji succinctly characterized how "this realm in-between" constituted a pronounced site of struggle over the politics of representation; the "second generation grows up on cultural languages which are not foreign to them, though they are still designated as foreigners" (Bannerji 1993, 146). Unlike my parents, I grew up always being a "sort of" foreigner. "Not quite" an immigrant, I am something like a post-immigrant. The "post" implies a differentiation between my experiences and my parents,' but the hyphen still braces me to their designations as migrant others. The hyphen, again, mediates characterizations through which my understanding of selfhood and otherness are procured. Recollections shared by Jyoti Seghal, a schoolteacher and a second-generation Indo-Canadian, sadly typify the consequences of such designations:

> The positioning of "otherness" is central to the way my identity has been formed. Even being conscious of identity might point to the "otherness" of my existence in a dominant culture of whiteness . . . I could never be too "comfortable" because I was aware of the difference; perhaps this was the intention of the Multicultural policy and the subverted message of "tolerance." I knew I was being tolerated. . . .
>
> I received and believed the messages of Indians being "backward," "poor," "ugly," and "smelling like curry." There certainly weren't many, if any, people

> in the media or in my school who looked like me. Accurate information on South Asians was also scarce. There was nothing to counter my feelings of inferiority at school. At that point, I didn't have the confidence to deflect the images received. (Sehgal 2000, 264, 266)

Racism attended our parents' migration; Seghal grew up being the other. From childhood, her sense of self was macerated by awareness of her otherness. Even attempts to reconcile her multiple heritages, Canadian and Indian, reified dichotomies between Canada, which symbolized civility and selfhood, and India, which symbolized otherness:

> I was not considered Indian in India but my emotions and desire to cope with those feelings were secondary to capitalizing on my experience to gain in the Canadian world. I was working against the prevalent and dominant images of Indians and India. Essentially, I was trying to present India as being on par with Canada. To be accepted by peers, I needed to use my experience and frame it in a "positive" way, comparable to the normative Canadian experience. At this point, I was well aware of the value (or lack thereof) of having an Indian heritage. I used the "backwardness" of Indian culture as the grist for jokes—I either glorified it or joked about it. Both methods supported the perceived superiority of Canadian culture. The framing of my experience from the dominant perspective fills me with remorse. I stripped people (my people, really) of dignity. At the same time, I know that it was done to neutralize or equate differences between my mends and myself at the time. (Sehgal 2000, 269)

Neither emphasizing nor denying differences between her heritages could mitigate her sense of otherness. Denying differences entailed arguing India conformed to standards of civility characterized by Canadian culture. Emphasizing differences entailed distinguishing herself from "other Indians" (frankly, by empathizing with whites who believed Indians deserved to be derided or, at best, tolerated).

"Others in Their Own Land: Second Generation South Asian Canadian Women, Racism, and The Persistence of Colonial Discourse," by second-generation Indo-Canadian sociologist, Angela Aujla, presented arguments and evidence richly contextualizing Sehgal's experiences. Addressing the "gendered racialization" of second-generation South Asian women, Aujla argued that colonial discourses, which justified Canada's historically racist immigration policies, had not been appropriately acknowledged or addressed by Canada's official policies of multiculturalism. Citing academic studies, historical documents, colonial literary texts, and contemporary headlines and editorials from a variety of mainstream Canadian media outlets, Aujla forcefully demonstrated why "South Asian Canadian women are in a predicament of perpetual foreignness—constantly being asked where they are from and having stereotypical characteristics assigned to them despite their 'Canadian-ness.' Though they are in their country of origin, they are not of it" (Aujla 2000, 43). As Aujla developed her argument, she confronted the same dichotomy that bound Sehgal's attempts to negotiate her identity. As long as colonial ideals mediate how cultural differences are named and engaged, being accepted as a Canadian will, at best, entail being accepted as an honorary white person. Official multiculturalism, Aujla argued, represents a still-born attempt to make notions of citizenship more culturally inclusive. State-sanctioned multiculturalism encourages feel-good notions of cultural difference (which is why multicultural events were and are almost always festivals of some kind or another) that risk reinforcing essentialist distinctions between "normal" Canadians and "ethnic" Canadians.

Sehgal and Aujla both address the stigmatizing affects of otherness, assessing consequences of internalizing specific beliefs about Indian cultural inferiority. To these consequences, I would add another pole of despondent otherness that can mire second-generation narrations of selfhood. Classical colonial discourses not only slur our cultural heritage as inferior, they impose static definitions of "culture" on our communities, leaving us little latitude to consider generational and gendered processes of cultural permutation. Colonial anthropologists, apparently, had had little interest in exploring how culture morphs through the history of a community, across generations and between genders. As cultural critic Glen Bowman observed, "anthropology's early development in the cradle of colonialism has . . . had a powerful influence on the way we have conceived . . . the character of the other as firmly affixed for the gaze of the anthropologist in a stable and unchanging cultural framework" (Bowman 1997, 36). Commonly, cultural change was understood in quasi-scientific terms: western civilization representing the evolutionary height of cultural development, the rest of the world representing peoples who would, by force or eventuality, catch up. Where does this leave us, the children of Indian immigrants? If India is stigmatized as "backwards," then I can try purging some of my otherness by denying my heritage and conceding that western civilization is more culturally evolved. If India is stigmatized, more sympathetically, as "exotic"—ancient and mysterious— then I can ease into my otherness more cozily, accepting my fate as a New Age cultural showpiece, a token of tolerance. In either case, I can never be an equal. My heritage remains locked in colonial fiction. The problem does not stop there. Essentialist formulations of identity not only render me "too Indian" to be a "real" Canadian, they also render me too "Canadian" to claim a substantive connection to my ancestral home. The gendered dynamics of this dichotomy, to which I will now turn, could and can be shouldered more onerously—more vividly, more violently—by second-generation women.

THE GENDERED AXIS OF ANCESTRAL "PURITY"

As Jasbir Puar noted, tired ethnographic formulation of authenticity and dif-ference, which risked rendering second-generation Indo-American and Indo-Canadian women "other" on both sides of the hyphen, were exacerbated by their distance from their ancestral homes.

> The list of calls of authenticity, depending upon situational and discursive social space, is endless and specifically impacted by competing, relational white/black, East/West, traditional/modem discourses embedded in second-generation constructs. Though distinctions between generations are problemat-ic, it is useful to point out that while immigrants can equate displacement with actual physical movements, subsequent generations must conceptualize dis-placement in metaphysical terms.
>
> Ultimately, the politics of loyalty predominate for the second generation in terms of loss, because of an inability to conceptualize "home" as previous generations do. Hence, I am not allowed to say or represent anything against my culture, because doing so implies internalized racism; I am not allowed to say anything in support of it, because doing so signals, in the context of Western supremacy, that I am deluding myself, that I am subjugated and oppressed by my heritage. (Puar 1994, 85)

Debjani Mukherjee, a clinical psychologist and a second-generation Indo-American, persuasively conveyed how colonial and patriarchal notions of difference could painfully taint Indian post-immigrant perceptions of culture and gender:

> South Asian American women are usually defined in terms of the other or in opposition to some other category. They are either not like South Asians or not like Americans. Add to this the layer of being a woman and we are left to deal with the cultural baggage and stereotypes ascribed to both categories of wom-en. In some contexts we are not the South Asian women who is seen as passive, obedient, subservient, a victim of sati, dowry death, and female infan-ticide. In other contexts we are not the American woman who is seen as loose, rude, not family oriented, a victim of rape, sexual harassment, and men who will divorce her. Many South Asian American women find themselves having to defend both 'worlds' or internalizing the pathologies of both. (Mukherjee 2000, 281–82)

As Mukherjee clarified, difference does not simply denote distinction, it connotes deficiency or deviance. Trinh noted that colonial discourses pre-scribe pursuing highly essentialized notions of authenticity as a "remedy" for this "deficiency." But what are the implications of believing that a selectively imagined India represents the authentic embodiment of an ancestral home against which diasporic communities must constantly measure their prac-tices, or that white America/Canada represents the authentic expression of

North American culture which all immigrant communities ought to emulate in our struggle for acceptance? Consider Trinh's insight:

> To raise the question of identity is to reopen the discussion on the self/other relationship in its enactment of power relations. Identity as understood in the context of a certain ideology of dominance has long been a notion that relied on the concept of an essential, authentic core that remains hidden to one's consciousness and that requires the elimination of all that is considered foreign or not true to the self, that is to say, not-I, other. In such a concept the other is almost unavoidably either opposed to the self or submitted to the self's dominance. It is always condemned to remain in the its shadow while making attempts at being its equal. Identity, thus understood, supposes that a clear dividing line can be made between I and not-I, he and she . . . between us here and them over there. The further one moves from the core the less likely one is thought to be capable of fulfilling one's role as the real self, the real black, Indian, or Asian, the real woman. The search for identity is, therefore, usually a search for that lost, pure, true, genuine, original authentic self, often situated within a process of elimination of all that is considered other, superfluous, fake, corrupted. (Trinh 1989, 415)

This bind is further tightened by patriarchal and orientalist interpretations of Indian culture and history that we inherit not only from racist Western media, but also from influential patriarchal factions within Indo-Canadian and Indo-American communities. Aparna Rayaprol, commenting on Priya Agarwal's ethnography of Indian diasporic communities in southern California, observed disturbing relationships between essentialism and patriarchy:

> Many of Agarwal's respondents attributed the gap in gender ideology (particularly with regard to issues of marriage and dating) between parents and children to the fact that for the parental generation, India is a "pure space" untouched by change. The rapid changes, particularly, in urban India are ignored by most immigrants and they construct an imaginary world where gender ideology is at its patriarchal zenith. (Rayaprol 1995)

In my experience, Agarwal's respondents' observations sadly typify how concerns regarding "cultural reproduction" could and can become highly charged, highly sexualized for many second-generation Indians. Patriarchal obsessions over chastity and purity, which often harshly curtail women's sexual freedoms, emerge with equal fierceness when censuring cultural practices that are not explicitly sexualized. As second-generation South Asians, the gendered metaphors—of violating the "purity" of Canadian and American culture, even as we struggle with fears that our Indian-ness is barely a bastardized version of our heritage—have had distinctly sharper material consequences for women than for men. The opening lines of Radhika Gajjala's Cyborg-Sita poems draw on Christian and Hindu imagery to illustrate how discourses of cultural and sexual purity, in our homelands and adopted lands, can be problematically conflated and born much more heavily by women. Gajjalla opens her critique of conflating sexual "purity" (with all its gendered connotations) with cultural "purity" by addressing us in a voice that identifies itself as "we," signaling a steadily-intensifying tension between its ambiguous multiplicity and its singular, chorus-like authority (Gajjala 2000, 213). Alluding to choruses in Greek tragedies, which often functioned as character-narrator hybrids, Gajjala positions this "we" as a character who, at times, believes it can speak as an "objective" (and therefore authoritative) narrator. But, by strategically reducing the third-person omniscient narrator to the perceptual field of first-person historical characters, Gajjala asks readers to question the seemingly transcendent voice of authority within their gendered narratives of identity. More specifically, as Gajjala sets up the introduction of her Sita character, she addresses identity narratives dealing with the so-called "pure" reproduction of lineage, biologically and culturally. Without mincing words, Gajjala asserts that these gendered anxieties about cultural-sexual purity narratives have been invoked to justify tremendous violence. In Gajjala's poem, Sita symbolizes women of Indian ancestry who do *not* maintain their cultural purity while living in exile—that is, the "forest," the West (Gajjala 2000, 214). Despite being held as the pinnacle of purity, Gajjala's Sita must eventually shed the cloak of purity, of tradition, and accept what she is. Neither "a woman nobly planned" (Wordsworth 1802) nor "a lovely lady garmented in white" (Shelley 1824) this Sita must do what many second-generation writers do: be more than a silent, objectified tool for cultural reproduction, constrained by colonial and patriarchal notions of purity and pollution. Gajjala's Sita must come to terms with her subjectivity; she must speak to wrest agency over her culturally-circumscribed construction of selfhood. She must resist internalizing, nurturing, and reproducing narratives of identity in which she is reduced to impassable otherness. Fundamentally, she must confront essentialist preoccupations attempting to arrest these efforts.

Although critiques of essentialism hardly seem innovative, second-generation "Gen-X" narratives can share empowering insights into parallels between our designation as cultural "foreigners" (here and in India) and the patriarchal interpretations of our heritage that remain fossilized in so many of our parents' imaginations. Rayaprol's and Gajjala's critiques, which explicitly addressed patriarchal pressures to maintain cultural "purity" shed much light on Sunaina Maira's observations about turn-of-the-century celebrations in New York commemorating India's independence from British rule:

> Orientalized images of artistic traditions drawn from a pre-modern, unsullied past were used to stand in for Indian culture, whereas a uniquely second-generation Indian American popular culture, based on music, dance, and fashion, is viewed as not truly Indian, even by those who participate in it them-

selves. This is not just a tension between "high" and "popular" culture, for it is tied to a vision of the home country—in this case, India—as the site of true culture and it relegates cultural productions created in the diaspora to secondary status. Indian films and film music, for example, are often a cultural pastiche yet are also viewed as "authentically" Indian expressions, as noted earlier, although perhaps not as virtuously "traditional" as classical music and dance. (Maira 1999)

The rhetoric of cultural purity—the "unsullied past"—wielded by constituencies of the Indian diaspora fuels patriarchal proscriptions which many second-generation South Asian women intimately confront. For these women, challenging patriarchal constraints entailed challenging essentialist interpretations of Indian heritage which granted those constraints legitimacy. Their feminist explorations of otherness, subjectivity, and agency generated imaginative, inspiring perspectives on cultural continuity that Indian diasporas *need*. If we ignore these writers' words, we risk resigning ourselves to glum, inflexible readings of our heritage. We risk locking ourselves into models of cultural identification, propagated by modem anthropology, that leave us little latitude to critique, claim, and contribute to our cultural inheritance.

Second-generation narratives—Gen-X and beyond—can provide a critical riposte to the sense of otherness that modernist anthropological discourses can continue to inculcate us. As these second-generation narratives wrestle with perspectives on cultural continuity, agency, and subjectivity, they demonstrate the futility of fixing identity into romanticized renderings of ethnic heritage or racialized renderings of citizenship. For these writers, using essentialist models of ethnographic description to represent the experiences of multigenerational, transnational communities is akin to dancing in a straitjacket. In contrast, these writers asked readers to consider how identity is constantly being articulated through a plasmic, yet politically-charged, process of negotiating multiple affiliations. A pronounced symbol of that negotiation is that gendered hyphen sitting tensely between "Indo" and "Canadian/American." That hyphen evinces correlative facets of cultural identity—such as the affects of migration on cultural identification, and the awareness of cultural heterogeneity within communities—that addle self/other dichotomies on which modernist ethnographic projects are premised. The remainder of this chapter considers how ethnographic subjectivity and agency, which are mediated by those self/other dichotomies, can be reevaluated in recognition of that hyphen.

HYPHENATED CONSEQUENCES

Bhuvana Rao argued that the epistemological foundations of "anthropology's early development" (Rao 1996) continued to have currency within the discipline, despite attempts to refocus ethnographic practice:

> Experimental ethnography questions the notion of the objectivity of ethnography, claiming that writing ethnography is a subjective enterprise, subjective to the cultural baggage of the ethnographer, where the ethnographer's biases should be acknowledged through self-reflexivity. The resulting ethnography can, therefore, never be an objective description of the culture. So, ethnographies should be read as semi-literary texts which are open to the interpretation of the reader. While this critique allows for a breakthrough in experimental ethnographic writing with special emphasis on the presentation of the voice of the subjects or the native, it simply alludes to the basic issue in question—that of how and why the knowledge of the "other" is created. In other words, it digresses from the heart of ethnographic methods: the business of fieldwork and the dynamics of the "data collection process." Epistemological issues in anthropology have not been considered perhaps because they question the very essence of anthropology—the business of studying the "other." (Rao 1996)

Though Rao questions the "very essence of anthropology," her observation about the turn to self-reflexivity in anthropology anticipates ethnographers' capacity to surpass "the business of studying the other" (Rao 1996). Laura Angel shares an anecdote from her days as ethnographer-in-training that cleverly illustrates how identifying the "self" as an ethnographic subject subverts the goals of traditional ethnography:

> While I was waiting to board a flight, a young woman who was also a student began a conversation. As every student does, she asked the inevitable question, "What's your major?"
>
> When I apologetically responded that my "major" was Anthropology, her eyes lit up. She proceeded to tell me that her brother studied Anthropology at Yale.
>
> "Oh, I commented," trying not to sound like an underachiever because I went to a lesser known school.
>
> "Where do you study?" She flipped her blond hair over her shoulders.
>
> "I study at The New School, in New York."
>
> "No, I mean which country?" she asked.
>
> "Country?" I was confused and I was sure I looked foolish.
>
> "Yeah, like my brother studies Thailand, he's been three times already. So, where do you want to study?"
>
> I pointed to myself and said, "I want to study here." (Angel 1993 in Visweswaran 1994, 140)

By identifying herself as a place—"here," as opposed to "me"—Angel challenges ethnographers to subject themselves to their own ethnographic gaze.

Indeed, Angel exposes and inverts the underlying synecdoche that allows ethnographers to signify "others" by the geographic and imagined locales those "others" inhabit (ethnographers who say they are studying Thailand, the politically and geographically demarcated place, means they are studying cultural practices among people whose identity includes multifarious ways of "being Thai"). As Angel's anecdote illustrates, the synecdoche that traditionally identifies the ethnographic "other" sounds awkward when used to identify the ethnographic "self." Perhaps this awkwardness registers more recognizably to second-generation writers because our ethnographic inscription resonates with the lively irony infused in Angel's synecdoche: traditional ethnography territorialized ethnic identity, but hyphenated, Indo-American subjects construct an ethnic identity that incorporates a heritage originating from a land outside the land they live in. By identifying herself as "here," Angel ironically de-territorializes her ethnographic subject and supports Devleena Ghosh's observation of anthropology's "increasing acknowledgment that cultures are not discrete, bounded entities" necessarily "fixed to particular localities" (Ghosh 2006, 248; see also Appadurai 1996, 48). Commenting on traditional anthropology, Susan Sontag argues, "For the anthropologist the world is professionally divided into "home" and "out there," the domestic and the exotic, the urban academic world and the tropics" (Sontag 1994, 74). Ethnographers like Visweswaran, however, subverted these professional divisions and begin addressing the ethnographic complexities of the hyphen that splits these worlds: "The Indian-American hyphen retains the imaginary of the nation-state, its mobile diaspora with increasing (if complicated) choices about whether to go or stay. It is a hyphen that signals the desire (and the ability) to be both 'here' and 'there'" (Visweswaran 1994, 116). For second-generation writers, vast networks of desires can be embodied in the hyphen, tempering migrations of synechdotal subjectivities between metonymies of "here" (familiar space, home—wherever that is) to "there" (foreign space—which seems, at times, to be everywhere).

According to Bowman, ethnographers could further reconceptualize traditional ethnographic relationships between "self" and "other" by acknowledging that the subjects of their ethnography—both "self" and "other"—may choose, and be inscribed by, several intersecting identifications: "The other then becomes like ourselves in so far as, like ourselves, he or she does not simply have an identity but builds up a repertoire of identities through identifications with subject positions set out in the discourses he or she encounters in negotiating his or her life" (Bowman 1997, 45). When ethnographers or ethnographically-oriented readers realize that their "other" has no single, primary, essential identity that can be identified, observed, and documented, they must also reassess their place in their ethnographic/literary engagement. How might this engagement stray from attempts to objectify otherness, to represent or read otherness "objectively," and instead fashion ethnographic analyses, as Crapanzano proposed (Crapanzano 1986, 51), exploring the dynamics of the *encounter* between ethnographic "self" and the ethnographic "other"? Abandoning essentialist identifications shifts the goals of ethnographic thinking in two key ways. Firstly, reducing an ethnography to a presentation of an encounter necessarily limits the scope of cultural knowledge contained within that ethnography. More importantly, limiting ethnographic analyses to presentations of a particular encounter identifies both parties in that encounter—the ethnographer/reader and the community they are studying—as subjects of the ethnographic scrutiny.

The "ethnographic humility" (Rabinow 1985, 1) evinced in hemming the goals of ethnographic analysis to the study of an encounter can expand our understanding of gendered agency within the complex, contentious, and continuous processes of identifying ourselves. These approaches help us appreciate how, in Diana Fuss's words, "a complex system of cultural, social, psychical, and historical differences, and not a set of pre-existent human essences, position and constitute the subject" (Fuss 1989, xi–xii). Take me, for example: I am a child of Indian immigrants, I am a Canadian citizen, a central-Ontarian, a Torontonian, a suburbanite, and an academic (this list, if allowed to go on, would grow quickly tedious). I use a different imaginative process to construct my membership within each of these communities. How I construct my identity within one community, however, heavily influences how I understand my identity within my other communities. Being a person of color has influenced how I imagine myself as a Torontonian, but being a Torontonian has also influenced how I imagine myself as a person of color (for people of color, living in an immigrant-dense and diverse urban center can be very different from living in a more ethnically homogenous city or community). All of my multiple identifications—Canadian, Torontonian, post-immigrant—are somewhat delicately made (though each for different reasons). Many of these identifications, far from pleasantly complimenting each other, often coexist within me nervously and antagonistically, competing for attention and allegiance. None of these imagined identifications can singularly accommodate all facets of my identity; none can comprehensively identify the single, deepest "essence" of who I am. Against calls for essentialist identity, Shaloni Mathur thoughtfully shared how her "identity is constituted by many provisional enunciations."

> As a middle-class woman of South Asian origin, born in India and raised in Canada, my entry into this culture is a product of a complex set of historical trajectories. I am accustomed to naming, labels and categories. My experiences have been variously contained, both willingly and reluctantly on my behalf, as those of an immigrant woman, a visible minority, an Indo-Canadian, an East Indian, of South Asian origin, as second generation (or is it first? I'm no longer sure), etc.

> *. . . Identity, I have learned, is a series of trade-offs, a strategic business of*
> *selecting the role that might best serve one's provisional ends.* (Mathur 1995,
> 273, 276 emphasis in original)

Ethnographically circumscribed identities, too, have provisional ends. To illustrate the point, consider the hypothetical example of an ethnography of Punjabi cultures in North America. This ethnography may contrast a Punjabi Hindu family in Dallas with a Punjabi Sikh family in Vancouver, but it must not assume that each family's Punjabi-ness represents an identification that always supersedes other identifications—being Texan, being British Columbian. Of course, that ethnographic study privileges the Punjabi identifications, but ethnographers must realize they do not simply represent subjects—as if subjects were *a priori* Platonic ideals waiting to be mirrored in writing. Ethnographies construct subjects (or, at very least, deal with constructed subjects). Mathur; for example, is an immigrant woman and a woman of color, but she would be constructed slightly differently in an ethnography about immigrant women than she would in an ethnography about women of color (or about Indo-Canadians, or about the South Asian diaspora, and so on). "The subject occupies different subject positions at different moments," argued Aihwa Ong, "and she cannot be different by an single discursive apparatus" (Ong 1995, 351).

Commenting on how particular Chinese-American writers negotiated their multiple identifications, Fischer argued a pluralistic model of identity construction can allow subjects to manage their many identifications with integrity.

> It is a matter of finding a voice or style that does not violate one's several components of identity. In part, such a process of assuming an ethnic identity is an insistence on a pluralistic, multidimensional, or multi-faceted concept of self: one can be many different things, and this personal sense can be a crucible for a wider social ethos of pluralism. (Fischer 1986, 216)

"Finding a voice" involves struggling to recognize one's multiple identifications, struggling to reconcile identifications that seem in conflict, and struggling to articulate identities that can complimentarily manifest (however imperfectly) these multiple identifications. North American feminists of color have illustrated this process of voice-finding quite powerfully over the past twenty years: one must identify fully as a person of color when identifying as a feminist (despite facing resistance from some Eurocentric white feminists), and one must identify fully as a feminist when identifying as a person of color (despite facing resistance from some patriarchal-minded people in our communities). As Cherríe Moraga states in *This Bridge Called My Back: Writings of Radical Women of Color,*

We are the colored in a white feminist movement.
We are the feminists among the people of our culture.
We are often the lesbians among the straight. (Moraga 1983, 23)

Rather than searching for an essential identity that transcends bitter differences, Moraga and Anzaldúa propose a deeper probing of marginalized subjectivities through a process of gathering divergent affiliations (naming ourselves) and harmonizing them into complex, empowering narratives (telling our stories). Moraga's and Anzaldúa's perspective on agency and subjectivity also subtly emphasizes the number of different bridges—indeed, bridges between bridges—that we attempt to construct between the communities to which we belong. No ethnography can hope to represent the entire lattice of intersecting narratives (not to mention half-built bridges) that constitute a subject. An ethnography of a hyphen critically tries to appreciate how that lattice simultaneously patterns, and is patterned by, the voices of dynamic subjects. Readers attempting to contextualize the culture milieu of second-generation South Asian women's narratives may want to remain attentive to the fears and desires modulating the hyphen and patterning the dynamics of cultural identification.

Homi Bhaba's perspective on "emergent identity" helped clarify how these fears and desires, particularly as they relate to experiences of marginalization, can be textualized into art:

> There is even a growing conviction that the affective experience of social marginality—as it emerges in non-canonical cultural forms—transforms our critical strategies. It forces us to confront the concept of culture outside object d'art or beyond the canonization of the "idea" of aesthetics, to engage with culture as an uneven, incomplete production of meaning and value, often composed of incommensurable demands and practices, produced in the act of social survival. Culture reaches out to create a symbolic textuality, to give the alienating everyday an aura of selfhood, a promise of pleasure. (Bhabha 1994, 172)

According to Bhabha, art produced in social margins is politically emergent—that is, it is produced in emergency, in incommensurable existential survival. Bhabha characterizes that emergency as the critical need to reconfigure symbols that alienate, that are potentially everywhere, into symbols that empower. Though Bhaba's perspectives shed light on certain circumstances that provoked the creation of these texts, he does not argue that cultural artifacts produced on the social margins are only strategies and tools for survival. Commonly, second-generation writers are not merely trying to survive personal stigmatization, they are critically interrogating and reconfiguring how gender, ethnicity, and nationality can be imagined. During moments of crisis and confrontation, these young writers brave giving up the security—and the fantasy—of occupying a single subject-position, and explore the possibilities of "occupying two places at once" (Fuss 1989, 19). Though East and West have been positioned antithetically (and antagonistically) in colonial discourses, these writers share imaginative and empathetic explorations of subject-positions that not only survive historical tensions between these "two places," but thrive as their voices increasingly evince the creative agency of identification. Survival connotes urgency and fear—as in the desperation someone might experience while trying to survive drowning. Urgency and fear certainly permeate many dimensions of South Asian post-immigrant women's writing, but turn-of-the-century, Gen-X, second-generation narratives of selfhood commonly evinced something more than conflicted cultural anxiety: these narratives evinced something lurking, subversively, in the empowering in-between.

REFERENCES

Ahmad, Aijaz. 1994. *In Theory: Classes, Nations, Literatures*. New York: Verso.

Angel, Laura. 1993. "Interviewing the Sef." Senior Thesis BA/MA Anthropology program, New York: New School for Social Research.

Appadurai, Arjun. 1996. *Modernity At Large: Cultural Dimensions of Globalization*. Minneapolis: University of Minnesota Press.

Aujla, Angela. 2000. "Others in Their Own Land: Second Generation South Asian Canadian Women, Racism, and the Persistence of Colonial Discourse." *Canadian Woman Studies* 20 (2): 41–47. https://cws.journals.yorku.ca/index.php/cws/article/view/7608.

Bannerji, Himani. 1993. "Popular Images of South Asian Women." In Himani Bannerji (ed.). *Returning the Gaze*. Toronto: Sister Vision Press. 144–52.

Behar, Ruth. 1993. *Translated Woman: Crossing the Border with Esperanza's Story*. Boston: Beacon Press.

Bhabha, Homi. 1994. *The Location of Culture*. London: Routledge.

Bowman, Glenn. 1997. "Identifying vs. Identifying With the Other." In Allison James, Jenny Hockey, and Andrew Dawson (eds.). *After Writing Culture: Epistemology and Praxis in Contemporary Anthropology*. London: Routledge. 34–50.

Chow, Rey. 1993. *Writing Diaspora: Tactics of Intervention in Contemporary Cultural Studies*. Bloomington: Indiana University Press.

Clifford, James. 1986. "Introduction." In James Clifford and George E. Marcus (eds.). *Writing Culture: The Poetics and Politics of Ethnography*. Berkeley: University of California Press. 1–26.

———. 1988. *The Predicament of Culture*. Cambridge: Harvard University Press.

Crapanzano, Vincent. 1986. "Hermes' Dilemma: The Masking of Subversion in Ethnographic Description." In James Clifford and George E. Marcus (eds.). *Writing Culture: The Poetics and Politics of Ethnography*. Berkeley: University of California Press. 51–76.

Dubois, Laurent. 1995. "Man's Darkest Hours: Maleness, Travel, and Anthropology." In Ruth Behar and Deborah A. Gordon (eds.). *Women Writing Culture*. Berkeley: University of California Press. 306–21.

Ebron, Paula, and Anna Lowenhaupt Tsing. 1995. "In Dialogue? Reading Across Minority Discourses." In Ruth Behar and Deborah A. Gordon (eds.). *Women Writing Culture*. Berkeley: University of California Press. 390–411.

Fischer, Michael J. 1986. "Ethnicity and the Post-Modern Arts of Memory." In James Clifford and George E. Marcus (eds.). *Writing Culture: The Poetics and Politics of Ethnography*. Berkeley: University of California Press. 194–233.

Fuss, Diana. 1989. *Essentially Speaking: Feminism, Nature & Difference*. London: Routledge.

Gajjala, Radhika. 2000. "Excerpts from the Cyborg-Sita Poems." In Kitchen Table Collective (ed.). *Bolo! Bolo!: A Collection of Writings by Second-Generation South Asians Living in North America*. South Asian Professionals Networking Association. 213–19.

Ghosh, Devleena. 2006. "INDIA@OZ: The Curry Pacific." In Stephanie Lawson and Wayne Peake (eds.). *Globalization and Regionalization: Views from the Pacific Rim*. Unversidad de Guadalajara; University of Technology Sydney. 239–62.

Hall, Stuart. 1995. "New Ethnicities." In Bill Ashcroft, Gareth Griffiths, and Helen Tiffin (eds.). *The Post-Colonial Studies Reader*. London: Psychology Press. 223–27.

Hussein, Nasser. 1989. "Hyphenated Identity: Nationalistic Discourse, History, and the Anxiety of Criticism in Salman Rushdie's Shame." *Qui Parle* 3(2): 1–18. http://www.jstor.org/stable/20685887.

Maira, Sunaina. 1999. "Identity Dub: The Paradoxes of Indian American Subculture (New York Mix)." *Cultural Anthropology* 14(1).

Mathur, Shaloni. 1995. "bell hooks Called Me a Woman of Colour." In Makeda Silvera (ed.). *The Other Woman: Women of Colour in Contemporary Canadian Literature*. Toronto: Sister Vision. 270–82.

Moore, David Chioni. 1994. "Anthropology Is Dead, Long Live Anthro(a)Pology: Poststructuralism, Literary Studies, and Anthropology's 'Nervous Present.'" *Journal of Anthropological Research* 50(4): 345–65. http://www.jstor.org/stable/3630558.

Moraga, Cherríe. 1983. "Theory in the Flesh." In Cherríe Moraga and Gloria Anzaldúa (eds.). *This Bridge Called My Back: Writings by Radical Women of Color*. Kitchen Table, Women of Color Press. 23–24.

Mukherjee, Debjani. 2000. "The Other in My Space: South Asian American Women Negotiating Hyphenated Identities." In Kitchen Table Collective (ed.). *Bolo! Bolo!: A Collection of Writings by Second-Generation South Asians Living in North America*. South Asian Professionals Networking Association. 260–77.

Ong, Aihwa. 1995. "Women Out of China: Traveling Tales and Traveling Theories in Postcolonial Feminism." In Ruth Behar and Deborah A. Gordon (eds.). *Women Writing Culture*. Berkeley: University of California Press. 350–72.

Puar, Jasbir. 1994. "Writing My Way 'Home': Travelling South Asian Bodies and Diasporic Journeys." *Socialist Review* 24(4): 75–108.

Rabinow, Paul. 1985. "Discourse and Power: On the Limits of Ethnographic Texts." *Dialectical Anthropology* 10: 1–13.

Rao, Bhuvana. 1996. "Anthropologist as Native and Other: Some Espistemological Issues in Fieldwork." *South Asian Research Graduate Journal* 3(2).

Rayaprol, Aparna. 1995. "Gender Ideologies and Practices Among South Indian Immigrants in Pittsburg." *South Asian Research Graduate Journal* 2(1).

Sehgal, Jyoti. 2000. "Seeking an Identity." In Kitchen Table Collective (ed.). *Bolo! Bolo!: A Collection of Writings by Second-Generation South Asians Living in North America*. South Asian Professionals Networking Association. 260–77.

Shelley, P. B. 1824. "The Witch of Atlas." http://knarf.english.upenn.edu/PShelley/witch.html.

Sontag, Susan. 1994. *Against Interpretation*. New York: Vintage.

Trinh, Thi Minh-Ha. 1989. *Woman, Native, Other: Writing Postcoloniality and Feminism*. Washington, DC: Georgetown University Press.

Visweswaran, Kamala. 1994. *Fictions of Feminist Ethnography*. Minneapolis: University of Minnesota Press.

Wordsworth, William. 1802. "She Was a Phantom of Delight." Text/html. Poetry Foundation. https://www.poetryfoundation.org/poems/45550/she-was-a-phantom-of-delight.

Chapter Five

Migration and Sexuality in S. J. Sindu's *Marriage of a Thousand Lies*

Maryse Jayasuriya

If migration always carries with it some degree of precariousness, this uncertain condition is magnified for LGBTQ immigrants and refugees from South Asia, particularly for second-generation immigrants who often are compelled to struggle against the expectations and assumptions of their first-generation parents and diasporic communities. S. J. Sindu's debut novel *Marriage of a Thousand Lies*, published in 2017, has confronted this double precarity directly. Sindu writes within the context of the Sri Lankan Tamil diaspora in the United States, offering a story that complements influential accounts of Sri Lankan Tamil diasporic life in North America like V. V. Ganeshananthan's *Love Marriage* and Shyam Selvadurai's *Hungry Ghosts*. My paper considers the complex interrelationship of nationality, gender, sexuality, and diaspora and the alternative understanding of what it means to be domiciled in varying contexts that this interrelationship implies in Sindu's rich and compelling novel. Sindu examines the intersection of immigrant and gay identities. Her protagonist comes to a realization of what she wants by staying firmly entrenched within what has traditionally been called the hostland, suggesting a mode of being domiciled that has implications for women's sexual and gender identities. Sindu's novel reveals the importance of resisting concepts of home that are imposed via the patriarchal family and nation-state and developing new concepts of home that are shaped by voluntary choices and by one's own sense of self and gendered identity. In this reading, a "hostland" is not just a place to which one moves; rather, it is a reality one creates.

GENDER AND SEXUAL IDENTITIES IN
SRI LANKAN ANGLOPHONE FICTION

Sri Lankan Anglophone fiction has alternated between repressing and celebrating diverse gender identities. While Shyam Selvadurai's critically-
acclaimed novel *Funny Boy* is a coming-of-age narrative that deals with
same-sex desire in a young Sri Lankan boy growing up during the early years
of the country's ethnic conflict, there have not been many Sri Lankan literary
works—either by diasporic writers or by those who are resident in Sri Lanka—that have focused on lesbian characters or enabled characters engaging
in nonheteronormative practices to provide their own perspectives. Punyakante Wijenaike's 1971 novella *Giraya* depicts an intimate, presumably
homoerotic, relationship between an aristocratic widowed matriarch and her
devoted servant.[1] The relationship is seen and conveyed to the reader through
the perspective of the former's horrified daughter-in-law, who describes it as
something "strange" and "abnormal." The 2008 novel by V. V. Ganeshananthan, *Love Marriage*, includes an episode about a close relationship between
an older, single Tamil woman in Jaffna and her protégée who works with her
in the same school, which draws comment and criticism from the latter's
family and community. The homoerotic relationships featured in *Giraya* and
Love Marriage do not end well since each of them includes power differen-
tials and elements of exploitation. The younger woman in *Love Marriage*
defrauds the older one and ultimately leaves her destitute while the servant in
Giraya, in a fit of jealous rage, strangles her mistress and then kills herself.

Mary Anne Mohanraj's 2006 novel *Bodies in Motion*, like *Love Marriage*, is a multi-generational novel, but it is even more episodic, focusing on
two Sri Lankan Tamil families and the variety of relationships of myriad
family members living in Sri Lanka and the diaspora. Mohanraj's work provides a more substantial treatment of the relation of diaspora to sexuality
than earlier works by Sri Lankan women. The novel includes a number of
nonheteronormative relationships that illustrate how women can and do
negotiate same-sex desire within the parameters of a patriarchal society.

One such is a brief but intimate relationship between two sisters-in-law,
Mangai and Sushila, who have a passionate week together following Sushila's arranged marriage to Mangai's brother Sundar in 1948. Even though
Mangai declares her love for her new sister-in-law and wants the two of them
to elope, Sushila does not believe that there is any possibility for the two
women to survive within such a relationship—their being together would
mean that they would "lose caste, lose family, lose the future" (33) in an era
when few opportunities existed for women to work outside the home and
support themselves. Sushila pragmatically insists that her place is with her
new husband: "I care for you, Mangai. But if they found us, they'd drag us
back in shame. They might do worse. [. . .] There's no place for us" (34). She

advises her sister-in-law to enjoy whatever opportunities for fulfillment that might come her way: "That's all we can do, Mangai. Take a little pleasure when we can" (35).

Since the novel is an intergenerational and episodic one featuring a huge cast of characters spanning many decades, we do not get much more from Sushila's perspective. We only hear in later episodes—mainly from her husband's point-of-view—that Sushila emigrated with Sundar to the United States, had children with him, and remains married to him; it seems that she finds her own pleasure with her female "friends" while circumventing familial and social censure. Sundar reflects on Sushila's reserve with him and within their intimate relationship even as he recognizes that his wife is by nature a warm and passionate person—the coldness and distance are reserved for him. Sushila's husband realizes that right from the beginning of their marriage, "there was more than maidenly shyness in her response to him" (148). Sundar gradually comes to the realization that his wife has betrayed him by saving her passion and her pleasure for others: "She will dance with her friends, his sisters—not immodestly, of course. Only with women— never with men. But she will laugh freely, will be flushed with pleasure, will lean toward the women [. . .] Exuberant, yet unobjectionable, as always. But the public does not always reflect the private, and he has always known what really goes on" (148). He "had done his best to never know the truth. He had no real evidence; he had tried not to know—yet he was sure. He knew" (149). Sundar struggles constantly with the discrepancy: he clings to the belief that his wife can only betray him if she were to be intimate with another man; yet, even though Sushila has engaged only with women, he knows that she has betrayed him. He cannot seem to bear to even name the possibility—or admit the truth—of what he knows: his wife is a lesbian who has been forced to marry him and who has managed to find a way to fulfill her same-sex desire despite being married to him. There is tragedy here—a man who does not want to name or acknowledge what his wife wants and needs because that would mean changing his traditional notion of marriage. He prefers to turn a blind eye to his wife's relationships with women and endure his own jealousy—which he knows could result in violence and which he tries desperately to curb through his adherence to Buddhism—in order to maintain his marriage even though this course of (in)action makes both his wife and himself unhappy and distorts their personalities to a certain extent.

Sundar's sister and Sushila's erstwhile lover Mangai, meanwhile, is known as "the woman who had lived with her servant, Daya, for decades, in a house with only one bed" (273), as revealed later in the novel. Mangai mourns Daya's death by donning the white garments of a widow, thereby emphasizing the true nature of the relationship despite the inevitable backlash that she gets from her community. It seems that she did indeed follow

Sushila's advice and found fulfillment in an intimate and enduring relationship with another woman. In certain ways Mangai seems to have fiercely and
defiantly carved out a life for herself in Sri Lanka that is more satisfying to
her than the one Sushila has managed to build in the diaspora.

Leilani, another character in Mohanraj's novel, is a second-generation
immigrant living in the United States. While attending college in Chicago in
1966, she realizes that she is bisexual and—following an intimate experience
with a college classmate—decides to live on her own terms. "I would tell
them [her parents] that I was hoping to be a poet. I would not tell them how
many lovers (mostly female, a few male) I had had. I would tell them that I
might never marry" (103). Leilani is choosing to create the life she wants for
herself while judiciously disclosing only a limited amount of information
about that life to her family.

What Mohanraj's novel emphasizes is that same-sex desire exists and is
negotiated both in the homeland and in the diaspora. A major difference we
see in Sindu's novel is that a lesbian is the first-person narrator and is thus
able to articulate her experiences in a way that the previously-mentioned
novels are not able to because much of the same-sex desire is described
through other, often homophobic, perspectives.

ARTICULATING IDENTITY IN THE DIASPORA

Stuart Hall has asserted that there are two ways of understanding cultural
identity—a collective one and one that is in flux. "The first position defines
'cultural identity' in terms of one, shared culture, a sort of collective 'one
true self' hiding inside the many other, more superficial or artificially imposed 'selves,' which people with a shared history and ancestry hold in
common" (234). The second sense of cultural identity "is a matter of 'becoming' as well as of 'being.' [. . .] Cultural identities come from somewhere,
have histories. But, like everything that is historical, they undergo constant
transformation" (236). It is the former, essentializing idea of cultural identity
to which the diasporic community depicted in Sindu's novel subscribes:
these diasporics believe that homeland and hostland are fixed and static, and
to embrace one through assimilation is to betray the other. Gayatri Gopinath
has said, "within the familial and domestic space of the nation as imagined
community, non-heteronormative sexuality is either criminalized, or dis-
avowed and elided; it is seen both as a threat to national integrity and as
perpetually outside the boundaries of nation, home, and family" (263). These
nationalist discourses and practices are reproduced in the diaspora. Instead of
being a source of support, this type of diasporic community patrols its borders and imposes restrictions and limits and enforces its authority, which is
reflected and replicated in a microcosmic way within the family unit as well.

Author R. Radhakrishan has discussed "the reality of a double life for immigrants, the ethnic private life and the American public life, with very little mediation between the two" (122). He goes on to say that "The two generations have different starting points and different givens, which creates a history of rupture within the 'same' community" (123). As a result, Radhakrishnan has argued that first-generation and second-generation immigrants should not presume to know what the older or younger generation has experienced. The family and the community depicted in *Marriage of a Thousand Lies* are rife with these very presumptions.

In Sindu's novel, Lucky (aka Lakshmi), the first-person narrator, has grown up in a diasporic Sri Lankan Tamil family in Massachusetts, meaning that there is significant tension between the context of the place where she is domiciled and the place that has shaped her family. She sees a diasporic community that provides both support and constraint, and she finds herself having to negotiate her personal gender identity and same-sex desire in a context that makes this negotiation highly fraught. At the beginning of the novel, she seems to have found a satisfactory strategy that enables her to fulfill her own desires while still pleasing her tradition-bound parents and community—she has married Krishna, her Indian gay best friend from college. This marriage of convenience enables both of them to present the illusion of marital bliss in public while dating whomever they really want in private. This solution begins to unravel when Lucky returns to her mother's house to help look after her grandmother who is ailing after a fall. She reconnects with her childhood best friend and first lover, Nisha—daughter of family friends—who is getting ready for her own arranged marriage and who thus faces some of the constraints imposed by the heteropatriarchal spaces of the Sri Lankan Tamil diasporic community that Lucky has, for a while at least, been able to evade.

Sindu has reflected in an interview with Raj Chakrapani on the painful realities of gender in diasporic communities with which Lucky and Nisha have to deal, and she has commented on the way in which their particular gendered identities shape their engagement with their community:

> But, to me, what really sets the two apart is their gender. Lucky is much more masculine than Nisha, and that masculinity marks her and outs her. Even if she dresses feminine, Lucky is visibly queer by the way she sits, the way she holds herself. And because of that, she is always the outsider who is trying desperately to fit in but can't. This in a lot of ways makes life harder for Lucky, but in some ways, it's what saves her, too. She is kept from continuing in the kind of decision Nisha makes because she can't completely hide inside the lies.
>
> This also makes Nisha, to me, the more tragic character. Nisha's femininity allows her to pass. She never has to acknowledge her queerness unless she wants to. In some ways, this is a privilege. She is not micromanaged the way

that Lucky is. She isn't subject to the homophobia of her community in the
form of rumors and gossip. But this ability to pass also becomes her cage.

Sindu's reflection here is poignant, in that it suggests the multiplicity of
gendered experience and the ways in which the ability to conform on the
surface to heteropatriarchal gender norms can actually drive individuals to
conformity in their private lives. These tensions between conformity and
nonconformity and between the varying pressures that gender performance
can bring to bear on a character play out in the protagonist's family as well.

Lucky's own family is a dysfunctional one. Her first-generation immigrant parents reflect some of the reasons why people leave the homeland for
a hostland. Her father, who came to the United States as a graduate student,
has relatively recently left her mother, who came to the hostland as a refugee,
to marry the latter's former best friend—another Sri Lankan Tamil who left
the homeland following the loss of her first husband and son during the
violence of the July 1983 riots. Lucky's parents have become diasporics due
to both the exigencies of war and a desire for upward mobility; as a result of
their experiences they put pressure on their children to conform to parental
and cultural expectations. Lucky's eldest sister Shyma has given up her white
American boyfriend to agree to an arranged marriage to a diasporic Sri
Lankan Tamil man, thereby subscribing completely, if unhappily, to expectations. Lucky's second sister Vidya has rebelled by cutting her ties with her
family for a relationship with an African-American man with whom she has
had a child and to pursue her artistic ambitions; she sees no possibility of
negotiation or compromise with her family or community. Each of the family
members seems in some way to have internalized a particular notion of what
it means to be a Sri Lankan Tamil in the United States—one must either
conform to the expectations of the family and the community or flee.
Lucky's mother constantly rebukes her daughters for acting out and wonders
what she has done to deserve such disobedient offspring. "She did something
terrible in her past life and is cursed with daughters who don't listen to her.
One who runs away, another who never acts like a brown lady should act. Be
a proper woman. Have a child. [. . .] Stop being a deviant. Do you have no
shame?" (175). Lucky's mother consistently polices the boundaries that her
diasporic community has established for itself based on a static notion of the
culture that existed in the homeland at the point of their departure from it.

Yet Lucky's mother herself has suffered and sometimes been ostracized
as a divorced woman in the diasporic community—despite the fact that it is
her husband who walked out of the marriage and married someone else soon
afterward—and tells her daughter about the fate awaiting her if she is a
"manless" woman. She has experienced the double standards of gender prevalent in the diasporic community but instead of critiquing them or rebelling
against them, she subscribes to them more closely, in effect disciplining

herself as well as her daughters. "After your father left, I worked hard to be part of this community. I paid a lot for my mistakes. I don't want you to suffer like I did. [. . .] You don't know how hard it'll be until you don't have it. Our world isn't kind to women without husbands" (235). The home that she has created illustrates Rosemary Marangoly George's assertion that "the basic organizing principle around which the notion of 'home' is built is a pattern of select inclusions and exclusions. Home is a way of establishing difference. Homes and home countries are exclusive" (1). Lucky's mother imposes exclusions on her daughters even as she attempts to create space for herself in a community that excludes divorced women, and these exclusions are shaped powerfully by the Sri Lankan Tamil homeland in which she no longer lives but to which she is powerfully attached, even when such an attachment contradicts her own interests. It is possible that Lucky's mother clings to the diasporic community that is representative of the homeland due to the trauma that she experienced as a result of the ethnic conflict: perhaps she associates the diasporic community and the traditions that it maintains so strictly with the security and support for which she craves following the instability and atrocities resulting from the war.

The hold that the diasporic community has over Lucky—as the only community that she has known for most of her life—is such that she feels it is impossible to come out to them. As she puts it, "Let me tell you something about being brown like me: your story is already written for you. Your free will, your love, your failure, all of it scratched into the cosmos before you're even born. My mother calls it fate, the story written on your head by the stars, the gods, never by you. Everyone is watching you, all the time, praising you when you abide by your directives, waiting until you screw up" (15). According to Marangoly George, "membership [in the home] is maintained by bonds of love, fear, power, desire and control," a situation that Sindu dramatizes here (9). While Lucky is in college, her mother discovers intimate texts from a girlfriend on Lucky's phone; she stops putting money in Lucky's bank account, which means that the latter runs out of funds and becomes homeless for a spell. This is what finally results in her sudden and somewhat desperate decision to marry Krishna, who has been disowned by his own family back in India when he came out to them. As a result of this marriage of convenience, Krishna gets a green card while Lucky gets to please her family and community. Despite the fact that the marriage is one of the "thousand lies" referred to in the title of the novel, it is actually a partnership in which Lucky and Krishna are able to be each other's confidantes and be absolutely open and truthful with, and mostly supportive of, each other. Lucky and Krishna's "lies," then, serve the purpose of creating a more truthful lifestyle for the two of them within the constraints of a heteronormative diasporic community.

The same hegemonic ideas—in the way the term was defined by Antonio Gramsci— that we see in Lucky's mother also hold true for Nisha, who knows she is in love with Lucky and wants to be with her but feels that this option is foreclosed for her as the only child of her parents. "We're not like them [Americans]," she tells Lucky. "We have to think about our families. If we lived like them, we would lose everything" (135). Even though she has and continues to declare her love for Lucky, initiates physical intimacy with her, expresses the desire to elope with Lucky, and reveals that she attempted to live a lesbian lifestyle while in college, Nisha feels unable to be open about her sexual identity to her parents or community, stating "I don't want to spend my life fighting a war I can't win" (135). Nisha's actions—based on her pessimistic belief that her sexuality will never be accepted by family or community—are shaped by the precarious tension between her gendered identity as a gay woman and her identity as a diasporic Sri Lankan Tamil living in a conservative heteronormative community. As Lucky reflects, "My parents are the kind of people who talk politics but never mention gay marriage, who watch the news but change the channel at the mention of gayness. Shame, dishonor, embarrassment. Five hundred Sri Lankan Tamil families in the greater Boston area, and not one of them has a gay kid" (208). Lucky's reference to the "greater Boston area" reflects the complexity of the idea of domicile for these families: very clearly, many of these families in the Boston area are likely to have gay children, but within the imagined framework of a diaspora that locates its real existence elsewhere, there is no way to give expression to this otherwise evident reality. The passage also complicates notions of assimilation and authenticity: to embrace the sort of authenticity claimed by the "[f]ive hundred Sri Lankan Tamil families" is to flout the authenticity of her own sexual identity and to invalidate her own desires. Meanwhile, her individual sense of what constitutes authenticity is ineluctably in tension with the creation of a distinctive communal identity, one that she both values and resents.

One question that arises is why it is hard for Lucky and Nisha to break away from cultural norms adhered to within the diasporic community. Even as they critique these norms, they are unable to reject them completely or, in Nisha's case, at all. Even as they desire to be independent, they also feel obliged to cater to the demands of their immediate and extended families as well as to the community. From the beginning, Lucky has been encouraged, scolded, and pressured into conforming to gender expectations. She is made to wear feminine clothes against her will. Even as an adult, a married woman, she feels compelled to get her mother's permission when she needs to break the curfew imposed by her mother or get a shorter haircut. She is aware of the disparities and contradictions within her life and shows an awareness of cultural and historical factors that have shaped the community of which she is a member, albeit a marginalized one. She critiques the colonial influence in South Asia that shaped gender expectations in the region: "In ancient India, before the British outlawed the practice, temples employed and housed dancers. [. . .] These devdasis enjoyed the privilege of a married woman in society but answered to no man. They weren't expected to remain chaste or give up their careers to become housewives" (66). She is also interested in the ambiguities in Hindu scriptures that are often suppressed but provide potential for queer readings: "I am named after a Hindu goddess sometimes pictured massaging her husband's shins as he sleeps. [. . .] Every time Lakshmi's husband Vishnu takes a human form, she does too. But sometimes Vishnu incarnates as a woman, usually in order to seduce men. And then what does Lakshmi do? Sit up in heaven and try not to watch? Or maybe she does, maybe she finds herself drawn to his new soft curves" (64). Both Lucky and Nisha live simultaneously in the quotidian, everyday world of Boston, which allows for an acknowledgment of their relationship, and in the idealized world of the Sri Lankan Tamil diaspora, which has chosen to disavow their identities and those of other gay men and women. This tension illustrates Marangoly George's dictum that "home" and "homeland" can be enabling and restrictive in parallel ways. Lucky's reflections on the devdasis and on Vishnu and Lakshmi show how she works to bring those two worlds together by re-reading foundational texts and cultural practices.

Sindu has underscored that resistance to these sorts of restrictions take different forms for different people and have the capacity to shape the kind of home that an individual either creates or accepts. Sindu has said in an interview with Crystal Hana Kim,

> It was important to me for my characters to all make different choices when faced with similar pressures. All the women in the novel are dealing with cultural misogyny and patriarchal oppression, but they all choose different paths. Similarly, I wanted my queer characters to choose different paths. I know a bunch of people who have chosen, like Lucky, to have marriages of convenience. But I know a lot more people who are like Nisha, who aren't fully comfortable with their sexualities themselves and so they deny it. Usually those stories don't end well. I guess to me this novel is as much an exploration of that choice as it is a warning.

In this sense, the differing fates of Lucky and Nisha become integral to an exploration of the relation between sexuality and home that is not an uncomplicated celebration of either the culture of the homeland or of all the choices that women make in response to pressure from their community, but rather an opportunity to probe and evaluate these choices. Lucky's story illustrates the power of homeland narratives even as it proffers the possibility of a new understanding of home in its closing scenes.

Lucky is able to find an alternative home site through a group of Nisha's friends who are part of an all-women "rugby house," and the women she gets to know there form the first queer community that she has ever known. The unconditional acceptance and the unwavering support provided by the women enable Lucky to reconcile herself to the fact that Nisha will never leave the familial space and cannot be "rescued." Even though Lucky has been raised to believe that her fate is written on her forehead, she gradually begins to challenge this belief. She tells her mother that she will be getting a divorce and reiterates her reasons for making this break: "I want to be me" (270). She will no longer try to conform or to avoid the resulting confrontations with and censure of the diasporic community: "In every story there's what is written for you, and then there's what you write. I think of what to tell Kris. I think of Nisha in her wedding saree [. . .] Amma crying upstairs mourning a story I never wanted to write. Can we escape fate? Can we change it?" (271). Lucky's first step in changing her fate is to take her own wedding photograph off the wall and bury it. Doing this shows that Lucky is confronting the task of creating a new sort of diasporic identity, one that allows space for her gendered identity as well as her national origin and which reflects the complexity of her position as a woman who is both enabled and restrained by competing concepts of home. The "rugby house" itself allows Lucky to create an alternative mode of being domiciled, in which both "home" and "homeland" are redefined through elective affiliations among women.

Sindu presents two faces of diaspora that are crucial to understanding the relationship between migration and sexuality in much of South Asian diasporic literature. As Sindu shows, the presence of a cohesive diasporic community can come with its own restrictions and pitfalls. The novel reinforces the sense that questions of sexual and gender identity resonate in particularly powerful ways for second-generation members of the South Asian diaspora in the United States, and that new understandings of what it means to be diasporic may be necessary to meet the needs of younger generations for both security and inclusion. Lucky and Nisha may be physically domiciled in suburban Boston, but their sense of home is shaped by the remoteness of their ancestral homeland and by the intimate interiors of their own identity in ways that their location in Massachusetts both enables and undercuts. Ultimately, Sindu maps new territory in relation to our understanding of home, both building on and extending the earlier work of diasporic Sri Lankan Tamil writers like Selvadurai, Ganeshananthan, and Mohanraj. Homeland and hostland, ethnicity and sexuality, identity and desire, all intersect in Sindu's novel in ways that reinforce the complexity and elusiveness of home and the importance of seizing control of and revisiting this powerful concept.

NOTE

1. For a more extensive discussion of the sexual and gender politics in *Giraya*, please see my "Sexuality, Class and Consumption in Punyakante Wijenaike's Giraya."

REFERENCES

Chakrapani, Raj. December 11, 2017. "The Ability to Pass Becomes Her Cage: Talking with SJ Sindu." *The Rumpus*. therumpus.net/2017/12/the-rumpus-interview-with-sj-sindu.

Ganeshananthan, V. V. 2008. *Love Marriage*. New York: Random House.

Gopinath, Gayatri. 2003. "Nostalgia, Desire, Diaspora: South Asian Sexualities in Motion." In Jana Evans Braziel and Anita Mannur (eds.). *Theorizing Diaspora*. Maldon, MA: Blackwell. 261–79.

Hall, Stuart. 2003. "Cultural Identity and Diaspora." In Jana Evans Braziel and Anita Mannur (eds.). *Theorizing Diaspora*. Maldon, MA: Blackwell. 233–46.

Kim, Crystal Hana. June 27, 2017. "An Interview with SJ Sindu on her Debut Novel Marriage of a Thousand Lies." *Apojee Journal*. apogeejournal.org/2017/06/22/interview-sj-sindu-marriage-thousand-lies-june-2017-soho-press.

Jayasuriya, Maryse. 2011. "Sexuality, Class and Consumption in Punyakante Wijenaike's Giraya." *Margins: A Journal of Literature and Culture* 1.1.

Marangoly George, Rosemary. 1996. *The Politics of Home: Postcolonial Relocations and Twentieth-Century Fiction*. Berkeley: University of California Press.

Mohanraj, Mary Anne. 2006. *Bodies in Motion*. New York: Harper Perennial.

Radhakrishnan, R. 2003. "Ethnicity in the Age of Diaspora." In Jana Evans Braziel and Anita Mannur (eds.). *Theorizing Diaspora*. Maldon, MA: Blackwell. 119–31.

Selvadurai, Shyam. 1994. *Funny Boy*. San Diego: Harcourt Brace.

———. 2013. *Hungry Ghosts*. New York: Penguin.

Sindu, S. J. 2017. *Marriage of a Thousand Lies*. New York: Soho Press.

Wijenaike, Punyakante. 1971. *Giraya*. Paddukka, Sri Lanka: State Printing Cooperation.

Chapter Six

Reimagining Reluctance

The South Asian Diaspora and Global "Homing" in Mira Nair's The Reluctant Fundamentalist

Shuhita Bhattacharjee

In this chapter, I examine Mira Nair's 2013 film, *The Reluctant Fundamentalist* (Nair, Pilcher, Boghani, et al. 2013), as an adaptation of and in relation to Mohsin Hamid's 2007 novel by the same title—a post-9/11 novel written from a nonwestern perspective that Nair, as a South Asian female filmmaker rooted in the very turbulence the text describes, turns into a film in a post-2011 world. I will argue that Nair, located within the South Asian diaspora, and therefore part of the community most affected by situations of global violence and most invested in the questions raised by Hamid, adopts a less contentious and more geopolitically strategic position than the novel—advocating global peace, suggesting the moral relativity of agents on *both* sides of this conflict (East and West, South Asian/Muslim and American), and emphasizing the need for them to connect in order to recuperate the possibility of a global "Home" for the diasporic inhabitant of fractured spaces.

Nair films the novel in the aftermath of the killing of Osama bin Laden around which time the world was erupting with terrorist attacks, including those against India in 2008 and 2011, and tells a somewhat different tale. As the photo diary on this book-film transition, *The Reluctant Fundamentalist: From Book to Film* (henceforth referred to as *From Book to Film*), notes—it is the "coming-of-age story of a young man who strives to find himself" over a decade—a personal tale that is embossed over another turbulent geopolitical trajectory—that "between 9/11 and the killing of Osama Bin Laden" (2011) during which decade the "young man grows up" (Nair 2013, 88, vii).[1] In retelling this story, however, Nair creatively intervenes, more invested—

107

as a South Asian diasporic filmmaker would more likely be—in bridging gaps, remedying misunderstandings, and recuperating a sense of a global "Home" that transcends borders instead of longing for a remote and regional place of origin as "Home" and upholding a partisan agenda. The aim is not to perform a biographical reading of the film, but to engage in a historically and geopolitically informed reading of Nair's creative reworkings that likely draw on her sensibilities as a South Asian diasporic woman characterized by a set of understandable experiences, anxieties, and yearnings. I will show how, while the text is marked by an essential ambiguity, and enters into a much more philosophical introspection on the meaning of "fundamentals," the film makes a more contemporarily relevant point about the "war on terror" and responds to contemporary urgencies by prioritizing the offering of a moral solution to it—a solution that brings with it the promise of a comforting global "Home" for the wandering migrant. In Nair's cinematic rendering, avoiding any moral ambiguity, both sides are in fact endowed with justificatory moral impulses for their actions. This creative decision to underplay the hostility between the two sides, as well as the moral reprehensibility of each (and especially of the West) is designed to further the possibility of global peace. Additionally, the film also elides the more uncomfortable and open questions one encounters in the novel surrounding human proclivities toward intolerance, cruelty, and violence—attempting to re-channel the deeply philosophical motivations of the novel into a more practical geopolitical one.

Hamid's novel tells an intriguing tale of foggy moralities in the first person where Changez, a Pakistani university professor, speaks in a monologue to an unidentified and silent American interlocutor at a Lahore café about his own American dream and his resulting success on Wall Street, followed by his complete disenchantment with this heartless commercialism and a subsequent return to Pakistan. Changez talks to the American of being at the top of his class at Princeton, of being hired by Jim (the boss at Underwood Samson, a top-ranking valuation firm on Wall Street) amidst cut-throat competition between the very brightest, of being close friends with Wainwright, of falling hopelessly in what was essentially a doomed love with Erica, of being among the most valued and successful at his company, of being identified as the cultural and class "other" by Jim (who himself was an outsider to the privileged that he had contended with and won against), of then encountering doubts and realizing his misplaced loyalties, of heartbreakingly learning that he was furthering American (Western) neo-colonialism against the interests of his own nation while Pakistan continued to be in the throes of poverty and war (with India), and of finally returning home to Pakistan to teach in a university. The novel ends in an atmosphere of indistinct fear, lingering doubt, and impending violence without a clear sense of the moral allegiances or hidden motivations of either party—speaker or listener.[2]

Mira Nair converts this plot into a fast-paced thriller that begins with the kidnap of Anse Rainier, an American professor at Lahore University. Shortly after this the American rescue operation begins, and Robert Lincoln (Bobby), a journalist who we later learn is also a CIA asset, visits Changez (a Pakistani professor who teaches at Lahore University) at Pak Tea House with the ostensible purpose of interviewing him. However, Changez, while narrating the same story as in the novel, shows his awareness of Bobby's real purpose. As the teeming student crowd gathered around the Pak Tea House threatens to erupt in a violent frenzy when the Pakistani police and American CIA prepare to attack in an attempt to find Rainier, Changez and Bobby try to trust each other in the interest of ensuring a nonviolent end to this inflammable situation. Changez in the film, who it is clear by now is a peace-loving professor with no dubious terrorist connections, tries to help Bobby find Rainier when Bobby sincerely appeals to him for help and tries convincing him by citing the future of his students. However, cultural suspicions get in the way and Bobby suspects Changez of betrayal toward him and complicity with the kidnappers when he receives the mistaken information that Rainier has already been killed by the kidnappers. Bobby tries to threaten Changez and leave, shocking Changez who was still genuinely committed to a peaceful resolution. This gives way to turbulent outbursts in the mob and as Bobby is rescued by the CIA in a speeding car, he watches Changez's favorite student, Sameer, get killed by the forces, and after communicating with the other CIA officers in the vehicle finally realizes the unfortunate miscommunication and the fatal cultural distrust that had caused the breakdown of his pact with Changez—something that signals the larger defeat of the very possibility of cross-cultural alliance. The film ends with a hopeful note, however, with both protagonists internally lamenting this breakdown of trust and Changez speaking soulfully of the possibility of peace at Sameer's funeral.

The ultimate aim of both the novel and the film in one sense is to expose the shaky grounds on which the "war against terror" and allegations against "fundamentalism" rest, and to blur the lines between global heroes and villains. Both the novel and the film (drawing from the novel) show Underwood Samson initially to be an unproblematic meritocracy where employees are exhorted to "Focus on the fundamentals" (Hamid 2007, 98)—a phrase meant to implicitly remind them as much of the company's business basics as of the American ethic of commercial ruthlessness. To this world of apparent justice (where a racial outsider like Changez and a class outsider like Jim are provided equal opportunity to succeed), is contrasted the global specter of "Islamic fundamentalism" that is represented through uncomfortably familiar rhetoric. Both the novel and the film, however, are alive with an ironic undercurrent from the very start so that amidst the general atmosphere of unpredictability, suspense, distrust, and fear, one is unable to clearly align Changez with Islamic fundamentalism[3] or unproblematically condemn this religio-political force as the source of all evil. Instead, the reader/viewer realizes through Changez's monologue that the commercial fundamentalism that is embodied by America's inhumane, unthinking, and arrogant pursuit of profit beyond all other values and concerns is no different from the religious fundamentalism that is so universally singled out as the germ of all global crises. Mira Nair writes of how she used Underwood Samson "to explore the concept of economic fundamentalism alongside that of political fundamentalism" (Nair 2013, 57).[4] The illusion of a just and democratic meritocracy surrounding America falls through as the nation begins to show its prejudicial teeth in the aftermath of 9/11—in the novel ("even at Underwood Samson I could not entirely escape the growing importance of *tribe*") and even more graphically in the film (through humiliating strip-searches and interrogations) (Hamid 2007, 117). Changez realizes that he is a "modern-day janissary" awakened by the quiet reflection of the man at the helm of the last company he goes to evaluate on behalf of Underwood Samson (Juan-Bautista at the head of a publishing company in Chile in the novel and Nazmi Kemal at Basak Yayimci Publishing in Istanbul in the film) (Hamid 2007, 152). This moment is dramatized poignantly in the film through the song, "Mori Araj Suno" ("Hear me out, O Lord," composed by Faiz Ahmed Faiz, and translated in the Photo Diary) where he appeals to his Lord who promised him kingship of the entire world, saying to the Lord that he does not want this, what he needs instead is "a grain of respect," and then ends by saying to the Lord: "If this pact displeases You/Then let me go find another God" (Nair 2013, 154).

What makes Nair the most creative, sensitive, and invested conduit for the cinematic rendering of the novel is her personal history of divided belongings between Pakistan and India on the one hand with her father's house being in Lahore, and India and America on the other with her professional life charted mostly in the United States.[5] Hamid himself considers this a crucial factor in the way they bonded over the collaborative homework on the film project and in the way this led to the successful cinematic output. Speaking of the centrality of diasporic sensitivity in the composing of this novel and in the making of the film, he writes: "Mira profoundly and intuitively understood my novel, so I was confident about her being at the helm of affairs" (Nair 2013, 23). He further explains how he "really clicked with her as a person" because she is "someone who comes from South Asia and has spent many years [there]" but "has lived abroad for almost half her life" just like him (Nair 2013, 23). Charles Gant concurs in his essay when he explains how the novel's "themes of assimilation and alienation" in the story caught between Wall Street and Lahore "resonated . . . with Nair, who was born in

India, educated at Delhi and Harvard Universities and resides in New York"
(Gant 2013, 18). This diasporic hybridity of identity—something that Hamid
calls a "mongrel" identity—becomes the definitive biographical and creative
grounding for novelistic composition, engaged filmmaking, and intuitive acting with respect to *The Reluctant Fundamentalist* (Singh 2012a, 149).[6] Nair
herself suggests that the diasporic experience of being split between India
and America makes her more sensitive at registering the vibrations of violence, contingencies of loyalties, and fractures within identities—fragilities
likely to make her a committed advocate for global understanding. She delineates her divided identities, firstly between India and Pakistan, when she
explains how her father grew up in Lahore before 1947, and how even she
"[a]s a child of modern India" was "raised like a Lahori"—"speaking Urdu,
quoting the poems of Faiz Ahmed Faiz, listening to the ghazals of Iqbal Bano
and Noor Jehan,"—yet knowing that "there was a wall" between India and
Pakistan "that could never be crossed" (Nair 2013, xi). And then, she explains the second facet of her split allegiance—that between India and America—which unites her, she says, with Hamid: "I came from India to America
when I was nineteen and, like Mohsin, have lived more than half my life
outside the subcontinent" (Nair 2013, xii). Summing up the relationship between her fractured diasporic existence on the cleavage of different nation-
states and her creative vocation she says: "I believe I may have been put on
this earth to tell stories of living between worlds" (Nair 2013, xi). She explains the reason she related to Hamid's novels and his protagonist's feelings
of alienness and his search for "Home," showing the reader how she is
organically connected to the diasporic sensibility at the heart of the novel
(embodied both by its author and by its protagonist):

> In the bones of Mohsin's tale, I saw a dialogue between one side and the other.
> And it is this dialogue that embodies my own life story . . . Unwittingly, my
> films, my work and life came to be about the seesaw between these worlds [of
> India and America between which my life was split], in which I felt both an
> insider and an outsider. And like many of us who live hybrid lives, I railed
> against the line that was drawn a decade ago when Bush coined the "axis of
> evil" and built a wall of myopia between one way of life and another. (Nair
> 2013, xii)

The idea of alienness across split geographical locations and the yearning for
a "Home"/"homeland" beyond borders are not only characteristic of Nair's
own diasporic reality but are also foundational to the scholarly theorization
of the diaspora. Alison Blunt examines the idea of "Home" or "domicile" in
the context of the Anglo-Indian diaspora, studying the "geographies of
home" that she observes are articulated "on scales from the domestic to the
diasporic" and experienced as a "space of belonging and alienation" (Blunt
2005, 2). Even a cursory look at critics who examine South Asian diasporic

works—such as that of Mohsin Hamid, or by extension into the realm of cinema, Mira Nair—reveals the same preoccupation with the idea of "Home." Lisa Lau distinguishes "diasporic South Asian writers" (those of South Asian origin who write from the West, such as Hamid, or by extension, Nair) from the "home South Asian authors" (those of South Asian origin who write from within South Asia), and notes that the work of diasporic South Asian women authors is characterized by a "double-consciousness" (resulting from the South Asian "Home" of their imagination/memory and the alien West in which they are situated), and by authorial notions of identity that are intimately connected with "concepts of *home* and place, as the space of return and of consolidation of the Self, enabled by the encounter not with the other, but with one's own" (Lau 2005, 252; emphasis added). Maxey concurs about the focus on the idea of "Home" in the work of South Asian diasporic works, observing how it is used to "raise provocative questions about changing societies and the place of ethnic South Asians within them" and how also serves as an "important synecdoche for wider social and national concerns" (Maxey 2006, 29). In landmark works of scholarship more generally about diasporic narratives, figures like Homi Bhaba, Frantz Fanon, Paul Gilroy, James Clifford, and Stuart Hall have emphasized the need to surrender essentialist notions of the "Home" based on ideas of purity. Vijay Agnew notes, for instance, the need to challenge earlier templates of diaspora narratives with "their fixed notion of home," where "the homeland is perceived nostalgically as an 'authentic' space of belonging" and the place of settlement as "somehow 'inauthentic' and undesirable" (Agnew 2005, 195). Avtar Brah understands the idea of "Home" in the diasporic context in non-"essentialist" terms, seeing the diaspora as a process of "historical displacements" that bring into play a "multi-locationality within and across territorial, cultural and psychic boundaries"—so that the "diasporian subjectivity" while not "rootless" is still characterized by a "multi-placedness of home" (Brah 1996, 197). Offering a critique of "discourses of fixed origins," Brah speaks of how the diasporic condition is characterized by "a homing desire" which is "not the same as the desire for a 'homeland.'" This home that is marked by longing and multi-locationality is what lies at the heart of Nair's cinematic construction of a global and "multi-locational" home and expresses what is implicitly her own diasporic experience of alienness across fractured geographies and her own "homing desire" in a time of violent cultural clashes and displacements (Brah 1996, 197). In fact, Nair confesses in an interview that post 9/11 "so much has changed in New York that it does not give you that *homely feeling* which it did before" and that she had made this movie for her son who was turning twenty-one and was "looking for *a place to call home*" (*NEWS18*, "*Reluctant Fundamentalist* is for my son: Mira Nair").[7] Not only does this make evident Nair's intensely personal search and longing for a "home," it also makes clear her attention to a similar "homing desire" experienced by her son, understandably soaked in his South Asian diasporic inheritance and the contemporary transnational currents. Nair's deep and pertinent search for "home," both at a personal and a cinematic level, in the displaced and violent post-9/11 world, echoes therefore the migrant's desire to "feel at home" in the host country that Gabriel Scheffer recognizes as typical to the diasporic condition (Scheffer 2003, 7). The self-conscious intentionality at the heart of Nair's cinematic construction of a "Home" is thus a matter not just of politically-aware intellectual intervention, designed to achieve a more harmonious world order, but also of personal emotion and innermost longings. The many aspects of this "homing desire," including the intellectual and the affective, become clearer if we look closely at Chandra Mohanty's 1993 essay called "Defining Genealogies: Feminist Reflections on Being South Asian in North America." In the essay, Mohanty asks what "Home"—"crucial to immigrants and migrants"—really is, whether it is "a geographical space, a historical space, an emotional sensory space" (Mohanty 1993, 352). Transatlantic South Asian authors in particular, deconstruct the very idea of home in a linguistic and philosophical sense, locating it not merely in the geographical or the ancestral (Maxey 2006). Focusing on such a possible creative redefinition of "Home," Mohanty concludes that in diasporic experience, "[p]olitical solidarity and a sense of family could be melded together imaginatively to create *a strategic space* I could call 'Home'" (1993, 352; emphasis added). It is precisely this intelligent and *strategic* construction of a sense of a global "Home"—an "ethno-global vision" of home—that we see in Nair's cinematic recreation of Hamid's story of diasporic alienness, designed to cater both to geopolitical and personal ends (Agnew 2005, 147).

FROM NOVEL TO FILM: CINEMATIC REWORKINGS

I will study in detail the series of creative alterations to the novel that Mira Nair makes, transforming in many ways the inherent motivations behind the text. Let me begin by noting the way Nair insightfully develops the thematic impulses of the text to highlight the centrality of the diasporic experience of the migrant, Changez, but to also crucially show Bobby to be a migrant himself—thus universalizing the diasporic condition with its search for a home. Nair's Changez beautifully intuits the lost in-betweenness of diasporic existence that he imagines Bobby must be experiencing—similar to what he himself had tragically experienced during his American life away from home—a story he narrates with great pathos and drama. He imagines for Bobby, and accurately as the film suggests, what a displaced diasporic life might feel like in its rootlessness, confusion of loyalties, and absence of love. He says to Bobby:

> I see a man with hash under his fingernails who likely smokes it alone. I see the odd white man who lives in the old quarter and only ventures out to buy local fruit and local girls. He's been here so long his own blood family have forgotten him, and there's nobody here to replace them.

Changez narrates this reality—uncannily similar to his own experience of loneliness in a state of split existence—addressing Bobby in the Pak Tea House in the current moment. But it is filmed interestingly where Changez's narrative actually appears as a voice-over or off-camera commentary and the visual shows Bobby pensively pacing around in Lahore, implicitly living out the life that Changez is describing. Nair reimagines what it means to be in this state—the globally suspect state of being a migrant in the diasporic space[8]—and the truths it makes you realize such as the multi-locationality, fluidity, unreliability, and necessity of homes. As Changez says to Bobby at the end of these lines, expressing the shared truth that diasporic experientiality brings, trying to save him suffering and alienation: "I'm telling you something that it took me a long time to realize. Some truths take their time." In Nair's film, lurched in the diasporic state all-too-familiar for her, both the central characters are able to share a deeper "global imaginary"—i.e., the palpable realization of conflict and the urgent necessity for mutual understanding—and are therefore able to resolve to move beyond mutual cultural suspicion (Darda 2014, 108). It is precisely this shared diasporic experientiality between the two primary characters, grounded in the South Asian diasporic life of the filmmaker herself, that brings them together in the film in their desperate clawing at peace, and in their hopeful longings for a "Home"— however shifting and multi-locational—across the globe no matter where diasporic travels take them.

Moreover, Nair, with her split loyalties between India and Pakistan on the one hand, and India and the United States on the other, dilutes the vituperative rhetoric surrounding India that peppers the novel. Changez in the novel attacks what he portrays as India's militant political stance as "the more belligerent" one between the two neighbours, and lambasts the diplomatic and military support provided to India by the United States which he notes allowed India to act "with America's connivance" (Hamid 2007, 143, 148). The text shows the existing acidulous relationship between the two neighbors when the narrator says that after "armed men had assaulted the Indian Parliament" in 2008, "[o]pinion was divided as to whether" these men had anything to do with Pakistan" while "there was unanimity in the belief that India would do all it could to harm us, and that despite the assistance we had given America in Afghanistan, America would not fight at our side" (Hamid 2007, 121, 126–7). Pakistan is portrayed by Changez as the weaker neighbor ("vulnerab[le] to intimidation"), treated unfairly and forced to reside "within commuting distance of a million or so hostile [Indian] troops who could, at any moment, attempt a full-scale invasion" (Hamid 2007, 128, 127). Being of South Asian origin herself, Nair, on the other hand, fuses a more united/ collaborative South Asian identity in the face of the American "other." Her film registers the Pakistan-India tensions only contextually at the time of Bina's (Changez's sister) wedding. It shows her lament the fact that her wedding required planning for war contingencies ("bomb shelter contingency plan") and the narrator informs us further that around this time the partying became more "raucous" and the food more "delicious" as the war-related anxieties mounted. Referring only offhandedly to this India-Pakistan animosity, Nair instead sharpens the US-Global South binary, foregrounding the American cultural and political arrogance in the face of South Asian humility and creativity.[9] Thus, the film strategically shifts the location of Changez's second Underwood Samson assignment from Chile to Istanbul. This choice is explained in one way by the cinematographer, Declan Quinn, who says that "Istanbul was a beautiful city to set the publisher scene—a real blend of European and Muslim culture in an ancient city" (Nair 2013, 95). But I would argue that Nair goes beyond this attempt at showcasing the shared inheritance of the East and the West. The shift allows her to suggest a larger alliance of most overtly the Muslim world (Pakistan, Afghanistan, the Middle East)[10] and in the larger sense the global south, where India, Pakistan, and the middle east, among others, forge a common front opposed to the American cultural sovereignty worldwide). Thus in the film, Changez, after declaring that his own father is a Pakistani (Urdu) poet, addresses Nezma Kamal—who supervises the publishing firm in Istanbul and publishes as we see later books of Turkish poetry as well—using a significant personal pronoun in the plural ("our") to signify a shared politico-cultural community: "[Y]ou are a keeper of our culture in this part of the world." And to this cultural frontier is opposed the globally dominant Western alliance led and represented by the United States, and Changez celebrates its spectacular 9/ 11-downfall, speaking to Robert Lincoln (Bobby) with great relish about his "pleasure" at the sight of "arrogance brought low." At this level then, Nair's film becomes a commentary on America's putative cultural imperialism, and as the work of a South Asian diasporic filmmaker it seems to promise a larger South Asian (or Global South) alliance in the face of this behemoth.

But, on the whole, Nair's film adopts a much more *strategic* position in order to "strategic"-ally sculpt a "Home" across the diaspora, echoing Mohanty's idea of the diasporic "Home" as a "strategic space" (Mohanty 1993, 352). As a South Asian diasporic woman, caught not only personally but structurally in this space marked by fractured allegiances and persistent alienness, and by a yearning for "Home" and belonging, Nair's creative intervention is designed to carve a "Home" that is global and not partisan, based on a pan-hemispheral understanding and trust. Being a diasporic South Asian and additionally a woman, and belonging therefore to communities that are perhaps most affected (emotionally and practically) in situations of global crises, and intensely aware of what is at stake for South-Asia in the (Indo-Pak) infighting encouraged by Western/American intervention, Nair moves instead in the direction of global peace, suggesting wisely the presence of benign agents on both sides (East and West, South Asian/Muslim and American) and emphasizing the need for them to connect. Nair's most critical reworking, therefore, lies in the area of the moral commentary that it offers, significantly altering the inflection of Hamid's text. For generic requirements, as well as in answer to contemporary urgencies, the film essentially makes the same larger point as the text—problematizing the Western interpretation of "terrorism" and "fundamentalism"—but through a clearly resolved picture of chosen loyalties and political standpoints. As I will proceed to show in my reading that follows, there is no confusion of moralities. The west is not villainized in the least but almost valorized, and both sides are in fact endowed with justificatory moral impulses. While the novel ends with unresolved tensions, mutual suspicion, and unclear allegiances, the film shows the disastrous result of such cultural distrust and provides a geopolitical solution toward establishing peace and recuperating a global "Home" for the diasporic wanderer—addressing the most immediate realm of pragmatic and emotional anxieties for a South Asian woman caught in the creative and yet violent cross-currents of a warring post-9/11 diasporic space.

The novel dwells in an intense and recurrent atmosphere of suspicion and conspiracy with no clear heroes or villains, both at an individual level (neither the Pakistani speaker nor the American interlocutor are openly vilified) and in a collective sense (neither Pakistan/the Global South nor America emerge as devious). As Hamid explains, the preoccupation of the novel's mystifying form as well as its content is with "the tension which comes from a sense of mutual suspicion between America and the Muslim world" (Yaqin 2008, 46). But despite this obvious binary, there are no clear indications of authorial moral endorsement in favor of either side. As Claudia Perner notes, referring also to Alastair Sooke's essay, the "predatory imagery which peppers the passages in which the narrator directly addresses his American listener keeps the reader wondering who will in the end turn out to be the hunter and who will find himself to be prey" (Perner 2011, 29; referring to Sooke, "*The* Reluctant Fundamentalist"). The form of the dramatic monologue that the novel adopts fuels the atmosphere of suspicion and conspiracy further by revealing very little of the unsaid thoughts of the speaker and none at all of the interlocutor (that are unfiltered by the speaker).[11] The text is marked by an essential ambiguity and is significantly structured as a dramatic monologue—a genre that is by its very nature covert (unrevelatory of all perspectives) and that mystifies the extent to which the silent interlocutor agrees with the speaker. Charles Gant quotes the producer, Lydia Dean Pilcher, who observes: "The novel reads like a psychological thriller. It has the Hitchcockian quality of the ticking bomb; the intrigue of the situation that makes you keep turning the pages to see what's going to happen" (Gant 2013, 18). Through these tense meshes of the novel—thriller-like in its texture and potently suggestive in its empty spaces/silences—we are tactfully alerted to the inherent villainy and potential violence of both the Pakistani speaker and his American listener.

At a basic level, both the text and the film highlight the exploitative, predatory, commercial, and rapacious nature of the American marketplace (that includes the American academia and the American workplace)—Changez in the novel uses the prostitutional metaphor to emphasize the crass commercialism of the American academia ("Princeton raised her skirt for the corporate recruiters who came onto campus and . . . showed them some skin . . . I was a perfect breast . . .—tan, succulent, seemingly defiant of gravity") and Changez in the film speaks of the militaristic ruthlessness of American commerce (displayed by the "Navy Seals of financing" at Underwood Samson) (Hamid 2007, 4–5). The text, however, is unique in the emphasis it lays on the suggestively sly and threatening nature of the American interlocutor. In the absence of an overt moral motivation for his menacing presence in Lahore, the American figure in the novel acquires an ethically suspect bearing even for the reader. This man in the novel is (arguably) less than forthright or noble, pretending to be a common civilian when Changez strongly suggests and clearly intuits that he is an armyman or a spy (a possible CIA agent) on a covert mission. His fidgety and cautious demeanor that Changez refers to (texting instead of calling back a contact, reaching under his jacket for what he says is a wallet but which Changez is sure is a gun, and displaying nervous and invasive predator-prey behavior) arouses the reader's moral suspicions repeatedly (Hamid 2007, 2, 30, 5, 31). Even more shockingly, defying typical readerly expectations, this Western figure that looms visibly uninvited and ominous on the Lahore skyline is shown to be implicitly lascivious, such as when Changez suggests that, not unlike the typical simultaneous representation of Islamic conservatism and prurience, the American also lecherously ogles women (with an "intensity of . . . gaze" and gets "distracted") and one particular student from the nearby National College of Arts "ca[tches] [his] eye" (Hamid 2007, 16, 22).

The novel also portrays Changez, the Pakistani speaker, as equally unpredictable and potentially violent. There is a consistent emphasis on the Pakistani relish of visceral desires, however violent to humane taste or cultural propriety they may be. Thus, Changez declares the "inordinate pride" that the Pakistanis have in their food, calls the spread in the restaurants surrounding them a "purely carnivorous feast" that is "delectable" and that "harks back to an era before man's knowledge of cholesterol made him fearful of his prey" (Hamid 2007, 101). Unashamed of this proud predatoriness, and confident that "[t]here is great satisfaction to be had in touching one's prey" (Hamid

2007, 123), Changez explains with great satisfaction that the restaurants around were untainted by the presence of a "western dish" on their menus. He declares to his American interlocutor:

> These, sir, are predatory delicacies, delicacies imbued with a hint of luxury, of wanton abandon. Not for us the vegetarian recipes one finds across the border to the east, nor the sanitized, sterilized, processed meats so common in your homeland! Here we are not squeamish when it comes to facing the consequences of our desire. (Hamid 2007, 101)

And Changez is able to draw together the Eastern (Pakistani) and Western (American, represented by his companion) sensibilities, showing how the American has followed his advice to touch his prey because his "fingers are tearing the flesh of [the] kebab" (Hamid 2007, 123). He is able to show moreover, that despite the politically correct rhetoric of humanitarianism and libertarianism, the Americans are inherently given to the same decadent and ruthless pursuit of pleasures and instincts. Thus, speaking in a different context (of sexual desire), Changez points to how "savor[ing] the denial of gratification" is the "most un-American of pleasures" (Hamid 2007, 69). Changez explains how these are basic human instincts and tendencies, showing for instance how humanity in general is able to experience the finesse of women's delicate perfume and the carnivorous feast that surrounds them simultaneously. Changez says: "It is remarkable indeed how we human beings are capable of delighting in the mating call of a flower while we are surrounded by the charred carcasses of our fellow animals—but then we are remarkable creatures" (Hamid 2007, 78). Therefore, Changez, through his apparently unrelated comments on human approaches to food, is effectively able to indicate how questionable the claims to morality are that are to be seen on both sides (the east and the west). He shows that the American is no superior, only a hypocrite, in not following through to the full implication of his desire, something that the Pakistani is not scared of doing ("Here we are not squeamish when it comes to facing the consequences of our desire") (Hamid 2007, 101).[12]

Besides obfuscating the moral positionality of both sides, the novel continues to baffle us with many uncomfortable questions that it leaves interestingly unanswered—the question of the unavoidable temptation one feels toward violence against the arrogant enemy and the ultimate limits of one's tolerance when confronted with intolerance—questions that drive us to entertain the possibility for human weakness and cruelty. We see tense moments in the novel when Changez relishes the televised sight of the twin towers crashing (which I will discuss later in detail), or when at several points he seems to threaten his American listener with violence in return for what he perceives to be a covert preparation for attack, or when he stands undeterred on the precipice of physical violence after being accosted in the parking lot with a racial slur in the 9/11 aftermath (yelling back and grabbing the "tire iron" from his car, letting "the cold metal of its shaft . . . [rest] hungrily" in his hands, and "for a few murderous seconds" feeling "fully capable of wielding it with sufficient violence to shatter the bones of his skull") (Hamid 2007, 118).

Nair's film performs certain dramatic alterations. It changes the entire context, adding urgency, pace,[13] and a moral overtone to the situation by grounding the plot in the kidnapping of Anse Rainier. Charles Gant quotes producer, Lydia Dean Pilcher, who says, "We concocted different directions in terms of what the urgent situation was that was causing the conversation to be tense" (Gant 2013, 18). The sub-plot they finally constructed allows Bobby (Robert Lincoln), the "journalist and CIA asset," the moral (and emotional since he says Rainier was his "friend") motivation that justifies his and America's lurking (and clearly invasive and unwelcome) presence among the largely peace-loving student community that populates the Pak Tea House (Gant 2013, 18). William Wheeler, one of the three screenwriters, explains that the writing team decided that while the film will also shift between two timeframes, present-day Lahore and the American/Western experience in the past, in the film, unlike in the novel, "the present-day story would be a fully fleshed out espionage story with a beginning, a middle and an end" (Nair 2013, 22). Wheeler explains that this "required the invention of several new elements: the kidnapping of Anse Rainier, the presence of an American intelligence unit in Lahore and, most importantly, the character of Bobby Lincoln—the cinematic equivalent of the unnamed American in Mohsin's novel" (Nair 2013, 22). Charles Gant writes that "[t]he biggest conundrum of all" was to decide "how to represent the unnamed American stranger" and therefore, screenplay writers "Boghani and Hamid fleshed out [this] character" and gave him an unquestionably ethical framework in that he comes to Changez believing that he "can help locate a kidnapped American whose life is in imminent peril" (Gant 2013, 18). This aspect of his character is further expanded later in the film when Changez asks him how he went from writing so passionately against American intervention in the region to spying on behalf of the American CIA. This is when Bobby narrates the case of Ahmad Shah Massoud in the Takhar province of Afghanistan whom he had interviewed and supported because, despite the fact that "he had blood on his hands," Bobby thought that through Massoud's social work and his opposition to the Taliban "he stood for something, meant something to people" ("opening schools for girls, talking about democracy, resisting the Taliban"). But he got killed two days before 9/11 by the 9/11 attackers through the use of "a bomb in a video camera," a shocking fate that made Bobby reverse his position and acknowledge the need for American intervention in the region in order to preserve global peace (not just for the continued existence of the

West but also of the East). Simultaneously, Nair's film also gives Changez an indubitable moral grounding. The film makes Changez explicitly disavow his own involvement or that of his students in any kind of home-bred Pakistani fundamentalism, altering the texture and tone of the text crucially and positing the alternative narrative of a righteous, peace-loving, and noble Pakistan. Screenwriter William Wheeler remarks on how these changes were made and with what intention:

> Giving Bobby just and reasonable arguments for the US presence in Pakistan while at the same time maintaining the power of Changez's critique of that presence—in addition to his experience in Underwood Samson and the United States overall—would, we hoped, allow members of the audience to engage with the material through their own individual perspectives (Nair 2013, 22).

Besides the pragmatic concern of ensuring that all constituencies of the audience gets to relate to the film, there was, of course, the other significant need to further the prospect of global harmony and the possibility of cross-cultural communication and "Homing" by depicting a picture of moral goodness on both sides wanting (yet failing) to enter a peaceful dialogue.

In a decided move toward neutrality and conciliation, Nair's film also ignores some of the most mordant critiques of American politico-cultural predominance that Hamid offers. These harsher passages include the one where Changez is infuriated by the callous and arrogant privilege exercised by the Western friends he is vacationing with in Greece (who behave discourteously with their subordinates twice their age or overspend unthinkingly) by "wondering . . . what quirk of human history" allowed them to be "in a position . . . [so they could] conduct themselves in the world as though they were its ruling class" (Hamid 2007, 21). He also speaks resentfully of this injustice of history when he compares the "vast disparity" between New York and Pakistani cities and the economies of the two countries: "Four thousand years ago, we, the people of the Indus River basin, had cities that were laid out on grids and boasted underground sewers, while the ancestors of those who would invade and colonize America were illiterate barbarians" (Hamid 2007, 34). Nair's team's creative decision to temper the hostility between the two sides, and underplay the moral reprehensibility of both (and especially of the west) is designed to further dialogue and peace. This urgency of facilitating international cohesion—crucial, I would imagine—to a diasporic author who is most affected by and acutely sensitive to the gaping rifts between international borders, makes the philosophical uncertainty of the novel untenable and undesirable. It is also interesting to note that this attempt to creatively facilitate and cinematically showcase the human yearning for love/trust across distant/hostile borders (such as between Erica-Changez and between Bobby-Changez) was not only worked out at the level of the film's content. This impetus toward fostering relationships across hostile/distant cultural diversities also manifested itself through the selection of the people who would form a part of the filmmaking team—essentially people who had diasporic lives/backgrounds and who could therefore instinctively empathize with affection across hostile/distant borders. Thus emphasizing the centrality of diasporic sensibilities in the process of cinematic production both at the level of individuals (people on the sets who have had diasporic lives or experiences personally) and at the level of the team (the filmmaking team that is marked by people from multiple cultural contexts and often hybrid national allegiances—Mira Nair, Mohsin Hamid, Shimit Amin, Ami Boghani,Declan Quinn, Riz Ahmed, Kate Hudson, the many South Asian actors), Wheeler says: "Working with partners from such varied cultural backgrounds made our collaboration an attempt, like that of Changez and Bobby, to reach across cultural divides to try and discover the things that make us all human" (Nair 2013, 22). This returns us to our recurrent realization of how central Nair's (and her team's) diasporic entities were to their understanding of the matter of Hamid's novel and to their collaboratively rich filmmaking processes.

The film also sanitizes and practically reverses Changez's reaction at the televised sight of the twin towers falling. In the novel, Changez confesses that he "smiled" and was "remarkably pleased" at the sight (Hamid 2007, 72). The film, however, substitutes the pleasure with (in Changez's words) "awe" in the first place at, among other things, the "genius" of the attacks. Only later does he suggest that he felt also "a split second of pleasure at arrogance brought low" and in the experience of this emotion he clearly suggests the complicity of the American agent (by asking Bobby if he has not also felt this way" before "conscience kicks in." The film's moralizing and universalizing of the experience of Changez goes even further. While in the novel Changez frankly declares that he was "pleased at the slaughter of thousands of innocents" though this burdens him, as he says, "with a profound sense of perplexity," the film shows Changez effectively reversing this tenor. He clearly recognizes that he "should have felt sorrow or anger." He clarifies to Bobby that he is "not celebrating the death of 3,000 innocents" just as Bobby "would not celebrate the death of 100,000 in Baghdad or Kabul." Drawing Bobby into this analogy, he seems to posit a distinctly moral angle to this reaction. He makes this most explicit in the climactic comparison of the 9/11 attacks with a victory of good over evil, and significantly with a Christian fable that dramatizes this triumph of good over evil, by saying confidently: "David had struck Goliath."

Thus, as indicated earlier, while the novel makes us confront the uncomfortable question of human cruelty in the face of the intolerable "other" who challenges one's limits of ethical tolerance, the film dilutes this entirely. The issue of cruelty is raised only indirectly when Changez is shell-shocked at the sight of Erica's multimedia art exhibit ("I had a Pakistani once")—a pastiche of quotes and neon images from the history of her relationship with Changez that arguably stereotypes him as the iconic Pakistani and reduces their relationship to her experimentation at intimacy with the cultural "other." Repulsed by the art display, Changez responds violently. Hurt by his anger, she begs him to stop using the rhetoric of "attack" usually associated with terrorism—something that Changez seems to unproblematically oppose. She pleads repeatedly: "Please stop attacking me." Undeterred, Changez viciously reminds her of her callous and drunk driving that had caused the death of her lover (Chris) in a car accident, and thus heartlessly deals a severe blow to a grief that was already relentless and soul-crushing for Erica. Shocked and shattered, Erica points to Changez's inherent proclivity toward cruelty by lamenting: "Oh, I didn't know. I didn't know you could be capable of such cruelty." This mention of cruelty in the realm of interpersonal relationship is anticipated earlier through the professional domain when he unhesitatingly suggests the severe downsizing of a company in the Philippines to save it enormous costs—a harsh (and almost inhuman) move to which even his colleagues respond by saying: "Boy, that's brutal," or "That's too aggressive," and Jim congratulates him on his capacity for ruthlessness by saying: "You have a gift for this. A very lucrative gift"—a gift of ruthlessness that is connected implicitly by the film to violence as enormous as the 9/11 attacks when Changez speaks to Bobby of the "ruthlessness" of the 9/11 attacks. The film, however, does not dwell on the most provocative suggestions of cruelty as a basic human instinct with which the novel preoccupies itself. In fact, it invests significantly in communicating to its audience that Changez in his various classes as a university professor explicitly disavows violence, attempts only to search academically and personally for a "Pakistani dream" that "does not involve emigration," closely mentors his students to make them follow the same nonviolent path, and authoritatively instructs them through emissaries and in person to keep calm when the American forces and Pakistani police violently invade the Pak Tea House premises to track down Rainier's kidnapper. The film, to put it succinctly, refashions the American interlocutor as an ethical agent, a righteous spy sent to question and if necessary kill a Pakistani "fundamentalist," who ends up realizing the innocence and essential nobility of this supposed fundamentalist, Changez. Thus, the novel is a cynical philosophical reflection on morality and the possibility of unimpeachable moral choices in a world so fraught with hostility and with human fear and cruelty. The film departs significantly from this novelistic impetus to question the notion, possibility, and desirability of absolute morality. It becomes instead a practical response to the seething problems of the contemporary world. It does not dwell in moral uncertainties but serves a more immediate political purpose, answering to the current geopolitical necessity of assuaging cultural suspicions and building international peace, and to implicitly the more personal need of a South Asian diasporic woman for a global, albeit multi-locational, "Home" for the nomadic migrant. In the Photo Diary, Nair says that she has made this film about "the schism between official America and Muslim people" which "becomes more pronounced with each passing day" and that this is a story, therefore, "about how we, East and West, regard each other" (Nair 2013, xi). Pilcher, the producer, notes that Hamid's novel allowed Nair and herself to "honestly explore many of the political themes that besiege our world when East meets West and commerce clashes with culture" (Nair 2013, 29). Nair explains that the film gave her the chance to "create multilayered characters, . . . to see beyond the terrible stereotype that is constantly projected on our television screens and, if we have done our work right, to create a bridge between worlds that will not know each other unless we have a dialogue" (Nair 2013, xii).[14] It is to this larger global cry for change that the film seems to be responding through the creative departures it makes in order to nurture the possibility of a reassuring global "Home" for the South Asian diasporic traveller. Testifying to the personal and creative motivations of Nair, Ami Boghani, screenwriter and co-producer of the film, says that in view of the shifting geopolitical scene, "Mira tasked the writing team with keeping the film utterly contemporary yet resoundingly timeless" (Nair 2013, 21). The film thus responds to the resounding shifts within Pakistan and on the global scene, which registers in the film through significant additional episodes that do not appear in the novel. There is the portrayal of Changez's humiliating full-body strip search (at the airport when he returns from the Philippines) as well as his insulting arrest on the street and subsequent interrogation just because of his skin-color (that made him the closest lookalike for who was, to all appearances, a mad Bangladeshi screaming on New York streets—someone who had been telephonically reported to the police by a bystander but who managed to leave before the police arrived searching likely for an "un-American"-looking fellow). This more public and systemic racial profiling is paralleled in the film at the level of private relationships when Erica stereotypes him as a Pakistani in her multimedia art installation, and when she speaks of the mindlessness of the 9/11 and ends by throwing a question, as if to Changez, "How does that happen? . . . How did it happen like that?" To this he replies with proud indignance, "What makes you think I'd know?" It is with a view to the changing and turbulent contemporary developments, then, that the film inserts these tangible fragments of daily discrimination and torture, and aims not only to remedy the colossal global crisis but also to recuperate the possibility of transnational "Homing" by presenting a largely sanitized and moralized setting for the story and by showing us how precious lives such as Rainer's and Sameer's are lost if we persist with our stereotypical cultural suspicions.

Nair's film emerges, therefore, as the most illuminating, albeit complex, creative adaptation of the novel that one could imagine, infused with the generative richness of the filmmaker's South Asian diasporic sensibilities that echo the "mongrel"-like South Asian subjectivity of the novelist and his protagonist. Extending this fractured diasporic subjectivity to Bobby in the film and grounding the cinematic narrative in disturbing global displacement with its attendant feelings of alienness and longing for "Home," Nair universalizes the diasporic sensitivity to the West and the East, propelling both sides into a more acute pursuit of global understanding and transnational "Homing" than the novel's philosophically reflective tone could ever make possible. In doing so, Nair however, dramatizes the innermost impulse of the novel where Changez declares, "Something of us is now outside, and something of the outside is now within us" (Hamid 2007, 174). This statement echoes how Nair's split existence makes her feel "both an insider and an outsider" with shifting but real "Homes" across multiple geographic locations—a feeling and a "Homing desire" that is reflected through the figures of both Changez and Bobby, caught in the rootlessness of diasporic ruminations and therefore eager to find "Homes" in each other through cross-cultural understanding (Nair 2013, xii). Bringing these motivations to a climax, Changez's soulful prayer is heard at Sameer's funeral as the film closes, engulfing and including the audience in an earnest appeal for global cross-cultural peace:

> Do not take revenge in his name./Too much blood has flowed into this river.
> Do not curse fate./Allah holds our son in His embrace. . . .
> Pray for a future/Free of dictators and tyrants/Free of all invaders . . .
> Go tell the majestic sun to preserve its precious rays/We'll teach the core of our own beings to glow with its [own] light.

NOTES

1. As we know from Hamid's own essay, "Slaying Dragons," his own novel grew through seven years, starting in a pre-9/11 world and ultimately metamorphozing to include the 9/11 watershed when excluding it was no longer imaginable in the changed reality of a post-9/11 world (Hamid 2009, 230–31). It is only natural then that Nair's cinematic adaptation would also follow this impulse and take the story of the novel a few years further while making the film in a post-2011 world where Bin Laden had been killed.

2. A small part of my observations on Mohsin Hamid's novel overlap with a brief segment in the first chapter of my book, *Postsecular Theory: Texts and Contexts* (Orient Blackswan, 2020).

3. The offer to Changez to join the forces of Islamic fundamentalism as well as Changez's clear denial of this offer is shown more categorically in the film than in the novel. The novel, however, does show Changez explaining his aversion to violent religious fundamentalism and his dedication to his position of university professorship.

4. The novel, and especially the film, point to how terms such as "terrorism" or "fundamentalism" are instrumentalized by the West, i.e., the way they operate as "slippery and dangerous trope[s] in the hands of dominant geopolitical forces, military leaders, formations of

counter-terrorism, and the mainstream western media" and the way what is ignored is Western economic fundamentalism (the "the terror and violence of new forms of imperial sovereignty") (Morton 2010, 247). In the novel, Changez realizes that what is institutionalized through the West-dominated global developments is "the advancement of a small coterie's concept of American interests in the guise of the fight against terrorism" (Hamid 2007, 178). The film takes this up and shows that unlike what this "small coterie" does, the true interests of the West (America) as of the East (Muslim world) lie in global peace.

5. Strengthening the link between the diasporic sensibility of the author/actor and the author's production of a work of art or the actor's performance of a role, Nair even mentions the emphasis she laid on a diasporic background for the actor playing Changez so that he might best understand the feeling of alienness when caught between fractured identities and the desire for a home that is forever fluid and elusive. To play this character that is split in allegiances and emotions toward both America and Pakistan, Nair seemingly wanted a South Asian diasporic actor (or a South Asian actor with a divided identity) who would have an instinctive understanding of the text. Nair notes: "I was counting on a charismatic Pakistani actor—or certainly a subcontinental one—someone who could move fluidly between the languages and *disparate worlds with truthful ease*" (2013, 55; emphasis added). This process ended with the casting of British actor and rapper of part-Pakistani origin, Riz Ahmed, who was born to a British Pakistani family in London, and who was therefore able to play the role with "instinctive ease" after a wonderful audition (Nair 2013, 56).

6. This is the immigrant experientiality that Hamid claims for himself and describes interestingly as a "mongrel" identity in his interview with Singh, distinctive because of the mongrel's implied absence of "purity," and signifying an identity that is split much like Nair's between Pakistan, India, and the West (both the United States and UK for Hamid). Hamid describes his own "mongrel" identity saying that on the one hand, he has the predicament of being "someone with a Muslim-sounding name coming into the John F. Kennedy Airport"— "someone with avowedly secular politics and liberal values writing in Pakistan." On the other hand, he lives in Lahore "which is thirty kilometres from the border of India" and so "there is clearly a blurring that takes place" (Singh 2012a, 149–50.)

7. Mira Nair is quoted as saying this at the Penguin Books India Spring Fever 2013 held in New Delhi in a *NEWS18* article. (*NEWS18*, "*Reluctant Fundamentalist* is for my Son: Mira Nair")

8. Margaret Scanlan discusses the mainstream depiction of migrants as sinister and violent vehicles of terror and then discusses the work of postcolonial novelists like Hamid to show how works like *The Reluctant Fundamentalist* are located on the faultline of rigid mainstream binaries which they render blurry—such as the binary between Islam and the secular West (Scanlan 2010).

Post-9/11 postcolonial fiction, according to Singh, is able to reshape the figure of the terrorist from the typical American "images of the non-western, Islamic, bearded, turbaned, radical jihadi," with the "accompanying markers of illiteracy, fundamentalism, hatred, and violence," into the figure of "the disempowered refugee, the disenchanted immigrant, and the dissident citizen"—a figure that "mount[s] a critique of the neo-imperial nature of the war on terror" which is, says Singh quoting Elleke Boehmer, an "imperialist agenda inextricably entwined with the history of neoliberal globalization and America's place within it" (Singh 2012b, 29; Quoting Boehmer 2010, 14). It is interesting, therefore, that this figure comes to be epitomized, in Nair's recreation, not only by Changez but also, as I show above, Bobby— reimagined figures that now participate in this larger critique and thus help propel the movement toward global connection.

9. Hamid remarks interestingly: "An Indian director making a film about a Pakistani man. That's not an easy thing to do." He gestures toward the national rivalry and cultural animosity that exists between India and Pakistan but ultimately reminds us of the similarity she shares with the protagonist or himself in terms of her split and diasporic existence—growing up in India but bearing in heart her (father's) home in Lahore (Nair 2013, 81). This biographical context of split identities with fractured "homes" is ultimately marked by an emotional longing for a transnational "Home" across geographical and political space. Thus, we learn from the Photo Diary also of Nair's emotional connection with and organic belonging to Pakistan, which

in fact functioned as a primary motivation behind her decision to make the film. Nair visited Pakistan in 2004 for the first time, and went on an emotional tour to Lahore, a city with which she had family connection. After returning from Lahore in 2004 she says she "looked for a tale to tell of contemporary Pakistan, a tale one never sees." It was in 2007 that Nair read the unpublished manuscript of Hamid's novel and "immediately recognized it as the one" (Nair 2013, 11).

10. This is suggested by Hamid's text itself when Changez describes Lahore as the last great outpost of the Muslim world and elsewhere describes himself as having been on the other (eastern) side of the "wall against the East" that he sees in Rhodes—a wall that was built to guard "against the Turks" (Hamid 2007, 23).

11. In Harleen Singh's interview of Hamid, we hear the author explain how, in his novel, the "formal structure" of a dramatic monologue ("almost like a stage-play with one character speaking") plays a special role. It is because of this form that, "by creating half of a conversation, a conversation of which you only hear one half, and where the other party of the conversation is only present as an echo, a space opens up in the novel, a vacuum that the reader is invited to fill" (Singh 2012a, 225).

12. One might even argue that this desire that is referred to holds true also in the case of the desire for money/success that drives both Changez and the Americans, but that can ultimately only lead to disenchantment—the kind of disenchantment that, by the logic of the novel, only Changez encounters, and that the hypocritical American will never follow through on his desire enough to encounter.

13. Ami Boghani, screenplay writer and co-producer, says that Mohsin Hamid, L.A.-based screenwriter William Wheeler, and she herself had to synthesize "all of the weapons in . . . [their] collective mental arsenal to extract a powerful, fast-paced screen story from the novel's contemplative monologue, all the while manoeuvering to keep the essence of the story intact" (Nair 2013, 21).

14. Nair says: "I wanted to make a contemporary film about Pakistan, one that would break all misconceptions about the country and reveal it in a manner not seen before—as a simmering, confident nation caught between its ancient heritage and the demands of a globalized world" (Nair 2013, 11).

REFERENCES

Agnew, Vijay (ed.). 2005. *Diaspora, Memory and Identity: A Search for Home*. Toronto: University of Toronto Press.

Blunt, Alison. 2005. *Domicile and Diaspora: Anglo-Indian Women and the Spatial Politics of Home*. Oxford: Blackwell.

Boehmer, Elleke. 2010. "Postcolonial Writing and Terror." In Elleke Boehmer and Stephen Morton (eds.). *Terror and the Postcolonial*. Oxford: Wiley Blackwell.

Brah, Avtar. 1996. *Cartographies of Diaspora: Contesting Identities*. London: Routledge.

Darda, Joseph. 2014. "Precarious World: Rethinking Global Fiction in Mohsin Hamid's *The Reluctant Fundamentalist*." *Mosaic: An Interdisciplinary Critical Journal*, vol. 47, no. 3: 107–22.

Gant, Charles. May 2013. "Development Tale: Double Identity." *Sight & Sound*, 18–19.

Hamid, Mohsin. 2007. *The Reluctant Fundamentalist*. India: Penguin.

———. 2009. "Slaying Dragons: Mohsin Hamid Discusses *The Reluctant Fundamentalist*." *Psychoanalysis & History*, vol. 11, no. 2: 225–37.

Hartnell, Anna. 2010. "Moving Through America: Race, Place and Resistance in Mohsin Hamid's *The Reluctant Fundamentalist*." *Journal of Postcolonial Writing*, vol. 46, no. 3–4: 336–48.

Lau, Lisa. 2005. "Making the Difference: The Differing Presentations and Representations of South Asia in the Contemporary Fiction of Home and Diasporic South Asian Women Writers." *Modern Asian Studies*, vol. 39, no. 1: 237–56.

Maxey, Ruth. 2006. "'Life in the Diaspora is Often Held in a Strange Suspension': First-Generation Self-Fashioning in Hanif Kureishi's Narratives of Home and Return." *The Journal of Commonwealth Literature*, vol. 41, no. 3: 5–25.

Mohanty, Chandra. 1993. "Defining Genealogies: Feminist Reflections on Being South Asian in North America." In Women of South Asian Descent Collective (ed.). *Our Feet Walk the Sky: Women of the South Asian Diaspora*. San Francisco: Aunt Lute Books. 351–58.

Morton, Stephen. 2010. "Introduction." *Journal of Postcolonial Writing*, vol. 46, no. 3–4: 246–50.

Nair, Mira. 2013. *The Reluctant Fundamentalist: From Book to Film*. India: Penguin Studio.

Nair, Mira, Lydia Dean Pilcher, Ami Boghani, Mohsin Hamid, et al. 2013. *The Reluctant Fundamentalist*. Mirabai Films.

NEWS18. March 18, 2013. "*Reluctant Fundamentalist* is for my Son: Mira Nair." Press Trust of India, https://www.news18.com/news/india/reluctant-fundamentalist-is-for-my-son-mira-nair-597416.html. Accessed October 23, 2019.

Perner, Claudia. 2011. "Tracing the Fundamentalist in Mohsin Hamid's *Moth Smoke* and *The Reluctant Fundamentalist.*" *Ariel: A Review of International English Literature*, vol. 41, no. 3–4: 23–31.

Scanlan, Margaret. 2010. "Migrating from Terror: The Postcolonial Novel after September 11." *Journal of Postcolonial Writing*, vol. 46, no. 3–4: 266–78.

Scheffer, Gabriel. 2003. *Diaspora Politics: At Home Abroad*. New York: Cambridge University Press.

Singh, Harleen. 2012a. "Deconstructing Terrror: Interview with Mohsin Hamid on *The Reluctant Fundamentalist* (2007): Conducted via telephone on November 12, 2010." *Ariel: A Review of International English Literature*, vol. 42, no. 2: 149–56.

———. 2012b. "Insurgent Metaphors: Decentering 9/11 in Mohsin Hamid's *The Reluctant Fundamentalist* and Kamila Shamsie's *Burnt Shadows.*" *Ariel: A Review of International English Literature*, vol. 43, no. 1: 23–44.

Sooke, Alastair. April 18, 2007. "*The* Reluctant Fundamentalist." *The Telegraph*, https://www.telegraph.co.uk/culture/books/fictionreviews/3664515/Man-Booker-2007-Prize-The-Reluctant-Fundamentalist.html, Accessed April 6, 2018.

Yaqin, Amina. 2008. "Mohsin Hamid in Conversation." *Wasafiri*, vol. 23, no. 2: 44–49.

Part III

Domicile Significations

Chapter Seven

Negotiating the "Postcolonial Exotic" through Subversive Third-Person Narration in Jhumpa Lahiri's *The Namesake*

Lara Virginia Kattekola

Perhaps the most slippery vestiges of the colonial enterprise emerge as we consider the consumption of postcolonial literature by metropolitan audiences (i.e. Anglo-American readers) expecting to encounter cultural difference through familiar tropes of otherness. Here, the literary encounter between readers and writers replays the colonial Self/Other binary though in an atmosphere of celebratory fanfare that has catapulted many a postcolonial author into both commercial success as well as the uncomfortable, undesired role of an "authentic" cultural representative. Graham Huggan offers a significant scholarly contribution to the discussion of this commodification of cultural difference, focusing on the production and dissemination of postcolonial literature in the global literary marketplace. In his 1994 article "The Postcolonial Exotic," Huggan comments on the touristic mindset driving the postcolonial publishing industry: "Though publishers' agendas differ widely, they all know exoticism sells. African or Indian writing offers a window onto a different, exciting world" that "produces wonder, rejuvenating the sensibilities of a readership tired of provincial navel gazing; tired also of literature that reflects a society from which they badly need release" (26). Huggan's observations echo the atmosphere surrounding the popularity of colonial travel narratives and novels of empire written for domestic audiences in England and Europe who yearned to learn more of the "exotic" peoples and lands in the far-off colonies. Representing colonized peoples through the colonizing gaze, the "monarch of all I survey" perspective (Pratt 1992, 7), such texts judged and made colonized peoples knowable through the coloniz-ing culture's values (Spurr 1993, 16) thus perpetuating the fixed binary iden-tities of the "superior" colonizer and the "inferior" colonized subject (Ash-croft, Griffith, and Tiffin 2007, 209; Said 1978) and fueling the project of European imperialism (Pratt 1992; Said 1993).

Hardly oblivious to the marketplace demands on their work, postcolonial writers, as Huggan explains, "recognize the value of their writing as interna-tional commodity depends, to a large extent, on the exotic appeal it holds to the unfamiliar metropolitan audience [and that] they risk becoming complicit with the cultural imperialism they denounce" (24). The question of how they negotiate the marketplace minefield is answered through what Huggan calls a "strategic exoticism," the "means by which postcolonial writers/thinkers, working within exoticist codes of representation, either manage to subvert those codes . . . or succeed in redeploying them for the purposes of uncover-ing differential relations of power (32). Commenting that one option avail-able to postcolonial writers is to lay "bare the process by which those my-thologies are constructed," Huggan references the "semiotic markers of Oth-erness" in Salman Rushdie's *Midnight's Children* via "snake charmers, ge-nies, fakirs, and the like" that serve to challenge exoticist myths and stereo-types (27). Huggan expands his commentary on the postcolonial exotic in his influential 2001 book-length study of the same name in which he again discusses postcolonial writers' awareness and resistance of their roles as cultural representatives and enunciates their strategic efforts to make "*read-ers* aware of the constructedness of such cultural categories" (26; emphasis Huggan). What is important to note here is that Huggan's comments under-score how much writers' awareness of the conditions of the global literary marketplace inform the textual strategies they use to mediate readers' aware-ness of the constructedness of signifiers of Otherness. Huggan's comments should not be construed that *all* readers of postcolonial works read them for the same reasons (i.e., to seek exotic otherness); Huggan is careful to reiter-ate exactly this point when he later stresses the heterogeneity of readers (30).

Following Huggan's work, Sarah Brouillette also makes a notable schol-arly contribution to the debate on the commodification of cultural difference in her 2011 *Postcolonial Writers Writing in the Global Literary Marketplace*. Brouillette acknowledges Huggan's work for its groundbreaking attention to the global reach of the publishing industry's machinations and notes that both she and Huggan understand "that postcolonial literature evinces a com-plicated composing process "indulging, resisting, and critiquing its imagined consumption" (viii) in the commodified climate in which it is produced. However, Brouillette takes issue of the extent to which Huggan's analysis rests on the figure of an unspecified reader who needs to be taken to task for his/her exoticizing tendencies, which, as she explains (26), is made evident when he stresses that writers make "*readers*" aware of constructions of otherness. Brouillette resists what she reads as too neat of a division informing Huggan's work that sees knowledgeable writers exercising textual strategies aimed at reorienting and reeducating readers seeking easy access to the Other (26). While recognizing there are *"some"* readers, of a "predictable class and location" (16) who require such reorientation and reeducation, Brouillette interprets the writing and reception of postcolonial works in a more nuanced manner that calls attention to writers' and readers' cognizance of the touristic spectacle underwriting the global literary marketplace and registers the anxiety both writers and readers experience concerning their complicit participation therein (respectively, as producers and consumers of "exotic" texts). Brouillette refigures "strategic exoticism as involving "a set of literary strategies that operate through shared assumptions between the author and the reader, as both producer and consumer work to negotiate with, if not absolve themselves of postcoloniality's touristic guilt" (7). In her analysis of a Derek Walcott poem, Brouillette further illustrates strategic exoticism, saying it is not about teaching actual readers about their mistaken notions of other cultures, "much though it depends upon the construction of a figure in need of such instruction;" rather, "it indicates a set of textual strategies that communicates at all because the author and the reader likely share assumptions about the way culture operates, and concur in their desire to exempt themselves from certain undesirable practices" (43).

Whether or not we adopt a more or less pessimistic attitude concerning metropolitan audiences' consumption of postcolonial writers' works, both Huggan and Brouillette offer us important understanding of how the inescapable materialist conditions underwriting the "industry of postcoloniality" (5), to borrow Brouillette's term, inform the writing of postcolonial texts. Huggan's and Brouillette's work also underscore for us the far reach of colonialism's legacy into our everyday practices of reading and the ongoing implications for both writers and readers as they, respectively, write and consume postcolonial literature (and, by extension, any of those literatures that are typically labeled diaspora, transnational, etc., reflecting the lives and experiences of so-called Others—exoticized/ethnicized/racialized peoples). In what follows below, I attempt to highlight and gauge these implications through an analysis of Jhumpa Lahiri's 2003 novel *The Namesake*. My analysis presupposes Lahiri's self-consciousness of the material conditions of her authorship—as a celebrated writer associated with Indian/Bengali roots whose work is largely published for unfamiliar metropolitan readers. I identify formal and thematic devices Lahiri employs to negotiate the postcolonial exotic through which she exposes and disrupts the othering processes that are the legacy of the colonial Self/Other divide. Lahiri's efforts underscore how notions of otherness are hardly representative of some fixed, discrete ontological condition but are, rather, subjective interpretations and constructions informed by hegemonic discourses. In other words, Lahiri's novel illustrates

that otherness, as Jean-Francois Staszak explains, "is due less to the difference of the Other than to the point of view and discourse of the person who
perceives the Other as such" (43).

My analysis focuses on Lahiri's use of a reliable omniscient third person
narrator whose multi-perspective narrative focalizes chapter one through two
of the novel's main characters. This type of narrator, a self-effacing yet all-
seeing and -knowing authoritative presence who glides seamlessly from one
character's perspective to another without calling attention to him/herself,
easily allows audiences to enter the spacio-temporality of the fictional world
being presented to them and act as observers of the goings on therein concerning its characters and their experiences. Unlike a third-person limited
narrator or first-person narrator who narrate from the perspective of only one
character, and, thus, are susceptible to questions of reliability, or a noticeably
intrusive narrator who might come across as too overtly authoritative to be
credible, Lahiri's choice of a narrator is an expedient one, enabling her to
weave a narrative that negotiates the postcolonial exotic subversively, and,
thus, without seeming to convey a heavy-handed didacticism that might
make some readers, especially those expecting familiar tropes of otherness
and/or easy-to-digest reading experiences, resistant to the alternative ideals
that inform it. Likewise, the subversive, "no finger-pointing" aspect of Lahiri's choice of narrator can be interpreted to illuminate a less obvious benefit—namely to acknowledge her own self-consciousness of the touristic
underpinnings of the industry that makes the publication of her work possible
and to acknowledge that metropolitan audiences do not necessarily need to
be aggressively taken to task for their participation in that industry because
they are open to or very well may share her assumptions about "the way
culture operates, and concur [or would concur with her as they read her
work] in their desire to exempt themselves from certain undesirable practices."

Because Lahiri's narrator's qualifying comments on characters or events
are typically too subtle or far in between, they are barely perceptible (especially on a first reading) and because s/he frequently uses present tense that
show characters' actions in the process of unfolding without any narrative
commentary to qualify those actions, Lahiri's narrator gives the impression
of objective reporting such that his/her narration is not unlike a disembodied,
invisible hand merely pulling the curtain back of that proverbial transparent
window onto the fictional world. However, this narrator, like all narrators, is
not disinterested; his/her narration reflects the infinite choices available to
Lahiri in the construction of her novel concerning what will be shared, how
much will be disclosed, through whom it will be focalized, in what order it
may be arranged, how it vividly it will be described, etc.

The narrator's detailed representations in the early chapters of the novel
of two main characters, Ashoke and Ashima, the Bengali-born and raised

parents of the protagonist Gogol, raise questions concerning notions of otherness through a shifting narrative perspective. As I will show in my explication of specific passages, the narrator's use of psycho-narration to represent the thoughts and feelings of both characters and free indirect discourse in one account of Ashima, works to shift metropolitan audiences' viewing perspectives of these characters, dislocating audiences from a fixed spectator panoramic-oriented position to one that brings them at times within very close proximity of characters' bodies and interior consciousness. I argue that this "zoom lens" narration effect is not merely an authorial ploy to guide audiences into deeper empathy and identification with their fictional Others or reveal Other characters' complex, layered identities though it may certainly do these things. Rather, it illuminates Lahiri's textual efforts to create rhetorically-charged scenarios aimed at fostering metropolitan audiences' self-consciousness of either their own otherness and of the transparent hegemonic standards by which nonhegemonic people become constituted as the Other. In short, the effect of this strategic shifting narration aims to make metropolitan audiences, especially those seeking familiar tropes of otherness, become, as Kristeva would say, "strangers" to themselves (1991). As significant as these constructed self-consciousness inducing moments might be for audiences, they are fleeting and operate through characters whose identities themselves are shifting and whose perspectives are not sustained by the narrator for the novel's entirety (since it is a multi-perspective narrative). And these moments are, like any component of any literary text, subject to multiple interpretations by audiences and critics alike and/or can just as easily be overlooked. But, arguably, the transient qualities or double-sided or multi-factedness of these moments, too, are strategic textual interventions because they allow Lahiri to avoid projecting notions of stable truths or identities that would otherwise only serve to reinvoke imperialist attitudes. In sum, what Lahiri achieves through her shifting, evanescent narrative reflects much of the thematic concerns of postcolonial writing and theorization, which understands, as Helen Tiffin explains, "Decolonization" as "a process, not arrival . . . and an ongoing project [that] . . . invokes an ongoing dialectic between hegemonic centrist systems and peripheral subversions of them" (95).

NEGOTIATING THE POSTCOLONIAL EXOTIC

Lahiri's more recent forays into translating and writing in Italian complicates the postcolonial/South Asian diaspora/transnational authorial identity label under which she is generally categorized by literary critics, the publishing industry, and the reading public but the "exotic" status she represents to market readers likely still holds sway given the huge commercial and critical success she received for her Indian immigrant-themed 2001 prize-winning collection of short stories, *The Interpreter of Maladies,* and her follow-up 2003 novel *The Namesake*. In subject matter and theme, *The Namesake* ostensibly ticks many boxes on publishers' "exotic checklist," depicting as it does the lives of the Ganguli family, which comprises a middle-class, educated, Bengali-immigrant couple, Ashoke and his wife Ashima, who maintain their family ties and religious and cultural traditions while raising their American-born children, Gogol and Sonia, in suburban Massachusetts. Accounts of the couple's arranged marriage, Ashima's Indian culinary endeavors, the children's naming ceremonies, and the family's frequent travels to India including a visit to the Taj Mahal, afford unfamiliar metropolitan audiences the exotic representations of otherness they may expect of a novel written by a writer with Bengali roots. The novel's 2003 cover design (copyright Houghton Mifflin Company) itself caters to such audiences because it features aesthetic choices encouraging their "exotic" expectations before they ever even open the book. Tamara Bhalla referencing Manish Vij's 2006 satirization of another diaspora novel's "exotic" cover art, informs us how the incorporation of certain cliched visual elements such as the enlarged typeface and prominent positioning of authors' names rather than the titles of their work help "drive the publication of transnational South Asian literature (106)." Less ostentatious than the cover art of the novel Vij satirizes, which features a gold sari border and a woman's brown hands holding a mango ("Anatomy of a Genre," reprinted in Bhalla, 2012), *The Namesakes's* cover design still reflects visual elements that suggest a muted but marketable enough "exoticism" to attract metropolitan readers. Featuring a pale ochre-colored background and a gracefully curved, multicolored lotus stem bending across the book's spine onto the back cover where its large white blossom is positioned under a picture, of what many fans would likely consider a photogenic representation of the author herself, *The Namesake*'s front cover showcases the novel's *New York Times* bestseller status and Lahiri's Pulitzer Prize-winning authorship (earned for *The Interpreter of Maladies*) and presents her name in reflective metallic copper typeface larger than the novel's title. The effect of all these signifiers easily suggest, even tout Lahiri's celebrated status as an/Other writer who will make good in delivering a narrative about the "exotic Other."

Despite the novel's cover aesthetics and ostensible immigrant narrative subject matter, *The Namesake* is no mere simplified portrait of exotic otherness. Lahiri's status as a postcolonial/South Asian diaspora/transnational author writing mainly for metropolitan reading audiences is reason enough to examine *The Namesake* through the postcolonial exotic framework I have outlined above. However, analysis of the novel through this lens is apropos because the novel self-reflexively raises questions surrounding readers' consumption of books since all the main characters are, in fact, readers. We encounter, for example, characters reading books on trains (115, 185) and in bars (193), contemplating which ones to buy at Rizzoli (247) or Barnes & Noble (272), checking them out of the library (163), passing them around at a dinner party (239), listening to them being read by the children's librarian (50), reading them in a high school English class (88, 90), reading them to avoid interacting with peers (192), giving them as gifts (24, 74), boxing them for donations (288), housing them in floor-to-ceiling bookshelves (153), leaving or finding them in coat pockets (173, 273), leaving them on beds (163, 245), cherishing meaningful inscriptions written in them (229, 288), taking them on vacation (153) or losing them there (75), and reading the same ones over and over (31, 83). Tucked here and there into the narrative, these and other references to newspapers, magazines, textbooks, and travel guides reflect the reading culture informing these characters' lives as well as characters' affinity for reading and the regularity of their reading habits. They also help deflect the postcolonial exotic, subtly acknowledging metro-politan audiences' own reading practices, and inviting them to read charac-ters such as Ashoke, Ashima, Gogol, Sonia, and later Moushima (the daugh-ter of Bengali family friends whom Gogol marries) in rounder terms, *not* merely as racialized, exotic Others, but, rather, as readers not unlike them-selves. In doing so, they blur the Self/Other divide between metropolitan audiences and the characters. However, while these fleeting references help make the characters and their fictional world more readily accessible to audi-ences, they are not aimed at purely naturalizing characters within readers' frames of reference since Lahiri also uses them to occasionally suggest vary-ing degrees of individual preference and cultural difference. Even among references to books that would likely be familiar to metropolitan audiences including texts such as *The Little House* books, *The Hobbit*, *Pride and Preju-dice*, or *The Great Gatsby*, there are references to what could be perceived as less familiar and/or digestible book choices including, for example, a "vol-ume of Greek poetry" brought annually on vacation by a minor character (153), "five Bengali novels" Ashima reads repeatedly in her early years of life in the United States, Moushima's English translation of an unnamed French novel whose main characters are referred only as "He" and "She, " which Gogol reads to better understand his wife (245), Auerbach's *Mimesis* housed on the book shelves of the two comparative literature academic char-acters (267), or Graham Green's *The Comedians* (173), which academic Ashoke brings to read while away on a visiting professorship, and, of course, Nikolai Gogol's short story "The Overcoat," perhaps the most enigmatic of them all, which serves as the main intertext of the novel.

SHIFTING NARRATIVE PERSPECTIVES

The novel's subtle interplay of similarity and difference through characters' reading practices and preferences becomes more provocatively apparent through Ashoke, the character most deeply consumed with books. Unlike the fleeting references to other characters' encounters with reading, Lahiri's omniscient third-person narrator affords audiences an intimate understanding of Ashoke's reading history, habits, and experiences that spans nine pages in chapter one. Much like the opening of this chapter and other parts of subsequent chapters (which feature Ashima's early years as a newly-arrived immigrant and later years after her children are grown and her husband dies), Lahiri's attention to Ashoke positions audiences to identify with his character even though he is not, as it turns out, the protagonist of the novel. Only after Lahiri provides considerable attention to the lives and experiences of Ashoke and Ashima in the early chapters will the protagonist's story (that of their son Gogol) be divulged.

In the passage immediately preceding the narrator's detailed account of Ashoke's reading history, the narrator offers a brief discussion of Ashoke as an expectant father waiting at the hospital where his wife is about to give birth to their first child. This account is worth noting to contextualize the complex treatment Ashoke receives through the narrator's characterization of him as s/he moves through this character's reading history. As is the case of his/her general representation of all characters in the novel, the narrator presents Ashoke through two main kinds of narration. One of these is that which Dorrit Cohn (1978) in her *Transparent Minds* describes as psycho-narration, a form of narration in which the omniscient narrator describes for readers what a character is thinking or feeling while still maintaining his/her subjectivity as the narrating voice; the other is "behavioristic" narration mode, which as Saleem et al. (2017) explain, presents the characters by describing them and their actions by "only what is visible from the outside;" "descriptions of the inner thoughts and emotions of characters are omitted from the narration" (3).

As the narrator focalizes the scene through Ashoke's perspective, s/he begins the paragraph in present tense offering a few descriptive details pertaining to Ashoke's state of mind, actions, and physical appearance in the hospital waiting room. "He now desperately needs a cup of tea for himself, not having managed to make one before leaving the house. He takes off his thick-rimmed glasses . . . polishes the lenses with the handkerchief . . . His black hair, normally combed back neatly . . . is disheveled, sections of it on end" (11). Providing a sense of a less-than-usually composed self, informed by the conditions of rushing to the hospital, Ashoke's expectant father status is most assured by the narrator's observations that "He stands and begins pacing as other fathers do" (11). After noting that there are "handshakes all around" every time the door opens and a nurse announces the arrival of a new baby to one of the fathers, the narrator's tone changes considerably as s/he now begins to contrast Ashoke from the other fathers who conform to those familiar American tropes of new fatherhood because they are smoking cigarettes and wait with "cigars, flowers, champagne, or address books" (12). The narrator's explanation for the disparity is notably spare, ending the paragraph in three straightforward sentences: "Ashoke is indifferent to such indulgences. He neither smokes, nor drinks alcohol of any kind. Ashima is the one who keeps all their addresses in a small notebook she carries in her purse. It has never occurred to him to buy his wife flowers" (12). The distinction the narrator makes between Ashoke and the other more materially expressive expectant fathers leaves room for pause in terms of audiences' reception of this character. Familiar audiences (those acquainted with Indian cultures) would understand that Ashoke's indifference likely reflects his cultural norms, which do not express joys of impending fatherhood by way of cigars, flowers, etc. However, the restraint through which the narrator represents him in these last few sentences of the paragraph could be interpreted differently by unfamiliar metropolitan audiences who may feel distanced from Ashoke because he, notwithstanding his description in the beginning of the paragraph likening him to the other fathers, does not display those iconic, celebratory American accoutrements of new fatherhood that inform their frames of reference. In this comparison between Ashoke and the other fathers, Ashoke's thoughts and actions (or lack thereof) make him seem emotionally unenthusiastic and removed from his impending role of fatherhood while the other fathers seem more emotionally enthusiastic. Moreover, if we understand, as studies such as those conducted by van Krieken et al. (2017) have shown, that "linguistic cues" can play a role in affecting audiences' identification with characters and narratives, the repetition of the narrator's negative terms ("indifferent," "neither," "nor," and "never") could potentially help support unfamiliar metropolitan audiences' disconnect with Ashoke. As if to foster such a divide, the narrator continues to invite metropolitan audiences' further distancing from him in the next paragraph. Here, the narrator again invokes what seems to be another deliberate comparison between Ashoke and the other expectant fathers because s/he again calls up that American trope of the pacing expectant father, explaining that Ashoke returns to his newspaper, "still *pacing* as he reads" (emphasis mine). But this reference dissipates as quickly as it is invoked since, as it turns out, Ashoke's pacing here serves not to demonstrate his nervous anticipation of fatherhood, but, rather, functions as the narrator's conduit into Ashoke's childhood during which the young Ashoke has cultivated the curious habit of reading while walking.

If Ashoke's difference is enunciated in the hospital waiting room, the narrator's discussion of his childhood reading practices, with its emphasis on his ambulatory mode of reading, does little to diminish it because the narrator paints a more detailed picture of Ashoke's reading idiosyncrasies within the context of his childhood home and native Calcutta. Here, the narrator reveals what can be described as young Ashoke's extreme reading behavior: "Since childhood he has had the habit and ability to read while walking, holding a book in one hand on his way to school, from room to room in his parents' three-story house . . . up and down the red clay stairs" (12). Ashoke's reading concentration is rendered in near super-human terms through the narrator's series of unequivocal statements: "Nothing roused him. Nothing distracted him. Nothing caused him to stumble" (12). Such disclosures with their repetitive negative linguistic cues ("Nothing . . . Nothing . . . Nothing") continue to suggest to Ashoke's unrelatability to metropolitan audiences (or any audiences for that matter). Even when Ashoke is presented in slightly more sentimental terms, which note his grandfather's influence on his reading practices, the narrator maintains the gap between audiences and the character by further distinguishing Ashoke's behavior from those around him. Unlike his siblings who " play and laugh" on the roof, Ashoke remains "blind to the world" "curled up at his grandfather's side, listening to him read novels" (12). Continuing, the narrator, again demonstrates Ashoke's extreme reading. Taking his grandfather's advice to "read" and "re-read" all the Russians" because "they will never fail" him (12), Ashoke takes to reading *The Brothers Karamozov*, *Anna Karenina*, and *Fathers and Sons*, while walking on "some of the world's, noisiest, busiest streets" in Calcutta, thus nursing his mother's fears that he would one day "be hit by a bus or a tram, his nose deep in *War and Peace*" (12–13). Ashoke's deftness also distinguishes him from his younger cousin who, in mimicking Ashoke's reading behaviors, "had fallen down the red clay staircase . . . and broken his arm" (13).

While such revelations offer colorful details heightening Ashoke's idiosyncratic reading practices, the narrator begins altering the narrative mood and seemingly attempts to bridge the gap between readers and the character s/he has metaphorically invoked through the previous narration by returning to the topic of Ashoke's relationship with his grandfather to offer a rather poignant scene, which sees a now college-age Ashoke taking a lengthy train journey to his grandfather's house:

> Ashoke had never spent the holidays away from his family. But his grandfather had recently gone blind, and he had requested Ashoke's company specifically, to read him *The Statesman* in the morning, Dostoyevsky and Tolstoy in the afternoon. Ashoke had accepted the initiation eagerly. He carried two suitcases . . . one containing clothes and gifts, the second one empty. For it would be on this visit, his grandfather had said, that the books in his glass-fronted case, collected over a lifetime and preserved under lock and key, would be given to Ashoke. The books had been promised to Ashoke throughout his childhood, and far as long as he could remember he had coveted them

more than anything else in the world. He already received a few in recent years, given to him on birthdays and special occasions. But now that the day has come to inherit the rest, a day his grandfather could no longer read the books himself, Ashoke was saddened, and as he placed the empty suitcase under his seat, he was disconcerted by its weightlessness, regretful of the circumstances that would cause it, upon his return, to be full. (13)

A stark contrast to the "indifferent" adult Ashoke in the hospital waiting room and even the seemingly super-human teenaged Ashoke who reads and walks unscathed on the world's "noisiest, busiest" streets," the above passage renders Ashoke more sympathetically through this obviously more emotional representation that invites audiences not to read him in terms of difference but to emotionally identify with him. Emotional identification, as van Krieken et al. (2017) explain, can result in "affective empathy" that causes readers to recognize another's feelings and feel sympathetic toward the character or, even more extreme, emerge as an adoption of a character's feelings (8). Such potential identification even seems to be the narrator's aim given the emotionally inflected linguistic cues in the passage—"eagerly," "coveted," "saddened," "disconcerted," "regretful"—which reveal not just Ashoke's emotional state but the gravity therein because there is an obvious transition from the enthusiasm Ashoke feels concerning his prospective possession of books to the sadness he feels concerning the circumstances that will make it possible.

Given the heterogeneity of readers and innumerable reasons why they may read Lahiri's novel, it is impossible to make a definitive claim that the passage just discussed would indeed make all readers identify with Ashoke. But, given readers' general willingness to suspend their disbelief when they read fiction and in the wake of much narrative research attesting to the influence of narratives on readers done by cognitive psychologist scholars such as the above mentioned van Krieken et al., or Peterson et al. (2009) and Saleem et al. (2017, it is feasible to assume that metropolitan readers may likely identify to some degree with Ashoke's character as they read about the sad conditions of his train journey. But, irrespective of the certainty or uncertainty surrounding the readers' degrees of emotional identification, we can still discern the narrator's shift in narration from the "behavioristic" narration mode used to describe Ashoke's childhood reading practices to the heightened psycho-narration mode, which, if nothing else, brings Ashoke and his thoughts into much closer focus—not unlike a zoom lens closing in on the character. That the narrator includes the detail of Ashoke's movements with the suitcase—"as he placed it under his seat"—seems even to bring audiences inside the train compartment itself as opposed to watching him from a further distance such as the long shot perspective the narrator invokes while

Ashoke walks unscathed on Calcutta's busy, noisy streets that do not offer any distinguishing features about the streets other than their names.

THEMATIZING THE CONSUMPTION OF THE OTHER

Tempting though it might be to interpret the narrator's repositioning of audiences' perspective within closer range of Ashoke's emotions and actions as, perhaps, Lahiri's attempt to bridge the Self/Other divide, such a reading would serve only to illustrate a maintenance of that imperial construct since it would, in this case, be based on shared/similar emotional responses (those of the audiences' and Ashoke's toward the grandfather's blindness) and exclude those who might not share the same reaction. Moreover, since Ashoke is presented alternatively in terms of similarity and difference, illustrating various aspects of his identity as we have seen thus far in this first chapter and at other points elsewhere in the narrative, this episode of a sympathetic Ashoke cannot be privileged over his less sympathetic/accessible/neutral versions. Indeed, even as Ashoke's most interior representation is made available in the next passage, his character becomes increasingly complex, creating a narrative scenario that suggest that Lahiri is not interested in inducing metropolitan audiences' uncomplicated interaction with this Other character to bridge the Self/Other divide, but, instead, is aiming to go beyond it. In this next account, Ashoke is reading from a single volume of Nikolai Gogol's collection of short stories, the only book he has chosen to accompany him on his overnight train journey. Ashoke's profound identification with Akaky Akakyvitch, the protagonist of Gogol's "The Overcoat," is made abundantly clear:

> Each time, reading the account of Akaky's christening . . . Ashoke laughed aloud. He shuddered at the description of the tailor Petrovich's big toe. . . . His mouth watered at the cold veal and cream pastries and champagne Akaky consumed . . . in spite of the fact that Ashoke had never tasted these things himself. Ashoke was always devastated when Akaky was robbed . . . and Akaky's death, some pages later, never failed to bring tears to his eyes. In some ways the story made less sense each time he read it, the scenes he pictured so vividly, and absorbed so fully, growing more elusive and profound. Just as Akaky's ghost haunted the final pages, so did it haunt a deep place in Ashoke's soul, shedding light on all that was irrational, all the was inevitable about the world. (14)

If the previous passage noting Ashoke's sadness over his grandfather's blindness narrows the distance between audiences and the character, bringing them, as I suggested, right into his train compartment, the above passage has the effect of the zoom lens narration being extended to its fullest capacity so that audiences are thrust forward, practically within face-to-face range, of

Ashoke—almost with faces pressed onto that proverbial transparent window onto the fictional world. This vantage point makes Ashoke knowable to audiences through his emotional identification with the fictional Akaky whose dismal fate renders him (Ashoke) feeling "devastated" and haunted, and it makes him knowable through what van Krieken et al. would refer to as his "embodied identification" with the fictional world, because he experiences Akaky's story corporally—as indicated by the narrator's observations ("He laughed . . . He shuddered . . . His mouth watered . . . his eyes [teared]"). Such attention to his corporal and emotional state ostensibly suggest the narrator's invitation to audiences to identify with their foreign fictional Other Ashoke just as he does with Akaky, his own fictional Russian Other. Yet even as this representation might draw audiences into such identification, it simultaneously works to complicate it since Ashoke's consumption of Gogol's short story ironically registers metropolitan audiences' own consumption of Lahiri's work—as is most provocatively suggested in Ashoke's mouth-watering reaction to the fictional food and drink offered to protagonist Akaky. The rhetorical charge of this thematization of consuming the Other is further amplified in the narrator's qualifying remark, which notes that Ashoke's vicarious bodily reaction occurs "in spite of the fact that Ashoke had never tasted these things himself." This simple qualification tucked in between the more visually impactful descriptive statements also exudes its own doubleness not unlike a two-sided coin. On the one hand, and within the context of Ashoke's extreme reading practices, which prioritize the fictional world over his material world, the narrator's remark can be interpreted as an illustration of the considerable extent of Ashoke's reading concentration, which is so intense that it allows him to be corporally affected by the fictional food and drink. However, on the other side of the coin, and in anticipation of future passages describing Ashima's Indian culinary endeavors, the remark ironically alludes to metropolitan audiences' own potential consumption of the Indian dishes Ashima prepares, sometimes for days on end, in preparation for the parties she hosts for her extended family/friends.

Lahiri's thematic and formal attention to the consumption of the Other is most rhetorically powerful within the context of the audiences' shifting perspectives of the fictional world. The narrator's psycho-narration mode with its engrossing vivid details and linguistic cues describing Ashoke's life and reading history evokes, as discussed above, a zoom-lens effect, positioning and repositioning audiences, bringing them closer into the narrative space within increasing proximity to Ashoke's body and interior consciousness. But Ashoke's consumption of Gogol's story and the ironic potential of the narrator's qualifying comment ("in spite of the fact that Ashoke had never tasted these things himself") together disrupt the uni-directionality of the audiences' textual movement/perspective, creating, as it were, a two-way street. Whereas audiences have been invited to consistently look into the text—first from afar and then increasingly closer to Ashoke's corporal and sentient being, the dramatization of Ashoke's intense emotional and embodied identification/consumption of an/Other text (about his European Other, that is) simultaneously, if only momentarily, serves to make the text gaze back at its metropolitan audiences to induce their self-consciousness of their own consumption of Ashoke and *The Namesake*. The effect of this textual strategy creates an oppositional force, that aims to shift audiences out of their uncomplicated, uni-directional viewing position of the fictional world and redirect them to their own subject positioning in their own real world, *not* in the ways they may perceive their own selves, which they likely presume to be whole and contained, but, in their own alterity and split subjectivity, as the *novel's* others because they are its readers and consumers. In short, Lahiri's thematization of consuming the Other textually serves to induce readers' understanding of otherness as a matter of perspective—as not just something out there in the bodies of those whose cultural difference deems them the exotic, ethnic, or racial Other but also as something inherent within one's own self because the self is always the other to someone outside of itself.

Again, it would be impossible to know if or to what extent metropolitan audiences are affected by the textual provocations on notions of otherness through Lahiri's thematization of the consumption of Other texts. Moreover, since we can infer that Ashoke's consumption of "The Overcoat" reflects serious intellectual engagement rather than a satiation of simple hedonistic desires (because he reads the "elusive and profound" text multiple times, becoming enlightened "on all that was irrational" and "inevitable about the world" [14]), metropolitan audiences, in their quest to interpret Ashoke's interaction with the story, may remain blind to what I read as Lahiri's ironical gesturing of their consumption of her novel; or, they may forget it immediately after it is invoked. However, the uncertainty concerning how or if audiences even process the redirection of the textual perspective does not diminish the presence and self-reflexive quality of Lahiri's thematization of readers consuming Other books, which, as my interpretation above indicates, illustrates Lahiri's self-consciousness of the touristic spectacle underwriting the industry of postcoloniality. That Lahiri's thematization of readers consuming Other books is subversive enough to be overlooked is itself a textual strategy Lahiri employs. Like many other postcolonial writers, Lahiri understands how overt didacticism will not likely not influence audiences and is interested in destabilizing *not* supplanting imperialist truths, certainties, and practices; such aims require nuanced strategies that may very well lend themselves to double or more meanings. Lahiri continues to utilize such strategies as can be seen in the narrator's ongoing attention to Ashoke's train journey, which invokes more shifts in the narrative perspective.

Even after bringing audiences so deeply into Ashoke's emotional and corporal reality, Lahiri's narrator shifts the narrative perspective outward, pulling them away and outside of the train compartment to begin narrating, in unambiguous, time-stamped, location-precise, journalistic fashion, the tragic and deadly train crash that leaves Ashoke almost dead:

> Ashoke was still reading at two-thirty in the morning, one of the few passengers on the train who was awake, when the locomotive engine and seven bogies derailed from the broad-gauge line. The sound was like a bomb exploding. The first four bogies capsized into a depression alongside the track. The fifth and sixth, containing the first-class and air conditioned passengers, telescoped into each other, killing the passengers in their sleep. The seventh, where Ashoke was sitting, capsized as well, flung by the speed of the crash farther into the field. The accident occurred 209 kilometres from Calcutta, between Ghatsila and Dhalbumgarh stations. (17)

Injected with linguistic cues noting the "bomb exploding" sounds, the capsizing of train cars, and the images of passengers killed "in their sleep," this distant, panoramic narrative perspective renders a tragic account but is rendered in an objective, emotionally-contained tone, especially when compared to what follows next, which sees the narrator fluidly switching back into psycho-narration mode to reveal Ashoke's perspective of the agonizing sights, sounds, and smells, and the bodily sensations he experiences:

> Ashoke can still remember their shouts, asking if anyone was alive. He remembers trying to shout back, unsuccessfully, his mouth emitting nothing but a faint rasp. He remembers the sound of half-dead people . . . moaning . . . whispering hoarsely for help . . . . Blood drenched his chest and his right arm . . . . He remembers being unable to see . . . . he thought that perhaps, like the grandfather whom he was on the way to visit, he'd gone blind . . . . He remembers the acrid odor of flames, the buzzing of flies, children crying, the taste of dust and blood on his tongue . . . . He remembers believing that he was dying, that perhaps he was already dead. (18)

The narrator's linguistic cues, which note the repetition of the present-tense phrase "He remembers" five times, at once reiterates the credibility of this passage's details but likewise raises questions of their reliability because they are the narrator's explication of Ashoke's memories, *not* the narrator's own commentary, being expressed while Ashoke is experiencing events at the time of the crash. The ambiguity the narrator is illustrating even in this very dramatic scene continues to suggest Lahiri's reluctance of perpetuating a stable narrative meaning that could be privileged over other meanings and thus invoke imperialist structures and mindsets. However, the juxtapositioning of the narrator's "official" presentation of events with Ashoke's personal remembrances also lays out for audiences an opportunity not so much to decide which of the two is more valid but to become engaged with the text in ways they may not have anticipated and, namely, to become more conscientious concerning matters of meaning-making, or interpretative tasks. Another way of saying this is that Lahiri promotes what literary/literacy theorists (i.e., Rosenblatt 1978) refer to as a transactional model of reading that, as Graesser et al (1999), explain "assumes meaning is constructed between the author, text, and reader," and that "meaning is substantially influenced by reader's background, knowledge, cognitive elaborations, and emotional responses" (284). Graesser et al. distinguish this model of reading with other models such as the "translation" model, which assume that "meaning resides in a text and is independent of the author and reader" and the "transmission model," which "assumes that meaning is directly transmitted from the author to the reader" (284). Lahiri's invitation to readers to assume the transactional model of reading speaks to her reluctance to perpetuate imperialist discourses (in the form of a stable narrative truth). But Lahiri also offers her own "models" via the subversive strategies she uses (e.g., the different versions of the train crash or the thematization of consuming Other books) to invite readers to make meaning for themselves that take into account other possible perspectives/meanings to derive fuller understanding for themselves. In other words, Lahiri's narrative invites readers to do as Ashoke's grandfather asks Ashoke to do of the Russian novelists—to "read" and "then re-read" again." And even as Lahiri promotes the transactional model of reading, she, likewise, continues to illustrate that the meanings readers derive from texts may never themselves be stable or complete as can be seen in Ashoke's reading of "The Overcoat" which though "sheds" for him "light on all the irrational things about the world" still "in some ways" "made less sense each time he read it (14).

JUXTAPOSITIONING CULTURAL DIFFERENCES

As if to make readers more self-conscious of the complexities and ambiguities that need to be negotiated and considered to attain fuller understanding of her fictional world and, by extension the world at large, Lahiri confronts readers in a more obvious way *not* just about the different perspectives they may encounter in their meaning-making experiences but also the *incommensurability* of those perspectives to help them avoid perpetuating imperialist-oriented interpretations privileging one truth/meaning/interpretation over others. Lahiri's narrator offers this guidance through his/her representation of Ashima's experiences of the cultural differences she encounters as a new immigrant in her confrontations with American lifestyles. In some of these usually short episodes, the narrator narrates Ashima's experiences through a mix of behavioristic and psycho-narration modes to reveal Ashima's reactions to what she encounters. Sometimes, the narrator offers little description of these encounters and/or efficiently uses minimal but strategic linguistic cues to heighten the sense of Ashima's discomfort with the "strangeness" of the people she encounters, as in the case when Ashima attempts to borrow rice from her hippy, progressive landlords who live upstairs: "*but* the rice in Judy's cannister is brown. To be polite, Ashima takes a cup *but* downstairs she throws it away" (34; emphasis mine). In other episodes, Ashima's revulsion is registered blatantly through the narrator's words as in the case when Ashima feels "mild disgust" upon seeing a cat being able to sit on the shelf of the local newspaper store (29) or when she checks in on her landlord's children one day and experiences "abiding horror" upon seeing the messy apartment in which there are clothes "piled" on the bed, "dirty plates" sitting "on the counter," and nearly "empty" "whiskey and wine bottles" on the refrigerator, whose mere visibility "had made" her "feel drunk" (32). Still in other episodes, Ashima is reluctant to participate in the second-hand, yard-sale shopping culture in her middle-class community that sees even respectable academics like Ashoke's department chair wearing "fifty-cent" pants (31). On the outset, these brief disclosures, with no narratorial commentary, represent Ashima on face value, so to speak, and, thus, invite metropolitan audiences to interpret Ashima less sympathetically and even as a judgmental character because she views these experiences only through her own cultural frame of reference. However, after setting this stage, the narrator complicates this view of her, by creating a narrative scene that juxtapositions Ashima's own frames of cultural difference with American norms/practices. Specifically, this scenario reflects Ashima's reaction to her son Gogol's class trip to an old colonial New England cemetery during which students are instructed to make crayon rubbings of the names carved on the gravestones. Ashima's reaction comes after the narrator discusses the trip through Gogol's perspective that reveals his engagement with the activity because it brings him a sense of communion with the long dead and buried people who, like him, have unusual names. That the narrator details the process by which Gogol is able to see the names transferred from grave to his paper and uses many present tense verbs (e.g. Gogol "walks," "kneels," "wonders," and "shudders") as he makes his way through the graves brings audiences into close proximity of not just Gogol's mental state and body but also his profound, immersive experience, which leaves him "silent" on the bus ride home as he sits "with his rubbings rolled up carefully like parchment in his lap" (70). The narrator also heightens the singularity of Gogol's experience and positions audiences to emotionally identify with him by contrasting him with his fellow students who are "bored" by the art project and find other ways to entertain themselves (e.g. "pushing," "chasing" and "teasing" one another) and with his "teachers and chaperones" who "sit on the ground, legs extended, leaning back against the headstones" smoking (70).

While audiences have likely achieved some emotional identification with the young Gogol, it is interrupted immediately in the next paragraph, which reveals, unexpectedly, a contradictory reaction in Ashima:

> At home, his mother is horrified. What type of field trip was this? It was enough that they applied lipstick to their corpses and buried them in silk-lined boxes. Only in America (a phrase she has begun to resort to often these days), only in America are children taken to cemeteries in the name of art. What's next she demands to know, a trip to the morgue? In Calcutta, the burning ghats are the most forbidden of places, she tells Gogol, and though she tries her best not to, though she was here, not there, both times it happened, she sees her parents' bodies, swallowed by flames. "Death is not a pastime," she says, her voice rising unsteadily, "not a place to make paintings." She refuses to display the rubbings in the kitchen alongside his other creations. (70)

Within the context of Gogol's profound cemetery art experience, this passage's opening line seems to prompt audiences into a defensive stance as Ashima's interior consciousness comes spilling out on the page to literally question that which metropolitan audiences may not themselves deem questionable. The emotionally-charged interrogative commentary may itself elicit audiences' own complex, shifting perspectives because the narration renders standard American burial practices strange and Ashima's volatile response to the art project more understandable because of the Hindu cultural values informing it. While the experience of such a passage may well provide Lahiri's audiences with a startling opportunity to understand the complexity of this Other character's identity, it is also significant because it invites audiences to consider the larger questions surrounding cultural differences not just as they are being purveyed through Ashima's perspective here but also in the narrator's representation of Gogol's American teachers. The creative, pedagogical value that informs the teachers' crayon-rubbing art assignment as well as their relaxed behavior in the graveyard reflects the nonchalance they attach to death, at least when it concerns a cemetery dating from colonial time. Their attitudes concerning death sharply contrast with the ominous, foreboding attitude Ashima has toward it regardless of the time period in which it occurs. The juxtapositioning of these contrasting values is not Lahiri's way of critiquing one over the other—that Gogol himself derives a profound experience from the art project itself suggests this. But, rather, the juxtapositioning is itself the point; for in doing this, Lahiri's narrator carves out a contact-zone-like space (Pratt 1991) within the novel. This space acknowledges what Bhabha describes as the incommensurable "uneven, multiple, and *potentially antagonistic* political identities" of those who reside in "plural, democratic societies" that reflect "a range of different sorts of interests, different kinds of cultural histories, different kinds of colonial lineages, different sexual orientations" (1990, 208). It also makes visible what Bhabha describes as "the transparent norm . . . given by the host society of the dominant culture" which says "these other cultures are fine, but we must be able to locate them within our own grid" (208). Because such spaces are governed by hegemonic norms that are often framed as human or universal condition, hegemonic culture remains the transparent standard by which all other cultures are ruled and constituted as the Other. In revealing Ashima's volatile reaction to the art project, the narrator illustrates not just Ashima's resistance to that transparent hegemonic norm, which in her case puts lipsticks on corpses and sees nothing wrong with cemetery art projects, s/he exposes and makes visible that norm, where it had likely gone unnoticed by audiences as they read about Gogal's cemetery art experience. In this vein, the narrator's psychonarration of Ashima's interior consciousness in the emotionally-charged passage above, offers metropolitan audiences another potential moment of self-consciousness to reexamine how those hegemonic practices and values they may deem "normal" are in fact an expression of cultural difference and markers of otherness to the many cultures that have their own separate practices and values.

CONCLUSION

A more nuanced meditation on hegemonic discourses and othering practices also arises in Ashima's reaction to the cemetery art project if we look closely again at some of the opening sentences in the passage above: "What type of field trip was this? It was enough that they applied lipstick to their corpses and buried them in silk-lined boxes." These lines create ambiguity in the text because they are delivered through free indirect discourse, the narrative technique that conflates a narrating subjectivity with that of a character's, thus making it difficult for readers to distinguish whose discourse is being expressed. Lacking the third person singular pronoun indicator (i.e., *she* said) that would reference Ashima's subjectivity as shown elsewhere in the passage, these two sentences could represent either the narrator's subjectivity *or* Ashima's. We might be tempted to think the second sentence points more directly to Ashima's subjectivity—"It was enough that *they* applied lipstick to their corpses" (emphasis mine)—because the "they" here suggests a pejorative application that reflects the judgmental attitude Ashima implicitly demonstrates toward American lifestyles and habits as discussed above. But, even so, there is no conclusive way to attribute this sentence solely to Ashima. The following sentence in the passage also exudes ambiguity because even though there is a third person pronoun reference to Ashima the "she" appears in a parenthetical clause in the middle of the sentence—"Only in America *(a phrase she has begun to resort to often these days)*, only in America are children taken to cemeteries in the name of art" (emphasis mine). Because the lines surrounding the parenthetical clause can be read independently and contain no pronoun referencing Ashima, they, too, remain ambiguous concerning whose subjectivity they reflect. As such, the ambiguity of these lines and that of the two previous sentences leaves open the possibility that they may well express the narrator's subjectivity or, perhaps even, the coexistence of his/her subjectivity with that of Ashima's, which then leaves us to wonder how to interpret the narrator's identity. Is the narrator indeed the objective, reliable authority audiences will have likely, if subconsciously, presumed him/her to be? And, if the lines can be attributed to the narrator's subjectivity or shared subjectivity with Ashima (the "racialized/exotic Other"), does this then make him/her the reader's Other? The questions I raise here are not intended to cast doubt on the narrator and the events and characters s/he represented throughout the novel. I raise them instead to illuminate once again that, even within this emotionally-charged provocative discourse, Lahiri creates ambiguities that suggest her reluctance to perpetuate imperialist-oriented notions of fixed identities—even when it concerns that of the reliable, omniscient, third-person narrator, the stable narrative force in many a literary text. I also raise these questions to assert that the progressive potential of making meaning of Lahiri's fictional world and the material world beyond it lies in a "transactional" process, *not* blind acceptance of transparent norms and standards, but, rather, conscientious and self-conscious interpretative efforts and negotiation with the multiple and often incommensurable attitudes that abound therein.

REFERENCES

Ashcroft, Bill, Gareth Griffin, and Helen Tiffin. 2007. *Post-Colonial Studies: Key Concepts*, 2nd ed. London: Routledge.

Bhalla, Tamara. 2012. "Being (and Feeling) Gogol: Reading and Recognition in Jhumpa Lahiri's *The Namesake*." *MELUS* 37, no. 1 (March): 105–29. http://www.jstor.org/stable/41440715.

Bal, P. Matthjiis, and Martijn Veltkamp. 2013. "How Does Fiction Reading Influence Empathy? An Experimental Investigation on the Role of Emotional Transportation." *PLoS ONE* 8(1): e55341. doi: https://doi.org/10.1371/journal.pone.0055341

Bhabha, Homi. 1990. Interview with Jonathan Rutherford. "The Third Space: Interview with Homi Bhabha." *Identity: Community, Culture, Difference.* London: Lawrence and Wishart, 207–21.

Brouillette, Sarah. 2007. *Postcolonial Writers in the Global Literary Marketplace*. New York: Palgrave Macmillan.

Cohn, Dorrit. 1978. *Transparent Minds: Narrative Modes for Presenting Consciousness in Fiction.* Princeton: Princeton University Press.

Graesser, Arthur C., Cheryl Bowers, Brent Olde, and Victoria Pomeroy. 1999. "Who Said What? Source Memory for Narrator and Character Agents in Literary Short Stories." *Journal of Educational Psychology* 91: 284–300.

Huggan, Graham. 1994. "The Postcolonial Exotic: Rushdie's Booker of Bookers." *Transition* 64: 22–29.

———. 2001. *The Postcolonial Exotic: Marketing the Margins*. New York: Routledge.

Kristeva, Julia. 1991. *Strangers to Ourselves.* 1991. Trans. Leon S. Roudiez. New York: Columbia University Press.

Peterson, Jordan P., Raymond A. Mar, and Keith Oatley. 2009. "Exploring the Link Between Reading Fiction and Empathy: Ruling Out Individual Differences and Examining Outcomes." *Communications* 34: 407–28.

Pratt, Mary Louise. 1991. "Arts of the Contact Zone." *Profession.* New York: MLA 1991, 33–40. http://www.jstor.org/stable/25595469.

———. 1992. *Imperial Eyes. Travel Writing and Transculturation.* London: Routledge.

Rosenblatt, Louise. M. 1978. *The Reader, The Text, The Poem: The Trans-actional Theory of the Literary Work.* Carbondale, IL: Southern Illinois University Press.

Said, Edward. 1993. *Culture and Imperialism.* London: Chatto & Windus.

———. 1978. *Orientalism: Western Conceptions of the Orient.* London: Penguin

Saleem, Susanna, Thomas Weskott, and Anke Holler. 2017. "Does Narrative Perspective Influence Readers' Perspective-Taking? An Empirical Study on Free Indirect Discourse, Psycho-Narration, and First Person Narration." *Glossa: A Journal of General Linguistics* 2(1): 61. doi: http://doi.org/10.5334/gjgl.225.

Staszak, Jean Francois. 2009. "Other/Otherness." *International Encyclopedia of Human Geography* vol. 8: 43–47. Oxford: Elsevier.

Spurr, David. 1993. *The Rhetoric of Empire: Colonial Discourse in Journalism, Travel Writing and Imperial Administration.* Durham: Duke University Press.

Tiffin, Helen. 1995. "Post-Colonial Literatures and Counter-Discourse." In Bill Ashcroft, Gareth Griffiths, and Helen Tiffin (eds.). *The Post-Colonial Studies Reader.* London: Routledge. 95–98.

Van Krieken, Kobie, Hans Hoeken, and Jose Sanders. 2017. "Evoking and Measuring Identification with Narrative Characters—A Linguistic Cues Framework." *Frontiers in Psychology* 8: 1190. doi:10.3389/fpsyg.2017.01190

Vij, Manish. 2006. "Anatomy of a Genre." Reprinted in Bhalla, Tamara. 2012. "Being (and Feeling) Gogol: Reading and Recognition in Jhumpa Lahiri's *The Namesake.*" *Multi-Ethnic Literature of the US* 37.1 (March): 105–29.

Chapter Eight

Singing the Subaltern Woman

*Film, Feminism, and Qawwali in the
South Asian Diaspora*

Lauren Bettridge

I attended a *mehfil-e-sama* featuring Ustad Fareed Ayaz, Ustad Abu Mohammed, and qawwali party on a late Spring September evening at the sprawling riverside campus grounds of The University of Western Australia. The small auditorium where I had once attended lectures was transformed; clouds of incense hung in the air, ornate rugs decorated the small stage, and two beat-up Lahore Music House harmoniums sat patiently awaiting their masters. The men appeared on stage to a small yet rapturous audience. The party played the canon of qawwali classics, including *Dum Mast Qalandar*, *Mera Piya Ghar Aaya*, and *Chaap Tilak*. At the end of the two-hour-long performance, the organizer and some academics from the University's host institution presented Ayaz and Mohammed with a gift of appreciation. The Pakistani-Australian organizer told the men in Urdu and then in English, that while they were playing she felt as if when she closed her eyes she was back *home* (in Pakistan). Two days after the performance I was emailing a twenty-something Indian-American friend on the occasion of Diwali. She sent me the YouTube link to the video-clip for the song *Aaja*, by the Swet Shop Boys, writing that the song made her "desperately homesick" (in her case, for India). Such is the pull of home, and such is the power of qawwali.

I sketch these two vignettes to draw attention to the way two different South Asian women are connecting with two different homelands via two different interpretations of qawwali. It is my intention in this chapter to think through how the secular and sacred South Asian music form of qawwali performs South Asian diasporic female identity and/or (re)constitutes notions

153

of home, nostalgia and nation. By (re)reading qawwali, a traditionally male dominated form, this piece is interested in the ways qawwali and qawwali in cinema can speak to and speak of the diasporic South Asian (for the purposes of this chapter, "South Asian" refers to Indian and Pakistani women only, though I note and am interested in the potential for greater research into Sri Lanka, for example). For diasporas across the world music has long been a livewire of sorts to the homeland. But as an increasingly syncretic music form, qawwali offers insight into radical ruptures along the lines of gender, sexuality, national identity and religion that warrant investigation. My emphasis throughout will be on reinserting women back into the frame of qawwali.

Qawwali has long been an unambiguously male form; from the *pir* who controls the proceedings, to the singers and musicians themselves, to the male-dominated spaces they are frequently performed in, and the audiences, once also entirely male. Virinder S. Kalra writes:

> Predictably, it is the boundary of gender that all *qawwals* are willing to agree on, and this is pointedly remarked on by Nusrat Fateh Ali Khan in an interview with a female presenter at *Lok Virsa*: "Women do *qawwali* [in film songs] and this is totally wrong. It has been specifically said that women should not perform *qawwali*. They should not even listen to it. They should not take part in it because this is *mazbi* [religious]." Though women have long participated in shrine music, Nusrat is here referring to the normative tradition of all male Sufi gatherings in which the *pir* controls proceedings. (Kalra 2015, 107)

Kalra's reading is generous, as there can be no question that qawwali was traditionally a male dominion, and one prescribed by "masculinist and heterosexual parameters" (Gopinath 2005, 31). But as Indian and Pakistani performers like Abida Parveen, The Nooran Sisters, and The Manwa Sisters play qawwali concerts at home and across the world; filmi-qawwali goes through a resurgence in Bollywood; as women across the world are welcomed at *mehfil-e-samas;* and as modern-incantations of qawwali, like the Swet Shop Boys begin to take hold; it is useful to consider how qawwali forms part of a musical culture and aesthetic that female diaspora keeps alive.

MOTHERLANDS AND OTHERLANDS

Said wrote that "All nationalisms in their early stages develop from a condition of estrangement" (Said 1984, 1), and perhaps nowhere is this statement truer than for the Indian subcontinent. The countries of India, Pakistan, and Bangladesh are saddled with history of estrangement—each the product of a difficult labor; born of a line carved through the middle of the land. With the Indian diaspora the largest in the world (at over 15 million people) and the

Pakistani diaspora the sixth largest in the world (with 7.5 million people residing abroad), there is an immense South Asian diaspora. Rushdie writes in *Imaginary Homelands*, "Exile is a dream of glorious return. . . . It is an endless paradox, looking forward by always looking back" (Rushdie 1997, 11) and it is this paradox that frames this study. I do not mean to suggest that every person in the diaspora is an exile or an alien, nor do I ignore those that feel alien in their homelands; but rather, I consider notions like diaspora, home and alienness on a spectrum of fluidity. Christina Emanuela Dascalu posits that "the notion of the exile—working within the cultural frameworks of the oppressive situation—poses a distinct threat to colonial discourse" (Dascalu 2007, 11) and given that the female body is most often the site where contests surrounding colonialism and nationalism are fought (this is particularly true of Partition—where women were routinely kidnapped, raped and forcibly converted on both sides of the country line), I argue that studies into the South Asian female diasporic subject are vital. There are numerous complexities and contestations surrounding the very notion of diaspora and diasporic identity, as Faiza Hirjji Kassam writes:

> Although there are some commonly recurring characteristics that can be associated with the notion of diaspora, such as dispersal across more than one country, a collective nostalgia for a shared homeland, or the maintenance of bonds through cultural products and media, there is no essential model of what a diaspora is or should be. (Kassam 2007, 4)

As a result, this chapter considers intersections and often contradictory connections between the South Asian female diaspora and qawwali. As a music form and a culture, qawwali is increasingly taking up a greater space in the diasporic imaginary.

Traditionally, qawwali troupes would visit villages throughout India and Pakistan and nearby villages would travel great distances for the special occasion; or families would visit Sufi shrines on Thursdays and Fridays to hear qawwali. Qawwali now travels instantly onto mobile phones, laptops, and into the living rooms of the diaspora like never before. But as the form of qawwali modernizes, it also transgresses its traditional roots, becoming something new in the process. This chapter begins by reading two filmi-qawwalis featured in two Indian films (one a Bollywood film, the other a cross-over diasporic cult classic) and the way they permit a glimpse of queer female desire; then examines modern qawwali fusion in the form of hyper-masculine diasporic rap duo the Swet Shop Boys; and finally, examines how performances of qawwali across the diaspora can both dilute the originary form and offer a sacred space for female fans. Ultimately, through close content analysis and secondary research, this chapter seeks to understand the role qawwali plays in constructing an identity for the South Asian female diaspora and how it can play host to a (in)version of "home." While much academic research has centred on how, for example, the British South Asian diaspora engages with Punjabi *bhangra*, far less research has been done in reference to qawwali and how the diaspora, much less how the female diaspora interacts with the form. The way the subaltern South Asian diasporic female connects with qawwali and notions of home therefore, remains a largely unexplored territory.

THE HOUSE OF QAWWALI

Ghar is the Hindi word for *house* or *home*, derived from the Sanskrit *griha*. Qawwali singers, like Fareed Ayaz and Mohammed Abu, typically hail from a *gharana*. A term used in classical Hindustani music, *gharana* refers to an organized principle dwelling populated by musicians and/or dancers who are connected via direct familial lineage or by apprenticeship, and wherein residents are devoted to a particular musicological (or dance-related) ideology. Ayaz and Mohammed hail from the famous *Qawwal Bachchon Ka Gharana*, a qawwali *gharana* dating back to Delhi in the thirteenth century. By way of good housekeeping, it is necessary to briefly unpack the basics of the qawwali form. Fareed Ayaz once said in a performance at The Proms in 2017, "Qawwali is not singing, it is praying. Qawwali is an exercise to improve your soul" (BBC 2017, n.p). The word "qawwali" stems from the Arabic word *qual*, which means "to speak" or to "convey a message." A musical means by which a group of male musicians (called qawwals) sing Sufi messages to (traditionally male) devotees, qawwali emerged from the rich tradition of the Chishti Sufi Order in the thirteenth century. As its purpose is to bring both singer and audience closer to God, the practice of qawwali singing is closely aligned with both Sufiism and Islamic mysticism. In an interview on YouTube by the Ajab Shahar—Kabir Project, a group devoted to preserving and discussing the works of Kabir and other Bhakti, Sufi, and Baul poets in Bangalore, Fareed Ayaz candidly talks through his path to Sufism and modern Sufism's relationship to orthodox Islam. In it, he explains: "Sufism is beyond the religion. In fact, Sufiism is not an 'ism' but a therapy for humanity" (Ajab Shahar—Kabir Project 2016).

The art of qawwali is largely attributed to renowned Sufi poet, musician, and mystic Amir Khusrao (1253–1325), who was a disciple and devotee of Sufi Saint Hazrat Nizamuddin Auliya (1238–1325) of Delhi. Inspired by his master, Khusrao devoted all his later works to Nizamuddin, and is largely credited with having created both the qawwali and ghazal music forms (two highly revered music forms in India and Pakistan). Indeed, no *mehfil-e-sama* is complete without at least one of Khusrao's works, such is his influence. Traditionally, qawwali took place in the context of a *mehfil-e-sama*, a spiritual gathering occurring on the anniversaries of Sufi Saint's deaths at their shrines (these days however, all performances of qawwali generally are termed *mehfil-e-samas*—whether they occur at a university auditorium or a stadium). On Thursday nights (the day of remembering the deceased) and sometimes Fridays (the day of prayer) the shrines are often filled with the sound of qawwali. Broadly speaking, qawwali is a devotional music form that expresses the divine love between man and God. A song or performance of qawwali therefore, has a ritualistic spiritual purpose and that is to bring members of the order into a trance-like state that ultimately brings the audience and performers closer to God. To bring the audience into communion with God, the qawwal enters a kind of ritualistic spiritual ecstasy. As a communal music practice, qawwali invites an audience response and as a result live performances, whether they take place at a shrine or in an auditorium, are often joyous and interactive experiences for all involved. Traditional qawwali performances could go all through the night, with qawwals taking their cues from audience response and depending on the occasion of the *mehfil-e-sama*.

A qawwali ensemble typically comprises one or two lead singers; a chorus of qawwals who support the leads by hand-clapping and singing the refrains; a harmonium player; and a percussionist and/or a tabla. The songs are performed in a call and response style of singing and the performance is highly improvisational with performers taking cues from each other and their audience, often building the performance to a final stirring climax. The lyrics of a qawwali song often focus on a poetic and metaphorical expression of the Sufi's relationship and love for God, by employing more recognizable images like that of an earthly love between a man and woman. Qawwali music is often considered secondary to the all-important lyrics. Works by Khusrao, Rumi and Hafiz form the base of most qawwali repertoire, but increasingly, modern qawwals draw from diverse texts in Hindi and Punjabi. Musically, qawwali is linked to the Hindustani classical tradition, interweaving parts of *ragas* (melody) and *tagas* (metric patterns) and using a formal structure not dissimilar to the *khayal* genre:

> Like khayal, qawwali performances feature a mixture of evenly paced metric refrains and rhythmically flexible solo vocal improvisations, which make extensive use of melisma (singing of more than one pitch to a single syllable). Moreover, a significant portion of any performance is built from traditional solmization syllables (syllables assigned to specific pitches or sounds) and other vocables (syllables without linguistic meaning). It is during the improvisational sections—particularly within fast-paced passages called tarana—that the lead qawwal engages with and responds to the listeners, elevating them to a state of spiritual ecstasy through ever intensifying, accelerating repetitions of especially evocative phrases. (Gorlinski 2009, n.p.)

Most scholars on the subject agree that qawwali constitutes part of "Islami-cate culture" (Dwyer 2006, 143), that is, it is born from the confluence of Muslim and Indic-cultures, and intimately related to Islam in South Asia, but part of an aesthetic and performative culture in which non-Muslims, and particularly Hindus can participate and partake in with great enthusiasm. As Leonard and Sakata argue, qawwali as a music form is closely associated with Pakistan and Islam by international audiences because said audiences "recognize it as a Muslim devotional genre and easily associate it with Paki-stan, an Islamic country. Second, it is Pakistani musicians who have popular-ized qawwali far beyond the borders of India and Pakistan, beyond the South Asian Muslim communities, and beyond purely religious contexts" (2005, 89). Though certainly true, the form is also evocative of India, as one of the most famous Sufi shrines, that of Hazrat Nizamuddin Auliya (the saint who was Amir Khusrao's spiritual guide) is situated in Delhi, and is filled with the sounds of qawwali every Thursday night (in a popular tourist attraction); there are a myriad of popular Sufi festivals in India (one in Delhi, one in Rajasthan and increasing others); and because of the qawwali's long and fabled presence in Bollywood.

QAWWALI ONSCREEN

India is a nation deeply infatuated with cinema. As the largest cinema-going, cinema-producing, and cinema-consuming nation in the world; cinema is something of a national obsession in parts of the country. The entire Indian film industry produced some 1986 films in 2017 (Film Federation 2017, n.p), with Hindi film industry accounting for 364 of those. Therefore, when con-sidering output and tickets sold, the Indian film industry as a whole is easily the largest film industry in the world (Punathambekar 2005, 6). It is also clear that of the prolific regional Indian film industries, Bollywood, the cine-ma produced in Mumbai and spoken in Hindi and sometimes English, is the "largest player" (Mishra 2001, 3). As a form with a unique aesthetic, one Salman Rushdie refers to as "epico-mythico-tragico-comico-super-sexy-high-masala-art" (Rushdie 1995, 148), Bollywood is something of a hybrid wonder. Pivotal to a film's success (and, increasingly so) are the roughly six to seven song-dance sequences contained in the film. Largely extra-diegetic, the song-dance sequence is a space that offers up numerous pleasures like voyeurism, romance, and comedy, all contained in spectacle that permits glimpses of desires otherwise proscribed by the narrative of the film. By enabling the hero and heroine to perform their private and physical desires for each other in a public setting, the song-dance sequence is imbued with the potential to transgress the chaste, heteronormative values of the narrative.

Bollywood films as a result therefore, mobilize the song-dance sequence for vastly different (alternative) pleasures and meanings.

The influence that popular Indian music and Bollywood has had and continues to have on each other cannot be overstated. While music fans often lament (what they see as) the diminishing of high-art Indian music, Bollywood fans purchase and consume Indian-pop-Bollywood fusion songs from films like never before. With easily accessible song-dance sequences deployed via social media and available on YouTube before the film's release, the sequences are a hugely useful commodity for filmmakers. But while recent contemporary Bollywood continues to focus on pop-nightclub-style hits, Bollywood has long had an enduring love affair with the qawwali. One of the earliest filmi-qawwalis was in the Muslim Social *Zeenat* where the unusual all-female qawwali, *Aahen Na Bhari Shikya Na Kiye* written by Nakshab Zarachvi, composed by Hafiz Khan, and sung by Zohrabai Ambewali, Noor Jehan, and Kalyani, was a huge hit. But arguably the most famous filmi-qawwali of all time sees Rishi Kapoor bouncing around on stage to *Parda Hai Parda* in *Amar, Akbar, Anthony.* Kapoor performs on stage with a qawwali group, hamming up the hyper-romantic qawwali tropes to attract his ladylove. Another key trope for the Bollywood filmi-qawwali is the "battle of the sexes" style qawwali in which two duelling or opposing groups (usually one male and one female) dual with lyric hooks. This form however, is ultimately an expression of the hero and heroine's passion for each other, disguised in the form of pithy insults. It is therefore, ultimately a heterosexual courting ceremony.

Of the hallowed place of the qawwali in Bollywood cinema generally, Pavitra Sundar writes that, "Classic film qawwalis capitalize on the simultaneously scared and worldly connotations of the lyrics, even if the setting of the performance is resolutely secular" (Sundar 2017, 141). As the onscreen qawwali's popularity grew, and it became increasingly unmoored from its Sufi origins, and became the "filmi-qawaali" as Jayson Beaster-Jones and Natalie Sarrazin define it. The authors identify the key components of the filmi-qawwali as follows:

- it is a close-ended, non-improvisational form;
- it is usually imbued with a time limitation of six to eight minutes on average;
- additional orchestration, often represented through Western instruments, over and above the traditional harmonium, *tabla,* and *dholak* used in *qawwali*;
- instrumental interludes marking the separate sections of the song;
- the vocal timbres it represents are more akin to crooning rather than a chest-based voice production as far as *qawwali* is concerned;

- it reflects the notion of "cinematic unmooring" or the disconnection between the performer and the audience; and (perhaps most importantly) in
it, the metaphor of spiritual love gets transformed into human love,
through its visual representation as well as through the use of lyrical
tropes. (Beaster-Jones and Sarrazin 2017, 167)

As the eminent scholar on qawwali, Regula Burckhardt Qureshi contends,
there is "feedback loop" (Qureshi1986, 165) that exists between qawwali and
Bollywood cinema. Bollywood film music, Indian and Pakistani folk music
traditions and contemporary popular music all have had, and continue to
have an effect on qawwali, with each influencing and (re)interpreting the
other. Scholars like Sundar argue that as the filmi-qawaali has become "item-
numberesque" and in the process, "the social graces and elaborately gendered courtship rituals associated with the genre in its mid-twentieth screen
iterations are rendered obsolete. Listening, for either pleasure or piety, gets
devalued" (Sundar 2017, 140). Sundar's argument holds true for the bulk of
recent Bollywood releases, however *Dedh Ishqiya* is a notable exception.

QUEER(ING) QAWAALI: *FIRE* AND *DEDH ISHQIYA*

Abhishek Chaubey's 2014 film *Dedh Ishqiya* returns its audience to the
opulence of the classic Muslim Social and then subverts the courtly tropes of
the Islamicate film to unearth queer female erotic possibility. The follow-up
to hit indie film *Ishqiya*, *Dedh Ishqiya* complicates the platonic prescribed
sakhi between its two lead female protagonists and offers up numerous queer
pleasures in the process. Interwoven throughout the film are frequent allusions to Urdu author Ismat Chughtai's ground-breaking queer text *Lihaaf*
("The Quilt"). Written in Urdu in 1942, *Lihaaf*, like *Dedh Ishqiya* and *Fire*,
radically situates same-sex desire within the home (and in both *Lihaaf* and
Dedh Ishqiya, the middle-upper-class Muslim home). Gayatri Gopinath
writes:

> The Quilt puts forth a particular conceptualization of female homoerotic pleas-
> ure that challenges colonial constructions of "oppressed Indian women," and
> exceeds and escapes existing theorizations of "lesbian" subjectivity. As such,
> it converges with the moments of queer incursion in the absence of "lesbians"
> that are apparent in Bollywood cinema. (Gopinath 2015, 144)

Dedh Ishqiya reweaves *Lihaaf's* approach to same-sex desire by picking up
new radical threads along the way. The film, firmly enmeshed in an Islami-
cate milieu, features a filmi-qawwali *Kya Hoga?* that subverts traditional
qawwali tropes by disorienting its audience to depict an earthy transgressive
romance between two women. These queer tropes also circulated around the

film, with Madhuri Dixit hailed a "gay icon" (Dedhia 2014, n.p.) for her role in the film.

Dedh Ishqiya also modernizes the classic Muslim Social by taking the tropes of the suffering tawaif and reinventing them. Instead of having the tawaif die or be condemned to a life of misery, the Begum and her handmaid drive off Thelma and Louise-style into the sunset with a stolen necklace in their loot. The film's promotional material largely consisted of trailers and taglines featuring the "*Seven Stages of Love*," drawing on Sufi tradition. The stages are as follows: *dilkashi* (attraction), *uns* (infatuation), *mohhabbat* (love), *akidat* (trust), *junoon* (madness), and *maut* (death). Initially, the stages form the yardstick for Khalujan (Naseeruddin Shah) to measure his relationship with Begum Para (Dixit) (and indeed for Babban's [Arshad Wasi] relationship with Muniya [Huma Qureshi]) but later in the film, when the two men drunkenly laugh in their room, both agreeing heartily that sex must surely come with each of the stages, the camera cuts to show Begum Para and Muniya laying on Muniya's bed giggling and tickling each other. It becomes rapidly evident that it is in fact the *female* union that subscribes to these seven stages. Further evidence of this occurs later when the men see an intimate shadow-play between the women, to which Khalujan and Babban say to each other "*Junoon!*" The film deliberately lulls its audience into a false sense of hetero-security by deploying a classic Bollywood romantic pairing in the two heterosexual relationships between Begum Para and Khalujan, and Muniya and Babban. It then shatters these notions in a great reveal, in which the audience discovers Begum Para and Muniya are actually in a relationship. The reveal is of importance, because it comes after a series of seemingly innocuous scenes of female bonding (that become in retrospect, homosocial bonding) between the pair.

Midway through the film, Begum Para and Muniya blindside the men and kidnap them. Having tied the men together in a decrepit house, the women happily revel in having pulled off their plan. There, on the second floor of the house (which has no wall, so provides the men a clear view of the bottom floor) the women celebrate their success by cavorting around the house, giggling and eventually collapsing into each other's arms. As Begum Para holds out her arms and Muniya runs into them, the camera moves away from the mid-shot of the women to focus on the adjacent wall. On the white-wall the camera shows their shadows in projection. The women embrace each other as the shadows slowly merge into one and they fall to the floor in an intimate scene. Khalujan smirks as he remarks to Babban, "*Lihaaf maang le?*" ("Shall we ask for a quilt?"), to which Babban knowingly smiles. By deliberately evoking *Lihaaf*, Khalujan silences any potential doubt about the women's desire for each other. For some viewers the shadow-play may come as a plot twist, because for the viewer unaware of *Lihaaf*, the women's desire may seem surprising (particularly as up until now Begum Para has been flirting with Khalujan and Muniya has even been sexually intimate with Babban). In this sense, *Dedh Ishqiya* caters to a niche audience because it requires an implicit knowledge of *Lihaaf* in order to understand the nuanced queerness on display. After the film's release, many viewers, whether accidentally or deliberately missed the queerness. Director Abhishek Chaubey said in an interview in *The Times of India*:

> Eventually, the hint was so subtle that if you got it, you left the theatre with a sly smile, and if you wanted, you could ignore it and still have plenty left with to enjoy. (Bhattavharya 2014, n.p.)

The oblique queer romance of the film perhaps speaks to the complexities of being *out* in modern India and South Asian diasporic cultures. But as Dua Kashish writes, the film also demonstrates "how self-censorship instead of being an act of yielding to stifling structures of censorship can also be directed to threaten the contours of the directives of censorship" (2017, 165). Therefore, Chaubey's play of revealment and concealment is a performance of self-censorship *as* an act of subversion.

Dedh Ishqiya's setting of Mahmudabad plays a far greater role than mere setting in the film. A city with contested Muslim heritage, Mahmudabad was one of the largest feudal estates in the kingdom of Awadh. The film draws deeply from the tropes of the Bollywood Muslim Social; there is a *shayari* showdown; a poetry-peppered gun-battle; nawabs; fake nawabs; nawabs pretending to be gangsters; Begums; ghazals; qawwali; and all the hallmarks of classical high Urdu Indo-Muslim culture. The premise of the surrealist mushaira cum *swayamvara* (itself a kind of cultural mash-up) heightens the sense of fantasy in the film—though this world once existed, it is now allegory. The characters therefore, exist in a filmic world filled with both fading, crumbling cultural relics of the past and yet all the technological trappings of a modern society. S. K. Singh explains of the unique setting, and of Begum Para's palace:

> The heteronormative arrangements of Begum Para's palace thus constitute the elaborate mise en scène, behind which female desire is enacted through a politics of intelligence, resourcefulness, discretion, and anonymity. Through this strategic negotiation, which is also a tactical necessity, the female protagonists are not only able to con the con men in the movie, but also imagine alternative subject positions that recognize the need for both pragmatism and expediency as well as deconstructing heteropatriarchal economies of desire. (Singh 2018, n.p.)

By occupying an alternative subject position, Begum Para is herself a global body, an intrinsic part of a cinematic universe director Chaubey calls an "alternate world" (Indian Express 2003, n.p.). This world, Krupa Shandilaya argues, "reconfigures Bollywood's imaginary of the small town, which has largely been seen as a provincial backwater untouched by the modernizing influences of the city" (Shandilaya 2017, n.p.). By constructing the small-town home as a space that permits and nurtures queer female desire, the film transgresses Bollywood's heteronormative and increasingly urban imaginings. While *Dedh Ishqiya* imagines the loci of queer desire in the (Islamic) home and is very much set in India, its subversions are notably queer and, as a result, global. Of Begum Para and Krishna (the heroine from the original *Ishqiya*), Madhavi Biswas contends that the:

> Bodies of these women are constructed as global bodies that express local concerns. The two female characters are a fascinating amalgam of local realism and genre construction. Both Krishna and Begum Para are small-town women who are defined in global terms. (Biswas 2018, n.p.)

The small-town "India" in *Dedh Ishqiya* is inherently Islamic (therefore "other" in terms of both sheer religious populace in India, and in terms of Bollywood representations) and in this way, Chaubey is able to experiment with queer-play perhaps more than he would have been able to in a "straight," urban Bollywood film. In functioning as an elegy to an Urdu world past, *Dedh Ishqiya* deploys an alien domicile of sorts.

The qawwali *Kya Hoga?* sung by Master Saleem, a Punjabi playback singer who is the son of famous Sufi singer Ustad Puran Shah Koti, is picturized on Khalujan's crushing defeat at the *mushaira*. *Topi* in hand, eyes downcast, Khalujan removes the rose from his button hole as Jaan Mohammed (Vijay Raaz) the moustachioed Urdu-spouting villain, celebrates his win (Begum Para's hand in marriage). Hoisted into the air, flowers garlanded around his neck, riding a wave of elation, Jaan Mohammed's beaming smile dissolves into a shot of a crowd seated and anticipating a performance. *Kya Hoga?* was written by poet and Bollywood lyricist Gulzar, who was himself born in British-India and whose Jhelum-home is now in Pakistan. As the unmistakable vocals of Master Saleem begin, the camera cuts to a high angle over an ornate balcony and a crystal chandelier to show fourteen qawwali singers seated on a small raised stage, arms outstretched to the sky singing in unison. As they perform, the camera shows several women dotted around the edges of the male-dominated room, before showing extra-diegetic action in which Muniya and Babban (who ruins the plan) are scheming to kidnap Begum Para (in a double-cross by Muniya). Khalujan sits beneath a tree crying as Jaan Mohammed joyously showers the qawwali singers with money and is showered in red rose petals in return, Begum Para forlornly readies herself in the mirror preparing for the wedding, and Muniya cries as she embraces Begum Para (and when her plan has gone awry). What is instantly clear from the women's impassioned embrace, is that they love each other. The song, features classic qawwali lyrics such as:

> I have sacrificed my life for her, I have come, having returned all the favours,
> I had picked the stars, but she robbed the entire sky.

While alluding to Khalujan and Babban's theft of the necklace, and then Begum Para and Muniya's own subsequent thievery, the qawwali functions here also as a vehicle of queer desire.

In updating and radicalizing the text of *Lihaaf*, *Dedh Ishqiya* imagines the queer relationship as preferable to the heterosexual relationships on offer by Khalujan and Babban. Where *Lihaaf* imagined the queerness largely a result of Begum Jaan's illness and as a substitute for a preferred heteronormative relationship, *Dedh Ishqiya* takes it further. Sarah Waheed writes:

> Lihāf is a cultural artefact, embedded within the larger narrative of Dedh Ishqiya; it is certainly not a film whose principal subject matter is same-sex love, such as Deepa Mehta's controversial English film Fire (1996). Nor does Dedh Ishqiya describe the two women's relationship in terms of lack, as in Fire, ie, "there is no word in our language for us," but inscribes the relationship in terms of fulfillment. (Waheed 2014, 24)

As Waheed writes, the Deepa Mehta film *Fire* features a queer romance that is defined by a lack, but the film remains groundbreaking. Financed largely by Canadian institutions and featuring a majority Canadian production crew, the film was shot in Delhi with Indian actors and made by an Amritsar-born, Canada-residing female director. As such, *Fire* occupies a transnational-hybrid space; India-set and diaspora-made, or as Senthorun Raj writes, it is a "disparate cultural production" (Raj 2012, n.p.). *Fire* garnered instant controversy in India for its depiction of two housewives (who are sisters-in-law) living together in middle-class Delhi who have an extra-marital affair with each other and run away together. The film angered conservative Hindu political factions, because as Raj writes, "it was marked as an obscene diasporic production infiltrating a fragile Hindu cultural space" (Raj 2012, n.p.). But while *Fire* takes place in a middle-class Hindu family and is encircled by Hindu-centric tropes, it too draws on Sufiism and uses a qawwali as a means of visualizing a transgressive romance. Pivotally, it features the shrine of Hazrat Nizamuddin in Delhi as a place of refuge for the lovers.

The film's Hindu-centric tropes are immediately evident in the character's names; Sita (Nandita Das) and Radha (Shabana Azmi) are important names in Hinduism (in *The Ramayana* and as the wife of Krishna, respectively) and imagery. In the climax of *Fire*, Ashok (Kulbushan Kharbanda) pushes his wife Radha toward the stove and watches on as her sari catches fire and flames engulf her. She breaks free and runs away, and in her charred sari makes it to Hazrat Nizamuddin to meet Sita. The moment, much written about in Hindi cinema academia, inverts Sita's trial-by-fire moment in *The Ramayana* where she "proves" her purity to Rama, by having Radha (in Hindu religious texts, the wife of Krishna) endure it instead. Shalini Ghosh writes:

> Surviving the literal "trial by fire," Radha is reunited with Sita. In contrast to the protagonist of Valmiki's Ramayana, it is not Sita who undergoes the trial by fire. In a metaphoric reversal the trial by Fire is for Sita and not by her. Like her mythical namesake, Radha surmounts innumerable obstacles to be united with her lover. Yet the symbology is not just that of a Hindu mythical terrain but also that of Sufi Islam (Ghosh 2001, n.p.).

The terrain of "Sufi Islam" is important throughout the film, because the women take sanctuary in the space of Hazrat Nizamuddin at two key junctures during the film. The shrine functions as a sacred and alternate space (outside the home) where the women can enact their true feelings. In one scene, the film follows the women on a cycle rickshaw through the busy, crowded, and male-dominated back-lanes of Delhi, and then into the shrine where they make wishes (*mannat*) by tying strings to the wall of the inner sanctum. As they tie the strings the women exchange the following dialogue:

Sita: I wish we could be together forever. I'm serious, let's leave! See, Jatin has Julie, Ashok bhaiya has Swamiji and Biji has Mundu. They won't even miss us.

Radha: And how will we survive?

Sita: We'll start our own take-out, of course!

After the exchange, which takes place by the wishing wall, Radha and Sita sit cross-legged alongside other women (with their heads covered) clapping and listening to a qawwali party. The qawwals, the Nizami Khusrao Brothers, sing *Allah Hoo* which is one of the most famous qawwalis of all time. The lyrics espouse the love of Allah, but the line, "You are in me and I am in you" takes on a far greater meaning in this context, conflating a divine love with a transgressive, subversive, earthly love. Thus, qawwali and indeed the contours of Sufiism/Islamism grant the women space in which to enact their love for each other (or at least, to verbalize or visualize it), a space the film suggests is unavailable to the women in Hinduism. Sailaja Krishnamurti writes:

> The use of a mosque as meeting place does not signify that Islam might be more accepting of their love than traditional Hinduism; it does, however, evoke India's long history of communalist conflict, so that the mosque repre-

sents a refuge completely outside of the Hindu establishment. (Krishnamurti 2000, 26–27)

Significantly, the film ends with the lovers embracing at the shrine, which as Shalini Ghosh suggests, has a deeper meaning:

> Radha and Sita are reunited at the shrine of Hazrat Nizamuddin famed for his intense and homoerotic bond with the legendary poet Amir Khusro. The film ends with the women in embrace within this symbolic space. (Ghosh 2001, n.p.)

The symbolic (queer) Sufi space hosts a transgressive female relationship, much like the Sufi milieu does in *Dedh Ishqiya*.

Senthorun Raj writes of *Fire* that the "legibility of the film is reliant on the implicit undercurrent of a lesbian sexuality" (Raj 2012, n.p.), a comment that applies equally as neatly to *Dedh Ishqiya*. Both films toy with revealment and concealment as methods of queering domestic yet global space(s) and in both films the women subvert the typically heteronormative space of the home to enact queer desire via qawwali. Ratna Kapur suggests that the place of the "sexual subaltern in postcolonial India is complex and at times contradictory and is not evoked exclusively as an identity of resistance to dominant sexual categories" (Kapur 2002, n.p.). In this sense, the female couples in both *Fire* and *Dedh Ishqiya* resort to veiled references of their relationships, but as Gopinath contends, just like *Lihaaf, Fire*:

> refuses to subscribe to the notion that the proper manifestation of same-sex eroticism is within a politics of visibility and identity. Rather, it suggests that in a South Asian context, what constitutes lesbian desire may both look and function differently than it does within Euro-American modes of masculinity and femininity. (Gopinath 2005, 155)

In both films, the female couples draw on qawwali and Sufi tropes as a means of representing and enacting their transgressive romances, and of reinventing their domestic spaces. Raj explains in regard to *Fire*, that "for queer diasporas reading the film, however, there are unique slippages between sexuality, nationalism and the home space" (Raj 2012, n.p.). Deepa Mehta said of her decision to set *Fire* in India, thus: "Fire is a much more dangerous film than one that simply sets up lesbians living in an elsewhere" (quoted in Raj, 2012). But just as Abhishek Chaubey referred *Dedh Ishqiya* as an "alternate world," both films studied here transpose queer female desire onto another place, despite both being set in India, making both distinctly diasporic in their imaginings.

DRAWING THE "DIASPORIC DOTS"
WITH THE SWET SHOP BOYS

On the occasion of their release of the song *Aaja* from their (then) forthcoming album, *Cashmere*, the Swet Shop Boys released a press release that read:

> Directed by Sofian Khan, this homage to teenage love was shot in Flushing, Queens and Coney Island, Brooklyn—bridging the gap between our Indian and Pakistani communities the same way Qawwali has. Once we wrote the hook for *Aaja* we knew we needed Pakistan's talented Ali Sethi to sing on it, helping us connect our diasporic dots while remaining true to the style of Qawwali. (qtd in Chauhan 2017, n.p.)

The diasporic rap duo comprises Himanshu Suri "Heems," an Indian-American and Riz Ahmed "Riz MC," a Pakistani-British actor. Suri is a Hindu-Punjabi whose family hail from what is now Pakistan, yet who grew up in Queens, New York, and Ahmed is a Pakistani Muslim whose family have ancestral roots in India and whose hometown is London (Trewn 2007, n.p.). As a result, hybridity is one of their key aesthetics. Drawing on hip South Asian themes, the duo's songs are culturally savvy, irreverently interweaving hip-hop beats with Indian and Pakistani instrumentation (frequently sampling qawwali) and dealing in identity, specifically "that of the South Asian immigrant child whose dual-identity preluded them from ever wholly belonging to either" (Trewn 2007, n.p.). The pair are self-reflexive and self-referential, with songs designed to wink at their South Asian diasporic audience—in essence, the band functions as a kind of cool-immigrant-kid club. But, the duo has a cultural vernacular that runs far deep. *Zayn Malik*, a song about the popular Pakistani-British ex-boy-band member of One Direction, features the lyric "*Yo, I'm bumpin' André hey ya, hey ya/Now I'm bumpin' chal chaiyya chaiyya*" which sums up precisely the young milieu in which the duo deal in. OutKast's 2007 smash-hit *Hey Ya!* (André 3000 is one of the lead singers in OutKast and *Chaiyaa Chaiyaa* was an A. R. Rahman super-hit from Mani Ratnam's 1998 Bollywood film *Bombay* featuring Shahrukh Khan and Malaika Arora atop a moving train)—both were cultural phenomena. As Pranav Trewn writes, the duo makes a "knowing hat-tip to the concept of hybridity" (Trewn 2007, n.p.). The Swet Shop Boys have a unique cyber-diaspora of female fans who respond to their unique cultural references and in the discussion that follows, I tease out some of these impassioned discussions of the role "boys" play in constituting modern South Asian diasporic female identity.

Brown Girl Magazine is an online publication that was "created by and for South Asian women" in 2008 in Houston, Texas, with a mission to "empower and engage those who identify as South Asian women living in the diaspora with a hyphenated identity." In an article about her experience at a Swet Shop Boys concert and their new release, diasporic South Asian writer Suraiya Ali writes, referencing the "4/20 crowd" (a pop-culture reference to cannabis culture and to the night the artists deliberately played, April 20, 2017):

> To be completely honest, this concert was my first concert. I got there early, got right to the front, and screamed the entire time. It was, in many ways, life altering. The two are fantastic performers, their energy is invigorating, to say the least. The 4/20 crowd was, in all senses of the word, high on life. New music from the Sufi La EP debuted along with favorites from Cashmere.... It all seemed perfect—a 4/20 night in the illustrious Los Angeles with your favorite South Asian rappers, hot boxing a venue to their hatred of capitalist oppression and qawwali hip hop beats.... It sounds as good as a joint feels (Ali 2017, n.p.).

Ali represents the prevailing sentiment of the cyber-diasporic female fandom when it comes to the Swet Shop Boys and especially to the release *Aaja*, which draws heavily on the traditional tropes of qawwali. She also gestures to the way the duo performs a rebellion (by referencing drug culture, for example) of "traditional" South Asian culture.

The video to *Aaja* opens with a shot of both Heems and Riz MC seated qawwali-performance style on a Pakistani rug on an elevated stage. Riz MC wears a traditional *topi* and moves with the exaggerated hand gestures evocative of a traditional qawwali performance. Heems sits to the side, dramatically dabbing at his forehead with a handkerchief, instantly evoking classic qawwali performances. The clip is washed with a deliberate VHS visual effect; one that for the diasporic viewer instantly recollects the experience of watching the late 1990s Bollywood films the video references. After the shot of the duo, the clip follows its young hero, a South Asian boy, on his bike as he makes his way to work. As he sips mango juice and watches Ali Sethi (the singer of the sample featured in the song) on the TV screen at his work, the action intercuts between two key stories—the blossoming love story between the boy and a girl he meets while sticking up posters of a concert for *The Sufi Sensations—Riz & Heems*; and the qawwali concert itself where Riz & Heems are performing in front of a rapturous South Asian crowd. As the camera follows the boy, notably sticking a poster over another poster emblazoned with the name "Donald Trump" and a photo of him, he spies a girl in a hijab on the street and follows her into the halal grocery store where she works. As he enters the store, the pair locks eyes and the boy imagines her in a Bollywood style romantic sequence (split in two, one image features him sitting on a curb—and the other her, hijab off, hair blowing in the breeze in a glittery dress/top). The action then cuts to him showing her the flyer through the window expectantly, but she remains coy. Later she returns to her bus-stop where she sees the boy has plastered her stop in the posters for the concert, she smiles and the camera cuts to the pair at the concert holding hands and smiling.

In the article "How to be Desi in 2017: Riz MC and Heems are forging a new cultural reflection of South Asians in diaspora" self-described Pakistani-American writer and journalist Iman Sultan echoes Suraiya Ali's earlier response to the duo. Sultan begins by describing her experience growing up Pakistani in America as lacking "cultural mirrors" and her need to rebel against the "cultural behemoth" of Bollywood that "became increasingly commercialized and sexualized in a way that retained the trademark corniness by renounced the starry-eyed sentiment which made flicks like *Khushi Kabhi Gham*, *Kal Ho Na Ho*, and *Dil Chahta Hai* so great." She continues:

> Then a few weeks ago, now long resigned to this state of affairs, I watched Swet Shop Boys' "Aaja" and it felt like salvation. . . . The video's depiction of regular life in diaspora is not a loaded political statement, and it's not an aesthetic polemic of representation either. Its power comes from showing a mundane reality in full technicolour. . . . The video invokes nostalgia with nods to traditional South Asian cultural tropes but brings them into the current day with a thoroughly modern diasporic setting. (Ali 2017, n.p.)

By deliberately riffing on qawwali traditions, the clip evokes the diasporic sentiments that appeal so strongly to its diasporic and nostalgic female fanbase. The video creates a strong sense of (South Asian) place, lingering on neon signs for Halal BBQ written in Urdu, and on other cultural intricacies of the South Asian diasporic milieu (like mango lassis). The 1990s-esque VHS effect evokes a specific time in its thoroughly Gen Y audience's life as Sultan's final line demonstrates: "And yet, while the video is a powerful expression of diaspora, the homeland is never far away" (2017). Similarly, North American diasporic South Asian writer, Josika Gupta wrote a piece titled "Nine Reasons Why Swet Shop Boys are the Group the South Asian Diaspora Needs," in which she too considers the way the duo represents uniquely diasporic anxieties about identity:

> *Cashmere* reminds us that we can and should love our diasporic identity:
> In most mainstream media depictions, South Asians are shown as rejects. We're too weird, we try too hard, we're socially awkward—we're never "cool" and when that's all you see, it's easy to think that you don't matter. Swet Shop Boys show an alternative identity: they let us be "cool" by validating and finding joy in growing up between two cultures. Their confidence and security in their own identities feels a little like a revelation. It's only fitting that the album ends with the appeal: "you can't escape yourself, please love yourself, please love yourself." (Gupta 2017, n.p.)

The end of the video to *Aaja* contains a devotion to Qandeel Baloch, a twenty-six-year-old Pakistani social media star who was murdered by her brother in 2016. With a hyper-colored shot of plastic red roses in a vase, the words "In Memory of Qandeel Baloch 1990–2016" appear in the center of the screen. A professional provocateur of sorts, Baloch was lauded by her fans for regularly posting mischievous videos to her YouTube and Facebook pages. Her YouTube videos inspired many Pakistani girls keen to envisage themselves reflected in her meteoric rise to household name status and admiring of her brazen honesty. Born in rural Punjab to a large family, Baloch began posting videos and provocative pictures of herself in 2013. The Swet Shop Boys' focus on Baloch is doubly interesting because their lyrics (such as *"She said my phone full of girls and we link too much, I said I can't help myself, I'm a sexy mother fakir"* largely objectify and sexualize women based on ethnicity (*"Polish girl, check that Slavic, yeah she sweet like baklava"*). Baloch's murder drew the ire of South Asian women across the world and in Pakistan, particularly due to their outrage at her murder being considered an honor-killing, with her brother citing the shame she brought upon the family as his primary motive. New York writer and fellow Muslim Mehreen Kasana wrote an article about Baloch's death, considering how Baloch performed to unsettle her audience by challenging Pakistani social, gender and class mores:

> Prior to opining on the subjects of womanhood, autonomy, sexuality, marriage, conservative backlash and the duplicity of male-dominated establishment in her own fashion, Baloch was what many Pakistanis would consider "time-pass"—a *shughal* to crack yourself up with, throw a Facebook reaction at and eventually forget like other "provocateurs" such as Veena and Mathira—but she hooked herself uncomfortably deep inside the national male consciousness with her questions and statements. Whether it was poking fun at the clergy or daring "haters" to show themselves, Baloch used the virtual medium to express objection. That's when she became less of a *shughal* and more of a *masla*. A problem. (Kasana 2016, n.p.)

The article appeared on *Kajal Magazine's* website. According to its mission statement, the magazine "rebuffs the damning scrutiny of onlookers to create a space for the South Asian diaspora to raise their voices" (*Kajal Magazine* 2016, n.p.). The Swet Shop Boys also offer up a space in which an increasingly restless and rebellious (largely female) diaspora can assert their unique cultural identity. The "boys" and the young women quoted focus repeatedly on the notion of "home" in their songs and writings, respectively, which is important because both Riz and Heems are from Pakistan and India. There is, then, a sense of a shared homeland for this cyber-diaspora; a hark back to a pre-Partition subcontinent and a united motherland that is too potent an image for second- and third-generation South Asian women to resist.

"MERA PIYA GHAR AIYA":
QAWWALI COMES TO MY OWN HOME

As Fareed Ayaz, Abu Mohammed, and qawwali party began to play the familiar strains of *Chaap Tilak*, a group of around twelve young male students dressed in *salwar kameez* began to congregate in front of the stage. They began to wildly dance, showering the qawwals in $5 notes that they had clearly been saving up for the occasion as they did so. In Urdu, Ayaz jokingly asked the boys to sit and listen politely before whipping them into a frenzy, encouraging them to sing with him the famous lines: "*Chaap tilak sab cheeni re/mose naina milaike*" ("You've taken away all trace of me/with just a glance"). As the remainder of the small appreciative Tuesday night crowd erupted and Ayaz chewed down some *paan*, a young woman, shoulders bare, hair loose, and in a figure-hugging sleeveless salwar kameez began to dance joyfully on her own to the side of the stage, and to the side of the men. As the men began to play *Mera Piya Ghar Aiya*, she gestured enthusiastically for other women in the audience to join her and four women; one an older Pakistani-Australian academic, one an older Caucasian academic and the other, a younger Caucasian lady also dressed in traditional *salwar kameez* joined in. As a counterpoint to the young virile masculinity on display, here was a group of diverse women, dancing and enjoying an increasingly secular sacred form, in Perth, Western Australia.

The qawwals then began to play the song *Kangana* ("Bangles"), explaining to the audience half in Urdu and half in English how it featured in the Mira Nair film *The Reluctant Fundamentalist*. An Indian-American director, Nair has a later oeuvre that trades in uniquely diasporic Indian characters (films like The *Namesake, Mississippi Masala*, and the aforementioned, for example), though she had immense early success with *Monsoon Wedding* and *Salaam, Bombay*!, both uniquely India-set films. *The Reluctant Fundamentalist* (based on the novel by Mohsin Hamid) stars Riz Ahmed (a.k.a. "Riz MC" from the Swet Shop Boys) as a Pakistani who experiences the vast differences of living in America pre and post-9/11. The beginning of the film opens with a party at the lead's family home in Lahore where Fareed Ayaz, Abu Mohammed and qawwali party are playing. *Kangana* is a particularly interesting qawwali. A *Malkauns* raga from Indian classic music (typically a serious, meditative raga that is played in the lower octave and at a slower tempo), *Kangana* is sung in Brij Basha (the ancient Urdu) and contains lines in Farsi. The lyrics speak of a classic Hindu love story—a tryst between Krishna and Radha where playful Krishna snatches Radha's bangles and Radha pleads with him to return it. The song itself is simultaneously both secular (Hindu) and sacred (Sufi). As a *saadra* in raag Malkauns, *Kangana* sung in *dhrupad* style (an ancient Indian style) and set to a ten-beat *jhatpal* (a rhythmic cycle) in *madh lay* (a medium tempo). The song, "a midnight raag,

Malkauns, is said to attract djinns and spirits when rendered correctly at the right time" (Adnan, 2015), which is particularly important to its performance in the film. It perhaps goes without saying that the raag is rarely performed by qawwals at midnight, owing to the timing restrictions of concerts and performance etiquette common in "The West." As Sufi tombs and shrines are few outside Pakistan and India, qawwali and performances of qawwali increasingly perform a stitching together of homeland and host-land:

> Today, the new South Asian Muslim immigrants sponsor and attend cultural performances and other popular recreational activities that are almost as accessible as they were in the homelands. These activities provide many resources for the construction of immigrant identities and sometimes strongly influence the host society as well. (Leonard and Sakata 2015, 83)

These shifts form part of a wider change for the form of qawwali—and a move to a new form of commodified cultural syncretism. As Nabeel Jafri writes, "the commodification of qawwali goes hand in hand with the commercialisation of qawwali" (Jafri 2016, n.p.).

Some years before *Kangana* was met with rapturous applause at the University of Western Australia and appeared in Nair's film, it was featured on Pakistan's phenomenally successful music program Coke Studio Pakistan. Coke Studio Pakistan forms perhaps the strongest evidence of Jafri's argument that qawwali is rapidly becoming a commodity. A Pakistani made and produced television series, the weekly program features a selection of studio-recorded music performances by both emerging and established artists from Pakistan (there is also a successful Indian version). With performances taking influence from ghazals, bhangra, classical, regional folk, and pop, rock, and hip-hop, it is by far the qawwalis performed on the show that have had the most success. Coke Studio's popularity, both the Indian and Pakistani versions, is immense: for a few days in 2010 the show became the eleventh most watched channel on YouTube in the world and according to Riddi Shah, was also one of the most Googled terms in Europe (Shah 2010, n.p.). Coke Studio Pakistan forms part of:

> A highly complex global process at play where the "sub-altern" (Spivak, 1988) is trying to project its voice rooted in eastern music aesthetics yet comfortingly ensconced in a self-referential western structure of form that is like second skin to most of the audience targeted. (Dhanwani 2014, 16)

Both versions of the program present a particular version of Pakistani and Indian identity via qawwali. it is important to note that the qawwalis here are unmoored entirely from traditional settings—filmed in a modern studio (with stage lights, a black backdrop, brand new instruments, etc.) with slick production values and running for around twenty minutes. In an essay on the phenomenon, Rashmi Dhanwani writes:

> Unlike the more popular mainstream musicians who are familiar with the studio, the site for cultural production for most of the less mainstream musicians has traditionally been a place or worship (dargahs), villages and open-air performance spaces (for wandering musicians such as the fakirs). The "studio" site, then, as a laboratory for cultural production and collaboration, although thinly veiled, needs to be seen not as a neutral space but as the dominance of prevailing popular cultural production format. A subtle play of musical migration is in attendance here. (Dhanwani 2014, 14)

This migration is one that extends well beyond Pakistan (and India) and deep into the diaspora.

An integral component of both versions' immense success is down to its tech savvy (read: diaspora-savvy) approach to marketing. Access to the clips of the performances are hosted via the Coke Studio website for free. Videos are also uploaded to Facebook and YouTube for viewing immediately following an episode (English subtitles added to the videos have also served to increase reach), in a process that Dhanwani asserts, "allows for the reasserting of collective authorship in the domain of community heritage" (Dhanwani 2014, 10). This "collective authorship" is so large that the Pakistani version had over 7.8 million "likes" on their official Facebook page as of January 2019. By having MP3s and video files immediately accessible and free to download, Coke Studio functions as a kind of political soft power, stitching together historic wounds between India and Pakistan (as both programs are still popular in the other country). The program also has an immense reach in the diaspora, with countless YouTube comments and Facebook likes from across the world. The studio's online presence is part of an online-democracy, a liminal (cyber) space in which the diaspora and Indian and Pakistani residents (and indeed, "other" fans) can interact, share, and connect over music:

> While the fusion music that is being produced at Coke Studio echoes originary in identification, it also rejects in it an articulation of cultural difference. It allows for a creation of what Bhabha (1996) would call an "inbetween space." (Dhanwani 2014, 12)

Dhanwani also points out that the "position of the subaltern woman" has grown to be explicitly more visible on season six of Coke Studio Pakistan "with traditional male-voiced songs now being sung and reimagined through a female perspective" (Dhanwani 2014, 9). The female performers who appear on the program are usually dressed in modern or ethnic-fusion clothing and are impeccably made up in an image that runs counter to popular Western media imaginings of a Pakistani women. On Coke Studio India, young spirited women perform regularly on the show, including the Jalandhari qawwali singers The Nooran Sisters, whose performance in 2012 of qawwali-classic *Allah Hoo* clocked just under 8 million views. But in season seven, episode six of Coke Studio Pakistan, the version of Khusrao qawwali classic *Chaap Tilak*, featuring female qawwali singer Abida Parveen and qawwali-royalty Rahat Fateh Ali Khan became the most popular performance from both the Pakistan and Indian franchises, with 18 million views on YouTube as of early 2019.

Abida Parveen is by very definition—"female qawwali singer"—transgressive. Hugely popular across the diaspora for her performances, Parveen is a devoted Sufi. The singer first performed in the United States in 1993 and has done numerous tours since then, saying in an interview with Nosheen Iqbal in *The Guardian*:

> I want this to be peace and love, I go to India so much because of this reason—we used to be one country. I go to Mauritius, Singapore, America, it's my job—I am an ambassador for the heart and will of our Pakistan. This is my destiny. (qtd in Iqbal 2013, n.p.)

Like Fareed Ayaz and the Swet Shop Boys, Parveen envisages qawwali as a device to aid India-Pakistan healing. In an enlightening chapter, Fawzia Afzal-Khan argues that Parveen and fellow female Pakistani singers Noor Jehan and Deeyah "challenge fundamentalist understandings of Islam via a Sufi-inspired "queering" of a heteronormative worldview that wishes to separate nature and culture, body and mind, as well as the divine from the human" (Afzal-Khan 2014, 32). Similarly, Gopinath explains how a performance by Parveen at an Outdoor Summerstage concert in New York City in July 1999 functioned as a "web of affect that served to bind and connect the queer men in the audience to each other and to Parveen herself" (Gopinath 2005, 60). She writes that at the concert the female audience remained largely seated, while the men gathered at the front of the stage—and as a result, "the queer listening and dance practices that revolved around Parveen's performance enabled a male homosocial space to translate quite seamlessly into a homoerotic one" (Gopinath 2005, 59). Gopinath herself contends that there is a notable absence from her analysis: the woman. She writes that Parveen's performance "can hardly be seen as a utopian site but rather as one that is contradictory and unstable, imprinted with hierarchical power relations organized along gendered lines" (Gopinath 2005, 61). In a sense, this chapter has sought to partly redress such imbalance; finding that in the decade since Gopinath's seminal work, women have in fact, entered the frame of qawwali. By tracking queer threads in narratives in Indian cinema like *Fire* and *Dedh Ishqiya* and finding transgressive, hyper-modern performances of qawwali (like the Swet Shop Boys), this chapter has found moments of radical rupture. Just like Parveen transcends her gender and self, she also transcends notions of nationhood. In this sense, Abida Parveen, the subaltern qawwali singer, embodies what this chapter has sought to explore: that qawwali *can* be transgressive for the female diaspora—permitting performers and audience/listenership alike to transgress and digress borders, and a form that increasingly welcomes the other into its home.

REFERENCES

Ali, Suraiya. 2017. "Swet Shop Boys: A Discussion on Representation, Politics and Entertainment." *Brown Girl Magazine*, June 14, 2017. https://www.browngirlmagazine.com/2017/06/swet-shop-boys-discussion/.

Afzal-Khan, Fawzia. 2014. "From Melody Queen to Muslim Madonna: Pakistani Female Singers Transcending the Secular/Sacred Divide." In Ketu H. Katrak and Anita R. Ratnam (eds.). *Voyages of Body and Soul: Selected Female Icons of India and Beyond*. Cambridge, UK: Cambridge Scholars Publishing.

Ajab Shahar—Kabir Project. 2016. "'What is Sufism?': Fariduddin Ayaz," Filmed September 9, 2016. Video, 0:35. https://www.youtube.com/watch?v=GFTOZQsNyi4.

BBC Music 2017. "BBC Proms: Highlights from the Classical Music of India and Pakistan Prom," Filmed September 4, 2017. Video, 8:22. https://www.youtube.com/watch?v=kNsG2NPA6_8.

Beaster-Jones, Jayson and Natalie Sarrazin, eds. 2017. *Indian Film: Memory, Voice and Identity*. New York: Routledge.

Bhattacharya, Roshmila. 2014. "Abhishek Chaubey on Dedh Ishqiya's unexpected end." *The Times of India*, February 14, 2014. https://timesofindia.indiatimes.com/entertainment/hindi/bollywood/news/Abhishek-Chaubey-on-Dedh-Ishqiyas-unexpected-end/articleshow/30207325.cms.

Biswas, Madhavi. 2018. "Romancing Widows: Insecure Women in *Ishqiya* and *Dedh Ishqiya*." (Conference paper extract). South Asian Literary Association 2018: Precarity, Resistance, and Care Communities in South Asia." http://www.southasianliteraryassociation.org/2018-conference-program/.

Brown Girl Magazine. 2018. "About Us." https://www.browngirlmagazine.com/about-us/.

Chauhan, Nikita. 2017. "Swet Shop Boys Mix the Profane with the Sacred in 'Aaja' Video." *A Nation of Billions*, March 3, 2017. https://nationofbillions.com/swet-shop-boys-mix-the-profane-with-the-sacred-in-aaja-video.

Coke Studio Pakistan. 2016. "Afreen Afreen: Rahat Fateh Ali Khan and Momina Mustehsan, Episode 2, Coke Studio 9." Daily Motion. https://www.dailymotion.com/video/x4pbxhj.

Dedhia, Sonil. 2014. "Madhuri Dixit: I don't mind being called the new gay icon." *Rediff Movies*, February 20, 2014. http://www.rediff.com/movies/report/slide-show-1-madhuri-dixit-i-dont-mind-being-called-the-new-gay-icon/20140220.htm.

Dhanwani, Rashmi. 2014. "Coke Studio: Remapping Translocality—Investigating the 'transnational' in its labour, technological and economic relations." https://www.academia.edu/7064955/COKE_STUDIO_Investigating_the_transnational_in_its_labour_technological_and_economic_relations.

Dua, Kashish. 2017. "Self Censorship in *Dedh Ishqiya*: Desexualization of Lesbianism as a Means of Countering Cinematic Hetero-normativity." *Lapiz Lazuli: An International Literary Journal* 7, no. 1 (spring). http://pintersociety.com/wp-content/uploads/2017/09/Dua-Kashish-9.pdf.

Dwyer, Rachel. 2006. *Filming the Gods: Religion and Indian Cinema*. Oxon: Routledge.

Film Federation. 2017. "Indian Feature Films Certified During the Year 2017." http://www.filmfed.org/IFF2017.html.

Gopinath, Gayatri. 2005. *Impossible Desires: Queer Diasporas and South Asian Public Cultures.* Durham: Duke University Press.

Gorlinski, Virginia. 2009. "Qawwali." *Encyclopedia Britannica.* https://www.britannica.com/art/qawwali#ref109055.

Gupta, Josika. 2017. "Nine reasons why the Swet Shop Boys are the group the South Asian diaspora needs," *Gal-Dem*, March 31, 2017. http://nu.gal-dem.com/nine-reasons-why-swet-shop-boys-are-the-artists-the-south-asian-diaspora-needs/.

Hindustan Times. 2007. "Deconstructing Aishwarya." https://web.archive.org/web/20121022025859/http://www.hindustantimes.com/StoryPage/Print/255081.aspx.

Indian Express. 2013. "'Dedh Ishqiya' is a flight of fancy: Director Abhishek Chaubey," December 13, 2013. https://indianexpress.com/article/entertainment/bollywood/dedh-ishqiya-is-flight-of-fancy-director-abhishek-chaubey/.

Iqbal, Nosheen. 2013. "Abida Parveen: I'm not a man or a woman, I'm a vehicle for passion." *The Guardian*, July 9, 2013. https://www.theguardian.com/music/2013/jul/08/abida-parveen-sufi-singer-passion.

Jafri, Nabeel. 2016. "The lost-soul: Qawwali's journey from ecstasy to entertainment." *Herald*, June 23, 2016. https://herald.dawn.com/news/1153407.

Kalra, Virinder S. 2015. *Sacred and Secular Music: A Postcolonial Approach.* London: Bloomsbury Academic.

Kapur, Ratna. 2002. "Too Hot to Handle: The Cultural Politics of *Fire*." In Brinda Bose (ed.). *Translating Desire*. New Delhi: Katha.

Kasana, Mehreen. 2016. "Our Pathological Fear of Women." *Kajal Magazine,* July 18, 2016. https://www.kajalmag.com/our-pathological-fear-of-women-like-qandeel-baloch/.

Kassam, Faiza Hirji. 2007. "Resistance is Futile: Indian Cinema and Identity Construction Among Young South Asian Canadians of Muslim and Other Backgrounds," Masters diss., Carleton University.

Krishnamurti, Sailaja Vatsala. 2000. "Boundaries on Fire: Hybridity and the Political Economy of Culture," PhD diss., University of Victoria.

Lakhani, Nashmina. 2016. "Swara Bhaskar: I am a Feminist, Proud and Unabashed," *iDiva,* January 5, 2016. https://www.idiva.com/interviews-entertainment/swara-bhaskar-i-am-a-feminist-proud-and-unabashed/15120386.

Leonard, Karen, and Hiromi Lorraine Sakata. 2005. "Indo-Muslim Music, Poetry and Dance in North America." *Amerasia Journal* 31, no.1. https://escholarship.org/content/qt26m9d5bj/qt26m9d5bj.pdf.

Mishra, Vijay. 2002. *Bollywood Cinema: Temples of Desire*. New York: Routledge.

Nair, Supriya. 2010. "High on Coke Studio." *Open Magazine*, September 25, 2010. http://www.openthemagazine.com/article/world/high-on-coke-studio.

Punathambekar, Aswin, "Bollywood in the Indian-American Diaspora: Mediating a Transitive Logic of Cultural Citizenship." *International Journal of Cultural Studies* 8, no. 2. https://doi.org/10.1177/1367877905052415.

Qureshi, Regula Burckhardt. 1986. *Sufi Music of India and Pakistan: Sound, Context and Meaning in Qawwali*. Cambridge: Cambridge University Press.

Raj, Senthorun. 2012. "Igniting Desires: Politicising Queer Female Subjectivities in *Fire*." *Intersections: Gender and Sexuality in Asia and the Pacific* 28. http://intersections.anu.edu.au/issue28/raj.htm.

Rushdie, Salman. 1995. "The Moors Last Sigh." New York: Vintage.

———. 1997. *Imaginary Homelands: Essays and Criticism 1981–1991*. New York: Vintage.

Said, Edward W. 2002. *Reflections on Exile and Other Essays*. Cambridge: Harvard University Press.

Shah, Riddi. 2010. "Pakistani Pop Music Takes on the Taliban." *The Atlantic*, December 4, 2010. https://www.theatlantic.com/international/archive/2010/12/pakistani-pop-music-takes-on-the-taliban/67485/.

Shandilaya, Krupa. 2017. "Gender Politics and Small-town India: The Cinema of Abhishek Chaubey." In Aysha Iqbal Viswamohan and Vimal Mohan John (eds.). *Behind the Scenes: Contemporary Bollywood Directors and Their Cinema*. New Delhi: Sage Publications.

Singh, S. K. 2017. "Conning the conmen: Intelligence and female desire in Dedh Ishqiya." *Journal of Lesbian Studies* 22, no.1. https://www.ncbi.nlm.nih.gov/pubmed/28398150?report=docsum.

Sundar, Pavitra. 2017. "Romance, Piety and Fun: The Transformation of Qawwali and Islamicate Culture in Hindi Cinema." *South Asian Popular Culture* 15, no. 2–3. https://www.tandfonline.com/doi/abs/10.1080/14746689.2017.1407550?src=recsys&journalCode=rsap20.

Sultan, Iman. 2017. "How to be Desi in 2017: Riz MC and Heems are forging are forging a new cultural reflection of South Asians in diaspora," *Media Diversified*, April 1, 2017. https://mediadiversified.org/2017/04/01/how-to-be-desi-in-2017-riz-mc-and-heems-are-forging-a-new-cultural-reflection-of-south-asians-in-diaspora/.

Trewn, Pranav. 2017. "Swet Shop Boys Showed Me How To Embrace Both Sides Of My Culture." *Stereogum*, March 22, 2017. https://www.stereogum.com/1930498/swet-shop-boys-showed-me-how-to-embrace-both-sides-of-my-culture/franchises/sounding-board/.

Trikone. n.d. Facebook post. https://www.facebook.com/pg/TrikoneAustralasia/about/.

Waheed, Sarah. 2014. "An Archive of Urdu feminist fiction and Bombay's gannewalis." *Economic and Political Weekly* 49, no. 10. https://www.epw.in/journal/2014/10/commentary/archive-urdu-feminist-fiction-and-bombays-gaanewalis.html.

FILMS CITED

Fire. 1996. Directed by Deepa Mehta. India: Kaleidoscope Entertainment, Canada: Trial by Fire Films. DVD.

Dedh Ishqiya. 2014. Directed by Abhishek Chaubey. India: VB Pictures/Shemaroo Entertainment. DVD.

The Reluctant Fundamentalist. 2013. Directed by Mira Nair. USA: Mirabai Films, Doha Film Institute. DVD.

Chapter Nine

Song, Narrative, Belonging

*The Place of Song in the Oral Histories of
Sri Lankan Tamil Women in London*

Jasmine Hornabrook

In 1985, music teacher Maya was one of tens of thousands of people who left
the island nation of Sri Lanka for the UK due to the ethnic civil war that
lasted almost three decades. Maya grew up in the Hill country of central Sri
Lanka, surrounded by mountainous views and tea plantations, but with growing ethnic tensions and riots between the Tamil minority and Sinhalese majority in the 1970s, her family were internally displaced to Jaffna, the main
Tamil city in North Sri Lanka. After graduation she worked as a music
teacher around the island, but the dangers of being a Tamil woman amidst
ethnic civil war became too great and she decided to join her sister who had
already migrated to the UK. Maya's decision to leave Sri Lanka was quick
and she told me:

> within two days—I will never forget it—it just happened, I just came to Lon-
> don with an empty suitcase. I only brought my music books and a couple of
> saris. (personal communication, September 2013)

This empty suitcase reflected the forced migration undertaken by Maya in the
1980s. Having worked in Colombo, she could not travel home to North Sri
Lanka to say goodbye to her parents due to intense fighting in the region, and
the few possessions she could bring with her—the Carnatic music books and
her saris—were both emblematic of her Sri Lankan Tamil cultural background and the story of her profession. The Carnatic music books symbolized a vital ingredient in Tamil cultural identity and the *sari* is a garment that
epitomizes Tamil and South Asian femininity.

179

After arriving at Heathrow, Maya stayed with family and spent most of her time during her initial resettlement at the Highgate Murugan Temple, one of the first Saiva Hindu temples in London. There, she sat on the floor of the temple, surrounded by the deities and devotees coming to worship, and chanted mantrams and sang Tamil devotional songs in order to heal and feel at home. In particular, she sang songs composed by sixth- to eighth-century Tamil saints who visited shrines for Siva in South India and northeast Sri Lanka, who sang about their devotion to God and the landscapes that surrounded them. Many Tamil Hindu devotees participate in singing of these devotional songs as they are in the Tamil language, they evoke sacred sites of pilgrimage in Tamil Nadu and Sri Lanka, and devotees say they experience closeness with God through the musical sound of the songs (see Hornabrook 2018). The songs also describe classical Tamil civilizations during the powerful Tamil Chola dynasty and therefore the songs function as a symbol of sectarian and communal identity that go beyond the strictly religious to shape Tamil ethnic-national consciousness (Peterson 1989, 5).

Beginning to emplace herself through temple visits and ritualized singing, Maya started to sing Carnatic—South Indian classical—songs again too. Using inventive instrumentation, such as an electric keyboard with its notes taped down to function as the vital *shruti* drone to sing and play along with, Maya and other newly-arrived musicians joined together to perform Tamil and Carnatic songs as they were "desperate for a music concert" after their migration to the UK (personal communication, September 2013). Eventually, a priest at the temple offered Maya the facilities to give music lessons to others who had recently migrated. This led to her career as a music teacher in London, contributing to a South Indian Carnatic music scene in the UK that is widely attributed to Sri Lankan Tamil migration. Maya has described the Tamil diaspora as being "scattered" across the world, as it stretches from India, Southeast Asia, Australia, North America to the UK and other European nations, but through music, song and other cultural practices, the scattered population can "become one again" (personal communication, September 2013).

In this chapter, I explore how music, and particularly song, has been a vital component in the oral historical narratives,[1] or the storytelling, of displaced Sri Lankan Tamil women, and how singing in ritualized settings has become a process and a space of belonging in diasporic settings. Based on the histories, narratives, and current musical practices of first-generation Sri Lankan Tamil women in London, the chapter aims to understand the importance of singing and song in the lives and stories of resettled women in a diverse urban environment. This chapter examines the place and the function of song and singing as a means of belonging. In contexts of forced migration, dislocation and resettlement, the notion of not-belonging and of alienation and alienness are inevitably brought into question when examining ideas of "home" and "belonging." As "home" and "belonging" become unbound from place, experiences of alienation and "not-at-homeness" (Mummery 2018) therefore provide the backdrop to the process of creating belonging through singing, song, and storytelling. The narratives discussed here are situated in a context of international migration and resettlement in the pluralistic and foreign society of the former colonial ruler; they are also situated in gendered contexts, particularly of isolation in domestic spaces. The notion of alienness and the Sri Lankan Tamil case is further complicated as mass migration was the result of ethnic persecution and civil war; othering and otherness had, therefore, divided the "homeland" of Sri Lanka and its citizens throughout the twentieth century. A process of alienation from the Sri Lankan nation was well underway before migration and resettlement in the United Kingdom (see Daniel 1996). Sri Lanka's Tamil citizens experienced both internal and international displacement and alienation from the nation-state as a result of escalating ethnic tensions, institutionalized discrimination, and ethnic persecution in relation to their Tamil ethnicity. Both the refugees arriving into the United Kingdom from Sri Lanka and those already resettled faced little chance to return and had to embark on processes of mapping and claiming life-space in the hyper-diverse and urban landscape of London. Of significance here is Avtar Brah's distinction between the "homing desire" and the desire for the homeland, particularly as the Sri Lankan Tamil diaspora could not sustain the ideology of "return" to the "homeland" (1996, 16). Many first-generation women arriving in 1970s and 1980s Britain landed into high levels of societal and institutionalized racism and discrimination, anti-immigration movements, the rise of the political far right and racial violence targeting people of South Asian origin; further contributing to a collective sense of alienation and otherness from the newly-adopted nation-state. The plurality and multiculturalism of the United Kingdom similarly "othered" newly arrived refugees as "[t]he multicultural society places the diasporic subject in a category of difference" (Ramnarine 2007, 2). As the narratives will show, the space of established temples and the act of singing during processes of resettlement and isolation provided familiarity and intimacy thereby counteracting the alien and unclaimed (and unclaimable) spaces of multicultural Britain. These practices also transcend nation-state borders and national citizenship through musical, linguistic, and religious practices that were common to multilocal Tamil populations and through the diasporic imaginary. Such mass migration alone does not create "diaspora" (Clifford 1994, Safran 1990, Sökefeld 2006); self-imaginations of a transnational community and mobilizing structures and practices must be implemented for a diasporic formation to come into being (Sökefeld 2006, 270). The act of storytelling and the narratives and practices explored in this chapter reveal snapshots into individual contributions towards the social formation and imaginary of the Tamil diaspora. Through cultural practices and processes of building the self into the social, these individuals and their stories avert alienation and disconnection from the social realm in order to become part of the whole and to maintain significant social and cultural connections in contexts of displacement and diaspora. Through Maya's narrative and singing practices, she exemplifies how she contributed to the larger project of "becoming one again."

The focus on women's narratives here does not suggest that men do not participate in singing or use narratives of music and song to belong; to the contrary, there are many male participants in London who share the song repertoire. However, men's participation is often more public and documented than women's and, considering the specific associations of women, tradition, and the domestic space of the home, it is significant to explore the stories of women in relation to migration, diaspora, and alienation. The chapter began with Maya's story because it highlights a number of vital points relating to song, narrative, and belonging. Basing wider issues in narratives and anecdotes is a common tool in ethnography, but here I look at narrative in terms of the telling, and my retelling, of the individual stories of Tamil women in London and the importance of song and singing in these personal histories. These narratives emerged in ethnomusicological fieldwork interviews within which I explicitly researched Carnatic music, Tamil song, and the Sri Lankan Tamil diaspora in London, therefore song and singing inevitably came up in the discussion. What is of particular interest here is the way song and singing often arose in narratives of first-generation women. The ways they described songs and singing practices often linked with wider Tamil cultural discourse surrounding song, singing, and belonging and therefore connected with diasporic and spiritual imaginaries. Drawing from these stories, I explore how this individual, subjective experience of music and migration links and informs wider Tamil diasporic society and collective cultural identities. It is important to iterate the scales of diasporic experience from locally lived and encountered to an "imagined transnational community" (Sökefeld 2006). Similarly, diasporic identities are simultaneously local and global; "[t]hey are networks of transnational identifications encompassing 'imagined' and 'encountered' communities" (Brah 1996, 192). The narratives of songs and singing, therefore, are powerful in both lived, claimed, and physically-encountered space and in creating connections across geographical space and with diasporic imaginaries. The process and connecting power of these narratives and practices of song and singing reflect James Clifford's assertion of the "empowering paradox of diaspora": "dwelling *here* assumes a solidarity and connection *there*. But *there* is not necessarily a single place or exclusivist nation . . . [it is] the connection (elsewhere) that makes a difference (here)" (Clifford 1994, 22; see also Vertovec 2000, 147). The narratives explored here are, therefore, stories and practices of individuals situated in times of alienation, creating a sense of belonging at both local and transnational levels.

Following this introduction, I first introduce ideas around narratives, memory, and storytelling before providing some context of migration from Sri Lankan to the United Kingdom and the relationship between women and song. I then move on to focus on belonging through song and storytelling. Both the practice of singing and the retelling of personal histories involving song and singing, I argue, link individuals, their oral histories and their place in the world to cultural, historical, and social imaginaries. I refer to "storytelling" (see Arendt 1958, Jackson 2013) in order to understand how the retelling of life histories creates feelings of belonging and how these narratives bridge the self to society, linking personal story to shared history (Jackson 2013, 122; Hage 1996). With reference to Hannah Arendt's notion of storytelling as a bridge between private and public realms, anthropologist Michael Jackson suggests that "[s]torytelling works out a rough synthesis of individual and iconic subjectivities, such that self comes to be identified with and experienced as coterminous with one's culture, history, race or nation" (2013, 118). Political discourse can emerge when the generalization of subjectivity takes place from self to society, from personal story to shared history, from, what Ghassan Hage refers to as, "homely" to "sovereign" belonging (Jackson 2013, 122; see Hage 1996, 467–70). I focus here on the empowering, although not unpolitical, process of personal narration that connects individuals to wider fields of cultural practice and transnational and diasporic imaginaries. In particular, I explore how the inclusion and practice of song and singing in these narratives create a sense of belonging, familiarity and solidarity in Tamil diasporic communities. In doing so, rather than demonstrating alienation, marginalization and passivity, the telling of these narratives and participation in "homeland" cultural practices reveals the agency and empowerment of migrant women (see Tomalin 2014).

NARRATIVE, MEMORY, AND STORYTELLING

Storytelling can be both a strategy for transforming private into public meanings (Arendt 1958) and, more existentially, for sustaining a sense of agency in the face of disempowering circumstances (Jackson 2013, 34). Both meanings are relevant here, but to gain empowerment in experiences of forced migration and resettlement is a particularly pertinent strategy through life storytelling. Michael Jackson argues that, though storytelling and reconstituting events in a story means that individuals no longer live those events in passivity, instead they actively rework such events "both in dialogue with others and within one's own imagination" (2013, 34). An oral personal narrative is a construction that, like memory, can subvert particular moments of trauma and instead assert power through active retelling and linking with a broader social field. Likening the performance of music and dance to the performance of storytelling, Jackson goes on to say that "[s]tories . . . are a kind of theatre where we collaborate in reinventing ourselves and authoring notions, both individual and collective, of who we are" (2013, 35). For those who experienced ethnic persecution, forced migration, and resettlement in a foreign society and nation, an overwhelming sense of alienation and disempowerment can lead to strong assertions of collective cultural identity as a means of solidarity and empowerment. The storytelling of personal histories links individual experiences and stories to a shared history (Jackson 2013, 122; Hage 1996): stories create feelings of belonging by bridging the self to society. Viewing narratives in this way does not mean to deny individual experiences, feelings, and values; instead it enhances the connectivity and power of individuals through shared practices and resonates with the experiences of others. As Joanna Herbert has suggested, "whilst it is the individual who remembers, it is within the group that they situate their recollections" (2009, 24). I argue that the inclusion of songs and singing in these narratives strengthen feelings of belonging further and bridge the self and individual experiences to wider diasporic communities.

Life storytelling and oral histories are particularly important in gaining access to the stories of the alienated and the marginalized, particularly female refugees and migrants. Referring to the study of the 1947 Partition of India, Pippa Vridee argues that oral histories connect women's stories and history, providing "the human dimension, which is often missing in the dominant political histories. Through living people, oral history allows us to connect the present with the past" (2013, 60). Through the dimension of oral histories and narratives, we gain access to the individual and everyday accounts of how people survived times of trauma and transition, while also highlighting significant cultural, religious, and social values. Oral histories specifically contribute individual voices to dominant historical narratives, with individuals' narratives allowing us "to venture into private female spaces and document histories which would otherwise remain hidden" (Vridee 2013, 60). Vridee's observations about oral history providing a meaningful connection between dominant histories and individual experience is reflective of the intersubjectivity and process of storytelling in connecting the private and personal with the public and, often, anonymous. However, Vridee argues how oral history has become even more important as women's voices are often marginalized and oral history, in particular, has the ability to uncover these voices, which would otherwise remain undocumented (2013, 53).

While overarching political histories continue to dominate over the stories of individuals, Herbert further highlights that oral history is an opportunity for respondents living in diasporic contexts "to express complicated issues and experiences that may have been difficult to articulate" (2006, 147) and that retelling such narratives can "enable forced migrants to express how their lives have been affected by the injustices of history" (2009, 24). Dominant emotional metaphors in personal narratives include food, landscape, and objects, and I argue song and music, particularly in communities yearning for their life in the "homeland" (Herbert 2009). Responding to Herbert's work and to oral histories, Seán McLoughlin suggests that "what begin as simple recollections of the stuff of everyday life can unlock the placed, embodied and affective maps of memory and identity which are at the heart of diasporic consciousness" (2009, 16). Acts of remembering, as Emily Keightley suggests, extend beyond the individual and enter a web of social communication and knowledge, that act on, and through, the social world: "Individuals remembering actively contributes to the multiple social and cultural frameworks within which we operate, endowing us with meaningful communicative material from which we can build social relationships, group affiliations and consensus" (2010, 58). Individual acts of remembering forced migration from Sri Lanka and processes of resettlement and healing in the United Kingdom through the practice of singing and song similarly contribute to multiple social and cultural frameworks. These acts and processes also connect the individual to collective memory and identity. Such remembering and retelling of singing and song actively contributes to diasporic cultural identities of the past, present, and future.

The everyday act of song and singing, particularly of Tamil devotional and South Indian classical songs used for religious ritual and for communicating with God is a significant metaphor and marker that, at first, appears as an everyday process but in fact functions to connect individuals with the wider community and cultural, religious, and social imaginaries. According to Santhirapala and Santhirapala (2015) and a number of devotees and singers, the performance of Tamil devotional songs in London is a vital part of retaining spatial and temporal connections with the "motherland." To refer to the practice of singing these devotional songs in personal histories is another means of settling into the diasporic "home" and connecting with the diasporic imaginary, while retaining connections with the Sri Lankan "homeland" and the sacred geography of South India. While the practices of singing and song are vital for a sense of belonging through the performance of songs themselves, I argue here that the inclusion of songs and singing in the oral histories and narratives of women further contributes to the active participation in the diasporic whole.

MIGRATION FROM SRI LANKA AND LIFE IN LONDON

The narratives to which I refer here are those of Tamil women who migrated as a result of matrimonial and forced migration from Sri Lanka to London.

Like many Sri Lankan Tamil people, Maya learned Carnatic music and practiced Saiva Hinduism as she grew up. Carnatic music is founded on a repertoire of songs in Tamil, Telugu, Sanskrit, and Kannada languages and based on a system of *raga* melodic frameworks and *tala* beat cycles. Despite being geographically associated with the whole of the South of India, the Carnatic music scene in London was largely the result of the displacement of thousands of Tamil people from Sri Lanka from the late 1970s. Many first-generation female musicians are based in London, both as vocalists and instrumentalists teaching and performing Carnatic music. As the Carnatic music system is based on a common repertoire of songs and as Tamil devotional songs are widely practiced, I discuss singing and song broadly in this chapter to include both Carnatic music and Tamil devotional music. The inclusion of both also reflects the reality of the mix of repertoire in both performances and in temple settings in London. Along with *Bharatanatyam* South Indian classical dance and the Tamil language, Carnatic music and Saiva Hindu religion characterized Sri Lankan Tamil cultural nationalism and identity in resistance to the Sinhalese majority culture during the twentieth century. These cultural, linguistic and religious practices were considered the "basic ingredients" of Sri Lankan Tamil cultural nationalism (Wilson 2011, 461) and are currently taught as "Tamil culture" in London's extracurricular Tamil schools.

In the 1970s, Sri Lankan education reforms reflected institutionalized discrimination against Tamil students, meaning that many students could not gain the higher education they aspired to and created a wave of students migrating to the UK for higher education. These reforms severely impacted Maya's career path in Sri Lanka. Often an aspiration of the Jaffna Tamil middle classes, Maya hoped to become a medical doctor but was unable to secure a place due to the decreased number of places for students of Tamil ethnicity in Sri Lankan higher education. She then decided to study music at the Ramanathan Academy of Fine Arts in Jaffna in order to become a music teacher. Having already experienced internal displacement within Sri Lanka, trauma from frequent riots, and institutional persecution, Maya reasoned that her change in path was destined. She told me "maybe God wanted me to learn music, that's how I took it" (personal communication, September 2013). In such narratives, the will of God is often referenced as a way of making sense of difficult situations and for the individual to find some resolution to these difficulties, all the while proclaiming their continued sense of faith. On the completion of her education at the academy, Maya became a music teacher and taught the next generation of musicians despite escalating tensions and civil war.

Anthropologist E. Valentine Daniel (1996) suggests that migration from Sri Lanka to the United Kingdom took place in three distinct phases. The latter two phases are linked with escalating ethnic tensions and eventual civil war: "phase one" refers to the elite who migrated to the UK in the 1950s but did not take part in distinct Tamil cultural practices; "phase two" consisted of mostly male students leaving for high education opportunities in the UK due to ethnic discrimination in the island's education system; and "phase three" consisted of refugees fleeing the island after the devastating anti-Tamil po-grom of July 1983, which resulted in civil war lasting until May 2009 (Daniel 1996, 155). Women migrated in all three of these phases, however, the ma-jority of first-generation women who participate in diasporic cultural prac-tices arrived in the UK as a result of phases two and three: women joined their husbands who migrated for education and employment opportunities in the 1970s during phase two; and many more women migrated as refugees after 1983 during phase three. Maya migrated to the UK as part of this third phase of migration. As the island nation went through escalating ethnic ten-sions throughout the twentieth century, Tamil cultural nationalism was con-solidated by the Tamil language, Carnatic music, *Bharatanatyam* dance and, often, Hindu religion (see Reed 2010; Wilson 2011). Many of Sri Lanka's Tamils looked to South India for solidarity as their ethno-linguistic, spiritual, and cultural home, and the subcontinent was referred to as "Mother India" in Tamil Sri Lanka (Russell 1982, 136). Chennai, as the capital of Tamil Nadu, became a significant center of Tamil politics, culture, and music from the early twentieth century (see Daniel 1996; Reed 2010; Wilson 2011). Many Sri Lankan students (female and male) completed higher education in Tamil Nadu, particularly those who wanted to advance their musical careers. As a result, personal connections with India tend to be strong among some mem-bers of the Sri Lankan Tamil diaspora in London, often leading to first- and second-generation members to refer to India, rather than Sri Lanka, as their "second home" after the UK. Such sentiments are not shared across the diaspora, as there are a number of Sri Lankan Tamil individuals and groups in London who disassociate from India and South Indian music as a result of the intervention of the India Peace Keeping Force (IPKF) in North Sri Lanka between 1987 and 1990 (see Krishna 1999). As a result, there are contradic-tory ideas of the cultural connections shared between members of the Sri Lankan diaspora and South India, despite sharing religious and cultural prac-tices and language with Tamil Nadu. Those practicing music and Saiva Hin-duism, however, tend to connect more readily with South India through socio-musical and religious networks, participation in Chennai's Margazhi music season and pilgrimage.

Tamil cultural identity has been constructed and reproduced through mu-sic and other religious, linguistic, and cultural practices in contexts of ethnic persecution, civil war, migration and resettlement. In particular, song and the voice have been mobile throughout these phases and have been integral to the emplacement of individuals and communities in London. Song and sing-ing are vital in Saiva Hindu rituals performing Tamil devotional *thevaram* songs, in Tamil popular music, and in Carnatic music. Songs are vehicles for the transnational performance and transmission of language, poetry, musical forms, aesthetics, and performance conventions and contexts. Practices of singing among Sri Lankan Tamil women in the UK often revolves around the devotional performance of the Tamil poetry of the Saiva saints which are set to Carnatic *raga* and *tala.* Women (and men) often sing collectively with others in a ritualized, temple setting or individually at home to perform *pooja*, a practice that connects with musical, religious, and cultural imaginaries. Such simultaneous musical practices in multiple diasporic locations reflects Mark Slobin's assertion that music is central to the diasporic experience "linking homeland and here-land with an intricate network of sound" (1994, 243). Music, song, and singing have the evocative power to connect across time and space in contexts of migration and diaspora and therefore hold a central significance in these narratives of belonging.

WOMEN AND SONG

Women, song, and the voice have been historical indicators of tradition, domesticity, and nation, particularly in South Asia. As the Sri Lankan Tamil diaspora heavily invests in, and connects with, Carnatic music as a cultural practice, it is necessary to discuss the position of women and song in the wider context of India and its diasporas. Positioned within the inner, spiritual sphere of the Indian nationalist project (Chatterjee 1989, 1993), women were essential in maintaining the inner self and the social space of the home, "imagined to be India's uncolonized interior" (Weidman 2006, 146). The spiritual sphere was placed in contrast to the male-dominated material sphere that reflects the world, the outer self, and the direct influence from colonialism (Chatterjee 1993). The emphasis on the social space of the home, spirituality, and ideals of femininity placed women to uphold the inner sphere of Indian culture as the "bearers of tradition" (Bakrania 2013, 17; Chatterjee 1989): as Falu Bakrania states, their "performance of femininity [w]as equivalent to national survival" (2013, 17). With regard to gender in postcolonial diasporic settings, Bakrania relates the idea of gendered domains of Indian cultural nationalism in the British-South Asian diaspora, with tradition and ethnic authenticity as the purview of women and modernity as the purview of men (2013, 5–6). Selvy Thiruchandran argues that in addition to feelings of diasporic double consciousness outlined by Du Bois (1989), the gendered identities of Sri Lankan Tamil diasporic women, in particular, may add another layer of consciousness. Thiruchandran says that this additional layer is that of "a Tamil feminine identity" where women are expected "to be modern (Western), to gain social acceptability," "to belong to a Tamil cultural identity while at the same time accepting reasonable levels of 'modernity'" and "to behave according to a Tamil feminine identity from the past" (2006, 18–9). These contradictory expectations of Tamil women indicate the complexity of women's expected roles in society. Women have therefore been positioned to show their ideal femininity through their role as bearers of tradition and through disseminating traditional "Tamil" cultural, religious, and social practices to subsequent generations,[2] while also demonstrating social acceptance in multicultural British society. With such cultural expectations and concepts of femininity relating to behavior, domestic space, and tradition bearing, Ketu H. Katrak (2003) importantly suggests that experiences of diasporic alienness and isolation are gendered and such experiences will differ depending on class backgrounds of migrant women.

Within South Indian music, the voice has been especially significant in Indian cultural nationalism during the mid-twentieth century and thus has become sonically iconic of India and South Asia; a sonic distinction from the music and singing of Europe. Amanda Weidman suggests that during the twentieth century it was not just a certain kind of voice that was valued, but the voice itself, "identified with chaste womanly behavior, came to be privileged as karnatic music's locus of authenticity" (Weidman 2003, 195). This voice was encapsulated by the South Indian Tamil artist, M. S. Subbulakshmi, who showed the domesticity, "sublime devotion," and Indian womanhood desired by Indian nationalism: she represented ideal "Indian womanhood" as a woman who devoted herself to the preservation of Indian tradition (Weidman 2003, 199) and domesticity: as a housewife who made flower garlands for the pooja room and knew nothing but music (Weidman 2003, 136). M. S. Subbulakshmi emanated a vision of ideal femininity within the Carnatic music world and beyond, with her attire of silk saris and jasmine flowers in her hair, devotional performances, and her iconic South Indian-style singing voice. M. S. Subbulakshmi's legacy lives on and the Tamil and Carnatic songs that she was known for singing are still highly popular and performed on a regular basis in concerts in the Sri Lankan Tamil Diaspora in London.

These aspects of femininity, tradition, and authenticity are powerfully represented in Maya's narrative, particularly in her story of migration and her suitcase, empty apart from her music books and a couple of saris. The narrative is striking in the way she describes that the only two material possessions in her suitcase represent essentials of South Asian and Tamil femininity that have emerged in times of transition, such as colonialism in India and Sri Lanka, ethnic persecution in Sri Lanka, and postcolonial migration. The saris and the music books reveal the two significant markers of her ideal femininity in terms of bearing the tradition through dress and through music. While there are a large number of professional and semi-professional male musicians and singers in London, connections and associations between women, the voice, and song in postcolonial diasporic settings are persistent. Male musicians still tend to be more visible in local and transnational perfor-mances, whereas many first-generation female singers and musicians priori-tize music teaching, domestic duties, and the transmission of song, singing, and music to subsequent generations. Associated with ideal "Indian woman-hood," the home too was a significant part of the nationalist project in the face of colonialism and pluralism. Fast forward to the Tamil diaspora in London, the concept of "home" becomes a contested and complicated space—is home in the United Kingdom, in Sri Lanka, in India, or in multiple locations in the highly-dispersed diaspora? And do women continue to assert their role as bearers of tradition in a postcolonial diasporic context in the country of Empire? I now turn to issues of belonging, emplacement, and the function of song and singing in the personal histories of Tamil women in London.

ASSERTING BELONGING THROUGH
SONG AND STORYTELLING

Song in the personal storytelling of these Tamil women in London reflects the importance of singing practices, in connecting with others around the world, and in portraying an idealized cultural identity. In this final section of the chapter, I examine the inclusion of song and singing in life storytelling and how these narratives position first generation women within a larger social framework of diasporic and spiritual belonging.

From her arrival in the UK in 1985 to our interview in 2013, Maya had seen a process of "scattering" and "regathering." She reasoned that the ethnic persecution, the internal and international forced migration, and dispersed resettlement that she and hundreds of thousands of others have endured have provided the opportunity for a new age of Tamil culture. She said that the postcolonial migration and formation of diasporic communities "will be a golden age to spread our culture, our religion, our civilization" (personal communication, September 2013). Despite her initial thoughts that life had come to an end for Sri Lanka's Tamil demographic through anti-Tamil riots, the outbreak of civil war, and the forced migration, Maya said that, in fact, a new life and a new hope had emerged through the dispersed and concurrent cultural practices in multiple locations: "The world has been one, then it has been scattered, now it is becoming one again, it's becoming one world" (personal communication, September 2013). Maya's comment here refers to the mass worldwide migration and the dispersal and scattering characteristic of diasporas, and relates to the discourse of universalism, prominent in many strands of Hinduism. The possibilities of travel, technology, and the circula-tion of goods and knowledge have enabled a unification of the world to which Maya refers. Maya played her own role in the reunification of the world "becoming one again" by singing in the first Tamil Saiva Hindu temple in London and in maintaining and disseminating mobilizing practices in London's Tamil diaspora. In order to regather her cultural, spiritual, and social life on her arrival in London, Maya visited the Highgate Murugan temple every Sunday to sing and worship. She recalled how she used to sit on the temple floor for hours, chanting mantrams and singing Tamil and Carnatic songs. As few musicians were in London, she became known for singing devotional *thevaram* songs for *pooja* rituals and spent hours singing these songs toward the deities. Like other musicians, Maya emphasized the importance of music in healing and overcoming the trauma of displacement. Referring to the Hindu belief of the inherent power of sound, or *nadam*, Maya chanted "om" and sang Tamil devotional and Carnatic songs in order to reach God and adjust to her new situation.

Maya's personal history places song and her practice of singing in the Murugan temple as the way she became emplaced and settled in London following forced migration. Fred Clothey (2006) proposes that ritual and group singing, in particular, is a means of "diasporic emplacement." Having written about the Indian Tamil diaspora in Mumbai, Kuala Lumpur, Singapore, and Pittsburgh, Clothey suggests that ritual practice in religious shrines is a significant way to emplace those who have experienced dislocation. He asserts that religion, and especially ritual, in diasporic contexts is a matter of "emplacement," "being placed in the context of the entire, of mapping one's place in life and cosmos" (Clothey 2006, 20). With reference to singing Tamil devotional songs in ritualized contexts, Clothey argues that interest in, and the performance of, these songs as a devotional act comes at a time of increased mobility, urban and professional constraints, and increased visibility of ethnic and religious pluralism. Such transitionary and challenging times give the sense that "one is living on the boundaries" and "the threatened loss of rootedness or personhood," but these songs from the past provide mooring in the present (Clothey 2006, 201). Through times of transition, therefore, singing these songs in ritualized contexts, or even the ritual of singing and the inclusion of singing practices in oral histories and narratives, contributes to the reconstruction of life-space after migration and during resettlement in foreign, diverse societies. For those who experienced ethnic persecution, the scattering of forced migration and the loss of their homes in Sri Lanka, the emplacement through familiar homeland cultural-religious practices is even more significant. The ritual of singing in a reconstructed cultural-religious context gave Maya a sense of place during her resettlement, but such musical and ritual practices also contributed to the prevention of social and cultural disconnection, which is pronounced in Tamil ideologies. Alienation and social, cultural, and ritual disconnection is prevalent in Tamil ideologies, particularly in the concept of *tosam*, the "deep, afflicting disorders of the body's natural harmony," which is caused by individuals distancing themselves from the reach of the rituals that maintain social and divine order (Fuglerud 1999, 78). By singing during resettlement and retelling stories of her temple singing, Maya emphasizes her social, cultural, and ritual connection and securely emplaces herself within the social and divine order despite her experience and narrative of displacement.

BELONGING/S

The narratives of performing Tamil song and Carnatic music in ritualized contexts indicates both the cultural connections sought at the time of resettlement and the construction of Tamil cultural identities in Sri Lanka and the diaspora. Constructed and perpetuated through the twentieth century during rising ethnic persecution and displacement and resettlement, Tamil, and Tamil diasporic, cultural identities were configured to reflect *Muthamil*—the ancient threefold cultural concept of Tamil poetry (*iyal*), music (*isai*), and dance-drama (*natakam*). As embodied knowledge, music, poetry, and dance were "belongings" that could be brought with refugees leaving Sri Lanka and arriving in the United Kingdom with few other material possessions. In Maya's words:

> What we brought with us is what we learned, our education, our knowledge, because everything else was taken by the government and the Sri Lankan army. Our houses, land, money, everything is gone. The only thing we brought with us is what we learned. So, we believe our wealth is our knowledge. (personal communication, September 2013)

The danger of ethnic civil war and the fierce fighting in the northeast of Sri Lanka resulted in many of Sri Lanka's Tamil population leaving the island and, with it, their homes, land, and material wealth. In narratives of loss and migration, the loss of homes, possessions, family, and friends is central to personal and societal histories. Song, based on poetry and music, also reflects the embodied knowledge and possessions that are mobile through migrating bodies, unlike material possessions that remain significant losses in accounts of forced migration. As Maya points out here, "the only thing we brought with us is what we learned," therefore music, songs, and other forms of embodied knowledge become more significant as the possession that refugees could take with them. The concept of *Muthamil* also has significance in these narratives, as *Muthamil* connects with a broader historical narrative of Tamil civilization, with the concept dating back to the time of the Tamil Sangam period. Song and singing then becomes a means of belonging in everyday practice and in storytelling, a vehicle for diasporic cultural identities, and a possession of embodied knowledge in forced migration. The power of stories and the things, memories, and activities brought out in storytelling must be acknowledged as a significant means of belonging, both in terms of the possession of an "object" and in terms of telling oneself into belonging within a much larger narrative. While Maya travelled to the United Kingdom with few possessions, her narrative of loss signals to a greater sense of being part of a much larger social field.

Belonging is a complex concept in diasporic settings and in the Sri Lankan Tamil diaspora in particular. Michael Jackson suggests that

> [t]o belong is thus to believe that one's own being is integrated with and integral to a wider field of being, that one's own life merges with and touches the lives of others—predecessors, successors, contemporaries, and consociates, as well as the overlapping worlds of nature, the cosmos, and the divine. (2013, 32)

In Maya's case, music was a vital feature in her migration and resettlement experiences. She used song to heal and to feel connected to, and integrated in, the life and people she left behind and those who were similarly scattered through forced international migration. Through her storytelling, she asserts her connections to the "imagined transnational community" (Sökefeld 2006) and she also reiterates to the second and subsequent generations the importance of song and singing in becoming part of a diasporic whole. Musical and cultural belonging gains importance in situations of forced migration, where experiences of colonialism and ethnic civil war further complicate and contest ideas of "home" and "nation." In terms of national belonging and citizenship, E. Valentine Daniel suggests that the Tamil refugees in the United Kingdom who experienced forced migration in the 1980s and 1990s were "nation-adverse" due to experiences of trauma, loss, and extreme pain. Daniel suggests that the idea of culture, nation, and therefore, citizenship and belonging, was not prevalent, and only a fluid, rootless future of constant movement was envisaged, where Tamil refugees would have to move around the globe, seizing opportunities to survive. One informant suggested to Daniel that "Tamil nationalism" didn't exist; what did exist, however, was "Tamil internationalism," in terms of not having any one place to belong (1996, 176). Many of Daniel's research participants were male, and therefore situated in a very distinct social and cultural role from that of women, who were expected to upkeep "homeland" practices and traditions. As the separatist politics of northeast Sri Lanka were, and still are, contested and polarized, I do not prioritize the nation in the discussion of belonging here. Rather, belonging is discussed in terms of overlapping similarities in Tamil ethnolinguistics and culture, Saiva Hindu religion, and the overall experience of displacement and resettlement of people from Sri Lanka to its many diasporic localities. Despite the aversion to ideas of "culture" and "nation" suggested by Daniel, music and song was, and continues to be, pervasive within

Tamil diasporas, traveling across the boundaries and concepts of the nation; through memory, through everyday musical and religious practice, through media, and through musical learning and performance.

ASSERTING MULTILOCAL BELONGING THROUGH MUSIC

The songs that Maya and others refer to in their narratives are regularly performed in ritualized settings in other localities in the highly dispersed Tamil diaspora. From the United Kingdom, to Switzerland, Singapore, Australia, and Canada, this concurrent multilocal practice is a significant facet of the contemporary performance of the songs. For instance, the popular devotional song, "Toddudaiya Seviyan," is regularly sung in London and is taught to second- and third-generation Tamil Hindu devotees and Carnatic music students. The song is also performed by Carnatic musicians in the Chennai music season and it has featured in Tamil films. In addition to its regular performance in the Saiva Hindu temples of London, studio recordings and live performances are digitally available worldwide. For instance, "Toddudaiya Seviyan" has been sung by the Oduvar temple singer, Sargurunathan, while on tour in Singapore and the recording is available worldwide via YouTube (see Ravi Glory 2011). The words of the song are retained, thereby following strict attempts to maintain continuity with the poem's composer, the seventh-century saint Sampanthar. The music of the song has been recontextualized from the Tamil *pannisai* music system to that of contemporary Carnatic music. Throughout these performances of "Toddudaiya Seviyan," the song's *raga* gambeera nattai and *tala* remain the same. The melody, however, is subject to variation based on from *whom* the song is learned rather than *where* the song is learned. The concurrent performance of this song reflects the concept of multilocal belonging (Ramnarine 1996, 2001). Tradition has close ties to particular localities; however, "the relationship between tradition and place is questioned when a single tradition is maintained, developed and changed by people in several different geographic contexts" (Ramnarine 1996, 133). Importantly for the case of continuity of Tamil diasporic culture in London, Ramnarine argues: "Even if members of that community remain unknown to each other, they share a common inheritance. This is a sense of relatedness . . . which encompasses . . . communities around the world" (1996, 151). Songs and singing are signifiers of multilocal belonging through shared inheritance, concurrent practices, and personal histories referring to singing and song in different localities. Musical practices and the concept of multilocal belonging reflect Avtar Brah's concept of diaspora that signals to processes of multilocationality across geographical, cultural, and psychic boundaries (1996, 194). Maya's narrative firmly situates the contribution of migrant women in this process of multilocationality.

These public performances and disseminated videos of multilocal singing practices are often portrayed by men. The songs and singing practices in women's storytelling are significant as the majority of professional and semi-professional Carnatic musicians are male, and the one London-based professional *oduvar*, or singer of Tamil devotional songs, is also male. Maya's, and other women's, narratives and storytelling is therefore a means of claiming a cultural practice that is less often visibly or publicly performed by women, whether these women are professional or amateur singers. The emphasis of song and singing in personal accounts is another way of announcing female presence and musical practice in the home and/or beyond public concerts or performances. The inclusion of individual singing practices within such narratives is also significant in terms of understanding the role of women in the custodianship and transmission of songs and singing practices in multiple locations, which otherwise appear as male dominated if taken from public performances alone. Narratives, such as Maya's, add a "hidden" and individual voice to the dominant history of the Tamil diaspora in London, that often refers to the establishment of Tamil schools, learning and performance of music and dance and cultural events. This history is often told through institutional historical narratives, such as those of temples, offering a dominant, historical text of the emergence of religious and cultural practices by Tamil communities in London (for instance, see Krishnamoorthy 1987 and Shree Ghanapathy Temple 2018). These texts rarely mention the significant role of individuals, and especially women, in transporting and disseminating songs and music on an everyday basis, in community formation and cohesion and in the construction of multilocal belonging. These narratives reiterate and reassert the role of women as bearers of tradition, demonstrating ideals of South Asian femininity and Tamil cultural citizenship. The interconnected relationship and iconicity between women, the voice and song in South Asia goes beyond aesthetics to postcolonial assertions of cultural authenticity (see Weidman 2006). The narrative of a woman singing Tamil devotional songs in the temple after the trauma of forced migration projects a self-representation of an ideal South Asian Tamil woman. Such a representation actively emplaces the singer beyond the singular site of a London temple and into the multilocal diaspora.

SPIRITUALITY

Maya's and other's narratives of devotional singing in ritualized settings overlaps to the field of the divine. The storytelling, narratives, and practices of singing in London signifies spiritual belonging in addition to, and beyond, diasporic belonging and emplacement. Through such narratives, women portray themselves as Tamil Hindus, who dutifully worship and demonstrate *bhakti*—religious devotion and attaining a shared space with God (Neumann 1980)—through their narrated actions. Narratives refer to the healing nature of song as well as the experience of spiritual belonging through singing. Singing to God in a ritualized temple setting during a traumatic and turbulent time, followed by a sense of resettlement, healing, and success, displays the power of *bhakti* devotion through singing in Maya's and other's accounts. The concept of *bhakti* performs a central role and purpose here. In a time and space of isolation and alienation imposed by migration, resettlement, and other personal traumas, a sense of belonging, comfort, and emplacement is found in the presence of God that is achieved through the devotional practice of singing.

A participant in the group singing sessions at the Sivan temple in Southeast London referred to singing and music as intrinsic and ever-present throughout her life story. As a child in northeast Sri Lanka, she learned Tamil devotional songs as a result of her homeland religious practices and she understood the concepts of *raga* through her lessons in the Carnatic violin. The experience of migration, marriage, and family life impacted her practice, but she started attending the temple singing sessions later in life in London. Having experienced ill-health and domestic isolation, she described listening to music and the act of singing as a way of healing and connecting with God. Her narrative referred to a sense of spiritual belonging and emplacement, and a connection with a wider discourse on singing, song, and spiritual experience. When talking about singing Tamil *thevaram* songs in London, the singer said she sings to develop her relationship with God. The voice, the songs, and the ritualized spiritual context in which song is performed contributes toward an experience of a virtual, spiritual space. In an interview, she said that singing the *thevaram*, particularly the songs she knows well in terms of music and lyrical meaning, take her to "a different world" where she can interact with the Gods (personal communication, April 2016). The singer said that she is taken away from the "material world" and its negativities and is taken up to a "higher spiritual place." The singer reflected on this transcendental feeling when singing *thevaram* in front of the deity and other devotees during *pooja* in the London Sivan Temple. She admitted her nervousness before singing as part of the temple's festivals, but once she started she "forgot" about her nervousness and experienced "one mind meditation," feeling at one with the music and the divine (personal communication, April 2016). The singer described her experience of becoming one with the music she sings and, in doing so, attaining a feeling of transcendence to a different world shared with the gods. This crossing from the "material world" to a "higher spiritual place," or the spiritual imaginary, results in, for her, a deeper understanding of her life (personal communication, April 2016) both to herself and in her retelling to others.

Through life storytelling and singing practices, the narratives of the first-generation women explored here signify the power of song and singing in contexts of migration, transition, and diaspora. While asserting the sense of diasporic and spiritual emplacement and belonging, these narratives serve to claim song and singing practices as the domain of women in often less visible settings. The voice, in its singing and its storytelling forms, averts alienness and is revealed here to connect people and places across time and space and between the individual, the collective and the imaginary.

CONCLUSION

Despite her empty suitcase, Maya's storytelling and possessions—the Carnatic music books and saris, her knowledge and musical background—reflect the iconic features of Tamil diasporic cultural identity and sense of belonging to which she subscribes through such a narrative. In a short story about Vietnamese refugees in the United States, Viet Thanh Nguyen writes "[i]n a country where possessions counted for everything, we had no belongings except our stories" (2017, 7). These stories shape the histories that are told to second and subsequent generations and that contribute to ideals of diasporic identities and vice versa. The performance of the songs and of life storytelling is a means of cultural connection, diasporic emplacement, and contribution to a more inclusive historical lineage.

The voice is a carrier of narrative and a carrier of song. The voices, stories, and songs are embodied belongings carried by individuals during migration, resettlement, and throughout their lives. Song, and the act of singing, is a vehicle for the mother tongue and "homeland" music, even if the oral histories are told in the language of the place of resettlement and in the context of displacement. Selvy Thiruchandran suggests that Sri Lankan Tamil collective identity has always been constructed through "being excluded as the 'other,' the inferior who is not entitled to full citizenship" in Sri Lanka and in the diaspora (2006, 11). While these narratives describe lives that have been marginalized, alienated, and isolated, the telling of the stories is a means of agency and empowerment through the reclamation of events that were experienced in passivity. The practice of singing in the lives of first-generation women in London and the telling of their narratives actively emplace these women across time and space.

Discussing individual female singers, Ruth Hellier suggests these women's singing involves "profoundly personal and individual experiential, sensory, and signifying processes that resonate with contexts ranging from local to global" (2013, 1). The resonance through song and singing connects individuals to society, from isolated spaces to imaginary and inhabited places. The performance of song in itself is a narrative in the making, but by relaying this narrative the song gains power in the teller's construction of their self-representation and the world they choose to represent. While ethnomusicology tends to look at musical practices and their place in the world, the centrality of song, singing, and music in individuals' narratives should also be considered. As Jackson has asserted, storytelling, like music and dance, is also a performance. Like musical practices themselves, the inclusion of song and singing in oral histories and narratives conveys the social and cultural value of music and similarly marks their position in both diasporic and non-diasporic societies. These narratives are vital markers of an individual identifying with society, to assert their part in "becoming one world again."

NOTES

1. I refer to oral histories, narratives, and life storytelling as overlapping concepts here. Oral history is significant as means to gain access to marginal historical voices; however, I am less concerned with historical accuracy than the ways people remember and retell their personal oral histories through narrative and storytelling.

2. Such cultural expectations are significantly challenged, particularly in British Asian music practices (see Hornabrook 2019).

REFERENCES

Arendt, Hannah. 1958. *The Human Condition*. Chicago: University of Chicago Press.

Bakrania, Falu P. 2013. *Bhangra and Asian Underground: South Asian Music and the Politics of Belonging in Britain*. Durham: Duke University Press.

Brah, Avtar. 1996. *Cartographies of Diaspora: Contesting Identities*. New York: Routledge.

Chaterjee, Partha. 1989. "Colonialism, Nationalism, and Colonialized Women: The Contest in India." *American Ethnologist* 16(4): 622–33.

———. 1993. *The Nation and Its Fragments: Colonial and Postcolonial Histories*. Princeton: Princeton University Press.

Clifford, James. 1994. "Diasporas." *Cultural Anthropology* 9(3): 302–38.

Clothey, Fred. 2006. *Ritualizing on the Boundaries: Continuity and Innovation in the Tamil Diaspora*. Columbia: University of South Carolina Press.

Daniel, E. Valentine. 1996. *Charred Lullabies: Chapters in an Anthropography of Violence*. Princeton: Princeton University Press.

Fuglerud, Øivind. 1999. *Life on the Outside: The Tamil Diaspora and Long-Distance Nationalism*. London: Pluto Press.

Hage, Ghassan. 1996. "The Spatial Imaginary of National Practices: Dwelling-Domesticating/Being-Exterminating." *Environment and Planning D: Society and Space* 14: 463–85.

Herbert, Joanna. 2006. "Migrant Memory and Metaphor: Life Stories of South Asians in Leicester." In Kathy Burrell and Pankios Panayi (eds.). *Histories and memories: migrants and their history in Britain.*. London: I. B. Tauris Press. 133–48.

———. 2009. "Oral Histories of Ugandan Asians in Britain: gendered identities in the diaspora." *Contemporary South Asia* 17(1): 21–32.

Hornabrook, Jasmine. 2018. "Songs of the Saints: Song Paths and Pilgrimage in London's Tamil Hindu Diaspora." *Asian Music* 49(2) Summer/Fall 2018: 106–50. doi:10.1353/amu.2018.0017.

———. 2019. "Gender, New Creativity and Carnatic Music in London." *South Asian Diaspora*. doi: 10.1080/19438192.2019.1568663.

Jackson, Michael. 2013. *The Politics of Storytelling: Variations on a Theme by Hannah Arendt.* Copenhagen: Museum Tusculaum Press.

Katrak, Ketu H. 2003. "Diasporic Alienness and Belonging: Selected Indian-American Cultural Expressions." In Sonita Sarker and Esha Niyogi De (eds.). *Trans-status subjects: gender in the globalization of South and Southeast Asia.* Durham: Duke University Press. 232–48.

Keightley, Emily. 2010. "Remembering research: memory and methodology in the social sciences." *International Journal of Social Research Methodology* 13(1): 55–70. doi: 10.1080/13645570802605440.

Krishna, Sankaran. 1999. *Postcolonial Insecurities: India, Sri Lanka and the Question of Nationhood.* Minneapolis: University of Minnesota Press.

Krishnamoorthy, C. 1987. "Hindu Association of Great Britain Souvenir." Highgate Hill Murugan. www.highgatehillmurugan.org/Temple%20History.pdf.

McLoughlin, Seán. 2013. *Discrepant Representations of Multi-Asian Leicester: Institutional Discourse and Everyday Life in the "Model" Multicultural City.* Research Paper WBAC 012.

Mummery, Jane. 2018. "Being Not-At-Home: A conceptual discussion." In Klaus Stierstorfer and Janet Wilson (eds.). *The Routledge Diasporas Studies Reader.* New York: Routledge. 230–34.

Neuman, Daniel M. 1980. *The Life of Music in North India: The Organization of an Artistic Tradition.* Chicago: University of Chicago Press.

Ramnarine, Tina K. 1996. "'Indian' Music in the Diaspora: Case Studies of 'Chutney' in Trinidad and London." *British Journal of Ethnomusicology* 5: 133–53.

———. 2001. *Creating Their Own Space: The Development of an Indian-Caribbean Musical Tradition.* Kingston: University of West Indies Press.

Ravi Glory. 2011. "Thevaram Thodudiya Seviyan. . . . By Satgurunathan." https://youtu.be/c6fRfH0kGa8.

Reed, Susan A. 2010. *Dance and the Nation: Performance, Ritual, and Politics in Sri Lanka.* Madison: The University of Wisconsin Press.

Safran, William. 1990. "Diasporas in Modern Societies: Myths of Homeland and Return." *Diaspora: A Journal of Transnational Studies* 1(1): 83–99.

Santhirapala, Rami, and Vatshalan Santhirapala. 2015. "Tradition: London: A Sri Lankan Citadel of Saivism." *Hinduism Today*, October/November/December. http://www.hinduismtoday.com/modules/smartsection/item.php?itemid=5636.

Sökefeld, Martin. 2006. "Mobilizing in Transnational Space: A Social Movement Approach to the Formation of Diaspora." *Global Networks* 6(3). 265–04.

Shree Ghanapathy Temple. 2018. "History." http://ghanapathy.co.uk/history/.

Thiruchandran, Selvy. 2006. *Stories from the Diaspora: Tamil Women, Writing.* Colombo: Vijitha Yapa Publications.

Tomalin, Emma. 2014. "Writing British Asian Women: From purdah and the 'problematic private sphere' to new forms of public engagement and cultural production." In Sean McLoughlin, William Gould, Ananya Jahanara Kabir, and Emma Tomalin (eds.). *Writing the City in British Asian Diasporas.* New York: Routledge. 179–98.

Viet Thanh Nguyen. 2017. *The Refugees.* London: Corsair.

Vridee, Pippa. 2013. "Remembering partition: women, oral histories and the Partition of 1947. *Oral History* Autumn: 49–62.

Vaswanathan Peterson, Indira. 1989. *Poems to Siva: The Hymns of the Tamil Saints.* Princeton: Princeton University Press.

Weidman, Amanda. 2003. "Gender and the politics of voice: Colonial modernity and classical music in South India." *Cultural Anthropology* 18(2): 194–232.

———. 2006. *Singing the Classical, Voicing the Modern: The Postcolonial Politics of Music in South India.* Durham: Duke University Press.

Wilson, A. Jeyarathnam. 2011. "Language, Poetry, Culture, and Tamil Nationalism." In John C. Holt (ed.). *The Sri Lanka Reader: History, Culture, Politics.* Durham: Duke University Press. 459–70.

Chapter Ten

Domesticating the Alien

Culinary References and Food Rituals in
Song of the Sun God

Shashikala Assella

Food has always been a contested terrain full of inclusive and exclusive trajectories charted on to its territory. Whether one belongs to the margins or the center is often determined and demonstrated through food choices and food habits—the diaspora constantly occupying liminal margins and fluid boundaries weave in and out of its many avatars when navigating alien terrains domiciled in Other spaces. Food being the most sought after and the most sensitive trope of discussion and self discovery, modern diasporic authors have been attracted to explore its many intricacies in their writing, especially while providing a platform to investigate paradigms of their own agency and selfhood, in and among different communities.

Shankari Chandran navigates the dialectics of heterogeneity of the Sri Lankan diaspora through her debut novel, *Song of the Sun God* (2017). Her position as a diasporic writer as well as her narrative voices in the novel, highlight the multiplicity of identity that enable diasporic writers to fashion and refashion their uniqueness in alien domiciles. England and Australia as narrative locations enable Chandran to explore alienness that is inevitably connected to the diasporic experience. Chandran further accentuates the cultural alienness of the Other even within Sri Lanka, by giving voice to Sri Lanka's ethnic minority: the Tamils. While this paper is not necessarily an exposition about Shankari Chandran's portrayal of the ethnic Other, it attempts to use food as a trope through which the domesticated female space both adapts to and resists diasporic differences when in their Othered spaces. *Song of the Sun God* is analyzed for its portrayal of domesticated and marginalized alienness that does not necessarily estrange the diasporic subjects from their host community. This complex relationship that emerges through the many negotiations women characters make throughout the novel, will be analyzed with comparisons drawn from other Sri Lankan writers, Ameena Hussein and Chandani Lokuge, who both write from the diaspora and from within Sri Lanka, respectively.

FOOD AS COMFORT

Garg and Khushu-Lahiri (2012) contend, "food associated with an ethnic community becomes the quintessential marker of identity" (80). This quintessential identity accorded through ethnic food grants an individuality to a community that decides to reside in an alien space due to sociopolitical reasons. The same uniqueness expressed in food practices and choices allows the diasporic individuals to establish their own personality away from perceived heterogeneous identity markers through individual culinary preferences and consumption. Shankari Chandran's *Song of the Sun God* explores this twofold individuality through a narrative that begins in a newly decolonized Sri Lanka in 1932. The novel unfolds the trials and tribulations of a large family that changes and expands with their transnational travels and personal desires and demands. In a country that is new and struggling to come to terms with its newly discovered ethno-social identity, Rajan, the patriarch of the narrative learns to let go of emotions and longings when his sister succumbs to an illness and his mother grieves in private. He learns to make *thosai,* just like his amma makes at a time when his mother is quietly grieving for the loss of her daughter. Thus, the *thosai* Rajan makes, allows him to find his mechanism to counter the deep grief he carries with him due to his sister's death, because the fermented rice pancake not only is his sustenance in a house where the mother is absent, but it also reminds him about his absent mother and her lullabies about the moon.

The same trope of finding solace through food, though not a new trope in diasporic fiction is carried forth in the novel, allowing the readers to engage with a long saga about a single family. While Rajan becomes the silent patriarch, who witnesses many ups and downs of his extended family, Nala, his wife navigates her ethnic and class identity through her food choices. Nala exoticizes herself, creating an alien identity for her own self even within Sri Lanka and also desires to consume the Other through her food preferences. Nala who is chastised by her own mother for not knowing "how to make a simple sarakku spice mix" (Chandran 2017, 25), becomes the owner of a "world famous butter cake recipe" (118) which she guards zealously. Nala's desire to differentiate herself is complemented with her desire to master the Other, in the form of butter cake. According to Huggan (2001), this desire to consume or exoticise the Other "can easily lend itself to various forms of exploitation and manipulation" (154), but in Nala's narrative, butter cake, while it differentiates her when in Sri Lanka, also is her own identity, because the cake recipe becomes her own identity, especially when she is in Australia, where she serves the "soldiers of the Australian Army [. . .] the best butter cake in the world" (Chandran 2017, 230).

MARKETING THE MARGINALITY

As Lau and Dwivedi (2014) argue with relation to Indian Women Writers' work "re-Orientalism is not exactly a choice, rather quite an *expected* outcome" (125) of our diasporic desires proclaimed through Anglophone writing. Re-Orientalism therefore enables the writers to articulate their marginalized position through their exoticized and Otherized narratives. Food therefore supplements this desire to domesticize oneself through alien means. Chandran's novel, while narrating the ethno-national divide that fractured the fragile social harmony among the Sri Lankans, emphasizes the importance of one's own ethno-social identity that defines one's class as well as one's individual identity and affiliation. Nala the matriarch of *Song of the Sun God*, while uninterested in the many intricacies of the culinary legacies passed on from her own matriarchal lineage, is able to create her own legacy of butter cake and improvise when needed in diasporic spaces. She provides her daughter Priya with her own means of sustenance and protection in the form of a freezer full of various curries when Priya has her first baby in London. Nala, whose class background does not equip her to be the domesticated culinary goddess, finds she is unable to be the true carer, because she is unable to cook. Undeterred, she uses her exotic Otherness in an alien space, by creating her own means of providing for her daughter through her network of "cousins in London who rescued her, each popping in with plastic containers of shark meat curry, sarakku okra curry, and garlic cooked in vegetables" (Chandran 2017, 132). As Nala navigates the various demands of her diasporic location, not only in London, but also when in Australia, by even venturing to make her own crab curry, the exotic descriptions about her food, full of spices, sarakku, and the once common, everyday food that has now turned out to be the Other, Nala becomes the exotic alien who has neutralized her existence to suit the diasporic space. While the exotic alienness differentiates her identity from the homogenized diasporic apartness, this same difference also allows her to domesticate her Otherness and establish her individual identity.

As Lisa Lau (2009) suggests in her discussion on "Re-Orientalism" diasporic authors especially the women writers write about their difference to "turn marginality [itself] into a valuable [intellectual] commodity" (Huggan

2001, viii). While this marginality may seem like an artificially imposed character trait that is forcibly learned to attract the attention of the host community as well as from their own diasporic community, the same marginality allows them to explore and nuance their complex lives more coherently. Thus, staged and performed marginality does not curtail the diasporic experiences of the modern women, but it rather enriches the desire to be different and unique, away from cultural homogeneity, for the new cosmopolitan women belonging to modern diasporic groups. Nala, the matriarch of Shankari Chandran's *Song of the Sun God*, and her daughter Priya perform their marginality in many forms to fit into and ascertain their individual identity when in diasporic spaces. Nala, who was used to "instructing Ayah back at home about how to make the [crab] dish" (Chandran 2017, 221), tries "to re-create the crab curry" (220) using her own means in Australia. Nala's mission to create the perfect crab curry in Australia not only emphasizes her own marginal exotic existence in Australia, since she has had to defend her own position as a colonized subject to the crab vendor, but also her uniqueness that defies the homogeneity ascribed to South Asian immigrants in Australia. She is not representative of all the other South Asians, let alone the other Sri Lankans. Nala's identity, fashioned through her own class, and economic position back at home, makes her stand apart from the rest of her own diasporic community: the Sri Lankan Tamils Nala therefore performs her own "marginality" not to please her host community, but to establish her own identity. Priya does the same, with her various food choices. She makes "sandwiches filled with spicy potato curry" (171) and has made her own daughter embarrassed by making "curried fish patties" (246) for mother daughter afternoon tea parties. Her insistence on recreating food from her own ethno social background at various significant occasions runs parallel to her sneaky McDonald treats to her young children, defying her religious and cultural beliefs. Thus, her individuality surpasses her own exoticism which "oscillates between the opposite poles of strangeness and familiarity" (Huggan 2001, 13). Thus as Lau and Dwivedi (2014) argue, re-Orientalizing themselves does not become a choice for these diasporic characters narrated through Chandran's narrative; rather, it allows them to establish their heterogeneity in the face of stereotyped homogeneity assigned to diasporic women.

While Chandran's narrators battle their difference and familiarity in diasporic spaces through food and other ethno-sartorial means, Sri Lankan Anglophone author Ameena Hussein uses food references unapologetically and not elaborated for the uninitiated to chart her own narrator's difference as an ethnic Other within Sri Lanka. When RaushenGul, the mother of the protagonist Khadeeja in Ameena Hussein's *The Moon in the Water* (2009) first starts school, she makes friends with a Sinhalese girl, by exchanging "*Muscat, Dodol, Sheenakka, Bowl* and *Dhoshi*" (Hussein 2009, 26) in return for dead butterflies. Mannur's (2009) treatise about Indian identity explored in fiction through culinary references marks that "more often than not food is situated in narratives about racial and ethnic identity as an intractable measure of cultural authenticity" (3). Hussein also emphasizes her narrative of cultural authenticity through food references. Despite being located in Sri Lanka and being an insider, Hussein's Moor narrators vie for recognition and acceptance as individuals defying a homogenized identity ascribed to the ethno religious Other. Thus, the desire to efface the ethno-social markings as the Other, is not only exclusive to the diasporic female but is a common predicament that needs to be contested by all the female characters, especially relegated to the margins due to various socio-ethnic reasons. Khadeeja's journey of self-discovery, amidst personal trauma and coming to terms with an altered sense of belonging, is peppered with her family's food choices and her own food choices. While her own mourning family gathers to remember Khadeeja's father, with religion and food on important Kaththam days consisting of "*nei roti* and turkey *badam* with chocolate pudding for dessert or *stringhopper kaliyavendu, porichcha koli* and *wattalapam*" (Hussein 2009, 40), Khadeeja finds her own estranged twin and connects with him through "packed lunch of chicken roast, *kadé paan, pol sambol* and beer" (69). Thus identity, drawn through culinary references establish one's ethno-social uniqueness while food choices explored through the same trope can establish one's own individual identity. Khadeeja finds happiness and bonds with her estranged twin through the nonpartisan all-time favorite of chicken roast, bread sourced from a local bakery, and coconut sambol. Her own difference is therefore established since she is trying hard to bridge the gap between her twin brother and herself. Their bonding, and their cosmopolitan identities are once again hinted at through their preference for beer as an accompaniment, and not necessarily the ethno-culinary choice of either tea or coffee. Thus, as Priya establishes her cultural identity in Australia through her aubergine curry, chilied chickpeas, and coffee trifle pudding, Khadeeja insists on bonding and finding her own space through her culinary preferences. Neither of the narrators, dismiss their cultural identity through their culinary choices, but also insist on finding their own voices through their food preferences.

FINDING "HOME" THROUGH FOOD

"[T]he word 'home' immediately connotes the private sphere of patriarchal hierarchy, gendered self-identity, shelter, comfort, nurture and protection," (George 1996, 1) notes Rosemary George (1996), exploring the politics of home as a space. Home, within the diaspora becomes a connotation not only for the patriarchal space of authority and protection, but also evolves into being the space that allows diasporic women to find their own individuality through their culinary practices and choices. Nala finds her own strength as an individual away from her cultural and ethnic affiliations within her small apartment in Australia. "As [Nala] opened the door to her apartment she was greeted by the smell of cooking, incense, and camphorwood. The familiar smells that told her she was home," (Chandran 2017, 282) but this sense of homecoming does not rely on the space as much as it relies on the memories it creates or invokes. Home for Nala and her children, both in and outside diasporic spaces means a place to invoke memories through its associations. Cooking smells thus invoke familiarity because culinary references invoked through memory ascertain one's space, place, and identity for those who are looking for acceptance, belonging, and uniqueness. The alien space of an apartment in a diasporic location in Sydney thus becomes the domesticated familiar space that can invoke emotions of comfort, nurture, and protection.

Spatially located culinary memories also become the means of invoking nostalgia and memories of belonging. As Partha Chatterjee (1990) articulates, the domesticated space of the home becomes a space to protect and nurture national culture, especially in a complex web that fuses home and female space together (239). This was true in the initial phase of the immigration process because it was necessary for the diaspora to preserve a homogenous cultural identity in the face of oppression directed at them from the host community. In a cosmopolitan society where transnational travel is much more frequent, home and especially the role of the female as the preserver of cultural memory through home loses its erstwhile importance. Despite Nala, Priya, and Priya's rebellious daughter Smrithi not using home as a space to preserve national culture, the same domesticated space becomes a location for them to establish their own individual identity through nostalgic memories. Nala thinks of her own "home" back in Colombo and identifies that "[h]ome was family" (Chandran 2017, 282). This identification, on the one hand removes Nala from a spatial affiliation further allowing her to find domesticated acculturation in her alien diasporic space. On the other hand, she looks for familiarity in the senses and the nostalgic tastes invoked by food. She "loved the small [Alphonso] mangoes [because] they tasted just like the ones back home" (283) therefore finding solace in the familiar memory invoked through sensory means, and not through spatial or temporal affiliations. Hence, home as a space loses its importance as fixity but becomes a point of interaction to invoke nostalgia, family ties, and culinary memories when the diaspora domesticates themselves in alien spaces.

Members of the diaspora located and domiciled in different spaces, redefine their culinary adherences and reevaluate their allegiances food practices. Easy transnational travel and cosmopolitan access to many different cultures and rituals allow the diaspora to move beyond the narrow definitions of ethno-cultural affiliations expressed through food. As Anita Mannur (2009) notes with reference to Indian diaspora's culinary affiliations to their cultural roots from North America "it becomes increasingly suspect to unflinchingly adhere to narrowly defined visions of national cuisines" (184), especially at a time when travel and access to different ethno-cultural food items is easier. Despite the ease of access to various other food sources and the ease of acceptance, diasporic communities, especially women seek comfort and familiarity through home-cooked meals. Shankari Chandran deftly weaves in these complexities for her characters and their food rituals through her extended cast of characters. When the daughters go into confinement, deliver their babies, and need nurturing, mothers and aunts come together to cook for them. As Nala calls on her extended family to support Priya's nutritional needs after her first baby, Priya carries "a 5Kg block of deep-frozen chocolate cake [. . .] and Tupperware containers of frozen aubergine curry" to London to nurse Smrithi when she has her baby. Priya also dispenses traditional food knowledge to Smrithi by rearranging "the spice cupboard [. . . reorganising] the fridge" and explaining that "the coriander and cumin in sarakku powder will heal and act as a natural antiseptic" (Chandran 2017, 300). All these complexities allow the female characters in *Song of the Sun God* to domesticate themselves in their alien spaces. Food not only functions as sustenance, a form of comfort, but also becomes a mode of maternal affection and care to be expressed and more importantly to create matrilineal bonds between close and estranged mothers and daughters.

DOMESTICATING THE ALIEN: FOOD AS AN IDENTITY

Alienness and domesticity are navigated and encountered by Chandani Lokuge who writes from Australia, but explores a different ethno-social narrative affiliation through her novel *If the Moon Smiled* (2000). Manthri and her family, hailing from a Sinhala Buddhist background migrate to Australia in the late 1980s to start a new life in Adelaide. Unlike Chandran's Tamil Sri Lankan family who find their space and place by bending their own family traditions, Lokuge's Sinhala family is unable to cope with the sudden changes and migrant demands foisted on them. Through the cultural displacement and the sense of dislocation felt by Manthri, Lokuge explores the various demands, alien locations, and cultures have on diasporic subjects. Manthri is comfortable within her known domestic space of her own home back in Sri Lanka, and is unable to find the same solace Nala and Priya find in their diasporic locations despite being alienated themselves. Manthri gives into her husband Mahendra's patriarchal demands and uses her domestic space not as a site to reconfigure her identity, but as a space of oppression veiled in duty and other familial demands. Thus, the diasporic space does not get familiar or domesticated for Manthri despite her culinary practices of cooking traditional food and inhabiting domestic spaces. Therefore, Lokuge's narrative demonstrates that, despite food being used as a means of establishing culture and tradition, it does not necessarily liberate or domesticate the alien diasporic subject. While Lokuge's narrator does not liberate herself either through the rejection of South Asian traditions or falls prey to the hyped assimilation of the diasporic subjects, Manthri's inability to ascertain her own worth and value in the diasporic space leads to her subsequent rejection of Australian values and diasporic lifestyle. This reaction of valorizing the diasporic space and ideologies and rejecting the South Asian traditions and values, as Inderpal Grewal (2005) has argued in relation to South Asian American fiction, has resulted in strengthening and extending the hegemonic belief of diasporic spaces as progressive and South Asian spaces as backward and static (x). Hence Manthri, while subscribing to the cultural biases of the diasporic hegemony and cultural alienation of immigrant spaces, contributes to the mainstream ideology of diasporic women's inability to weave themselves into the cultural practices and social rhetoric of their host community. While Lokuge's Australian narrative subscribes to the diaspora's alienation, Shankari Chandran writes about the same diasporic location of Australia and makes her female narrators revalue diasporic contribution and especially reinvent diasporic women's ability to move beyond the margins and integrate themselves into alien domiciles while retaining their own individual identity.

Chandran's *Song of the Sun God* also uses memory and nostalgia evoked through culinary references to grant heterogeneous identities to the various female narrators in the novel. When Smrithi was a baby, Dhara tries to feed her the familiar food of ghee and dhal with rice. Despite Priya's reassurances and Dhara's attempts, Smrithi refuses to eat her favorite food, because she was not fed by her own mother. Hence the same dhal, ghee, and rice, take on different meanings for Smrithi based on who is feeding her. Priya passes on the memory of her own father, her beloved cousin, sister, and her own childhood to Smrithi's children through *Faloodah*. "She remembered sitting with Dhara and Nandan on the back verandah, sipping its chilled milky pinkness with their father" (Chandran 2017, 386) and this memory allows Priya to have her own unique identity connected to her own family's quiet enjoyment of a drink inspired by Sri Lankan Moor community's food affiliations. This unique memory becomes a link that connects the family together, across generations when she tells her granddaughter that she "is going to make a drink [. . .] It's pink. You'll love it" (397). The quiet reassurance and confidence in Priya about the drink being a bridge between generations and even across heartaches and disappointments is reflective of the confidence diasporic individuals have of their own ability to bridge various socio-cultural gaps across the diasporic divide. This also allows destabilizing of the homologic affiliation usually perceived to be between ethnic identity and food practices by allowing multiple porous lines to be created with diverse influences and memories seeping into culinary preferences.

Domesticated and marginalized, alienness often allows female narrators to explore their insecurities and ultimately their strengths. This is evident in Amulya Malladi's *The Mango Season* (2003) where Priya the protagonist finds her strength through her interaction with her family's culinary practices. Priya's dislocated diasporic self, constantly craving acceptance from her family in India, reconciles and finds meaning through her own family's food choices and practices. In *Song of the Sun God*, Nala who feels marginalized and different in an alien location finds her own voice and her own strength through her culinary interactions. Nala finds herself more helpless than the usual immigrant due to her class and social position when in Sri Lanka. Having never cooked because she was able to have her own Ayah who took on all the domestic culinary duties, Nala "eventually became an inventive if not adept cook" (Chandran 2017, 386) because of her diasporic demands. Her alienness thus is twofold. One of being uprooted from her own comforts in Colombo and being stripped of her class status. The second of having had to reintroduce herself to the domestic duties of cooking and cleaning. These two challenges alter Nala into a progressive, if not quite a modern grandmother, who is able to support her grandchildren in their different pursuits. Thus, Nala evolves and domesticates her alienness to suit her own diasporic demands. As Ruvani Ranasinha (2016) argues with reference to contemporary South Asian women writers, they "decentre rather than reinscribe the centrality of the West in their collective critiques of first-world models of feminism and emphasis on different varieties of feminism" (7) Thus, Chandran allows Nala to reinscribe her individual identity through her means of appropriating the new alien culture. Instead of looking at either her own diasporic limitations or her host community's stereotyped homogeneity ascribed to her, Nala develops her own character, domesticating and appropriating her own marginalized alien diasporic existence, through her gastronomical choices as well as adopting various personal practices.

As Rajan (1993) posits in her feminist essay about the variety of cultural representations of women in India, there are no "non-contaminated" (8) spaces or identities that are reflective of one's own ethno-religious heritage. Diasporas too have evolved over the years with various other borrowed and adapted culinary practices to establish their identity through diverse forms of culinary expression. Celebrations therefore become a platform through which culinary identity can be explored and expressed. When Siva, Priya's husband gets elected as the president of the Rotary Club in Australia, the event is celebrated with "Foods of the World, Foods of Australia" (Chandran 2017, 342) where *dolma* is served alongside "fried sausage on a bed of Tip Top white bread and burnt onions" (341). Hybrid locations and multiple racial identities of the marginal communities in Australia come together through an amalgamation of culinary experience, which once again asserts the domesticized alienness that the diasporas have been able to claim as their own. While heterogeneity is still maintained through their individual prefer-ences, the ability to incorporate Tip Top bread into a culinary experience of other ethnic food bears witness to the diaspora's ability to integrate and incorporate their alien host culture into the diasporic experience. Thus, the space or the identity projected is not pure or exclusive. As Nala becomes an adept cook who is able to adopt herself to her diasporic demands, the other diasporic groups too move in and out of each other's ethno-culinary spaces, making them their own.

NOSTALGIA AND FOOD RITUALS

Food rituals also become a mode of evoking memory and also maintaining bonds while finding one's feet in alien landscapes. Dhara is advised by Priya to "go to Walthamstow in East London, bulk buy Sri Lankan food and restock Smrithi's freezer" (Chandran 2017, 317) when Smrithi had her sec-ond baby. Sri Lankan food in the freezer is not only a means of showing concern, but also becomes a means of establishing one's bond with one's familiar. Even when estranged due to family secrets that unravel not only their memories, but also their lives, both Smrithi and Priya engage in food rituals to maintain their bonds with each other. Dhara too insists on food memories, especially the memory of Priya's "amazing *lamprais*" (308) to pass on her own memories, as well as that of her family memories to Smrithi, the next generation. Food therefore not only supplements unsaid and unex-plored emotions, but is also part of the familiar heritage that is not defined by ethnic affiliations, but by one's own familiar spaces. *Lamprais*, which was a Dutch influenced dish that has been localized by the various ethnic groups in Sri Lanka, becomes the example to explore Priya's heterogeneity, separating her from the homogeneous identity ascribed to Tamil Sri Lankans drawn through their food rituals. The same individuality is apparent in Nala's butter cake recipe, which debunks the expected Tamil diasporic identity and help-less adherence to alien spaces and rituals. Both Nala and Priya, while retain-ing their ethnic identity as Tamil women from Sri Lanka, insist on their individual identity they have carried forth to their diasporic locations that assert their uniqueness.

Culinary preferences also become a space to explore memory and memo-rialization. Both Dhara and Rajan are remembered on the eighth day of their death through food offerings. Nala makes "*puttu, omelette* and coconut chilli *sambol*" (Chandran 2017, 355) to honor Dhara's memory while adding homemade vanilla ice cream and Sustagen fortified milk to the offering. Rajan adds a glass full of pink *Faloodah* with green jelly to the same offer-ing. This memorialization ritual allows the family members to not only per-form their religious duty but also to remember Dhara through her favorite food. Food, therefore, is ascribed a memorial and personalized value that surpasses its diasporic value as identity and sustenance. Gastronomical preferences of individuals thus become part of their identity, moving beyond its ethno-cultural values especially when used within alien diasporic locations. The same remembrance happens for Rajan when he passes away. His children remember him through his favourite prawn curries and chocolates. Memory and identity are evoked through food references and allusions ascribing more value to food than its nutritional role. These particular food items through which one is remembered, personalizes the experience, both to the deceased and to the living. The alienness of the diasporic space is forgotten, thus, in an individual appropriation of the location through rituals and food preferences that span cultures, regions, and spaces. While Sustagen as a nutritional supplement may invoke common Sri Lankan references particular to the urban middle class, *Faloodah* and its origin hark back to Moor culinary traditions in Sri Lanka. *Puttu* and various prawn curries speak of Tamil ethno-gastronomical preferences while omelette and chili *sambol* are common for a lot of Sri Lankans. Accordingly, more than ethnic individuality performed and highlighted through culinary references and images, Chandran insists on how the individual performs and negotiates various spaces within and without diaspora through her narrative. Her work, therefore, allows its various female characters to navigate and domesticate the alien space through culinary images and references.

CONCLUSION

"The figure of the *South Asian woman* could in itself be said to be a contested term in its imperious sweep across nations and communities. Differences of power mean that not only are 'we' referring to a heterogeneous figure, but also to an assortment of women who are more often than not positioned in contradistinction to each other" (Puwar and Raghuram 2003, 3) contend Puwar and Raghuram (2003) in their discussion on South Asian women in the diaspora with special reference to the academics. The same heterogeneity and varied identity are explored through South Asian women's diasporic fiction as well. While the term South Asian woman is contested with its multiple references and allegiances, the term Sri Lankan diasporic woman too can be contested. Difference in power hierarchies, the disparity in domestic presence and visibility together with class and socio-economic variants change Sri Lankan diasporic women's experience as explored through fiction. Chandani Lokuge's narrative voice examines a Sinhalese Buddhist upper-middle-class family's diasporic trials while Shankari Chandran's narrators hail from an upper-class urban Tamil background. Despite being located in the same diasporic location of Australia, the two writers examine unique diasporic experiences of navigating the alien domicile, through food and other rituals.

Domestic spaces in the diaspora become the locations through which the perceived alienness of the diaspora is destabilized. While the stereotypical diasporic female figure is rendered helpless and alien in a diasporic space, transnational travel and the easy access to many commodities allow modern diasporic females to navigate their different terrains with ease and with confidence. This confidence becomes crucial in defining and reforming their diasporic uniqueness, especially when navigating the alienness of the diasporic experience. *Song of the Sun God* captures the essence of negotiating alien spaces through the domestic, especially through the female characters who use food rituals and references to highlight their individuality as well as their ethno-social identity. Since the book explores the socio-cultural alienation felt by the Other within Sri Lanka as well as in diaspora, the narrative uses its culinary references, not to create homogeneous identities but to create heterogeneous individuals who use their culinary memories and heritage to supplement their diasporic identity. Thus, the narrative especially rendered through the women establish its own unique trajectory of finding and rediscovering one's own familiar through food practices, culinary choices, and gastronomic hybridity explored throughout the narrative. Food, especially appropriated within diasporic alien settings, thus subvert foreignness ascribed to the diaspora and establish alterity that allows the individuals to find their own voice and their own confidence. Hence the alien is domesticated and is appropriated to suit one's own demands. The diasporic female subjects thus find their own unique space through their own culinary preferences. While this is not a novel approach for South Asian diasporic writers, as a Sri Lankan diasporic writer from Australia, Shankari Chandran's attempt to voice the marginalized, while allowing the subjects to have autonomy and agency is exemplary. This is more significant because the Anglophone and diasporic fiction of Sri Lanka is yet to explore the full potential of food as a trope through which individual identity gets explored and established while retaining ethno-social underpinnings of the narrative.

REFERENCES

Chandran, Shankari. 2017. *Song of the Sun God*. Colombo: Perera Hussein.

Chatterjee, Partha. 1990. "The Nationalist Resolution of the Women's Question." In Kumkum Sangari and Sudesh Vaid (eds.). *Recasting Women: Essays in Indian Colonial History*. New Brunswick, NJ: Rutgers University Press. 233–53.

Garg, S., and R. Khushu-Lahiri. 2012. "Interpreting culinary Montage: Food in Jhumpa Lahiri's *Interpreter of Maladies*." *ASIATIC* 6(1)(June): 73–83. https://journals.iium.edu.my/asiatic/index.php/AJELL/article/view/237.

George, Rosemary. 1996. *The Politics of Home: Postcolonial Relocations and Twentieth-Century Fiction*. New York: Cambridge University Press.

Huggan, Graham. 2001. *The Post-Colonial Exotic: Marketing the Margins*. London: Routledge.

Hussein, Ameena. 2009. *The Moon in the Water*. Colombo: Perera Hussein.

Inderpal Grewal, 2005. *Transnational America: Feminisms, Diasporas, Neoliberalisms*. Durham: Duke University Press.

Lau, L., and O. P. Dwivedi. 2014. *Re-Orientalism and Indian Writing in English*. London: Palgrave Macmillan.

Lau, Lisa. 2009. "Re-Orientalism: The Perpetration and Development of Orientalism by Orientals." *Modern Asian Studies* 43(2): 571–90. doi:10.1017/S0026749X07003058.

Lokuge, Chandani. 2000. *If the Moon Smiled*. Victoria: Arcadia.

Mannur, Anita. 2009. *Culinary Fictions: Food in South Asian Diasporic Culture*. Philadelphia: Temple University.

Meer, A. 1989. "The Artist's voice since 1981." *BOMB* 29(Fall). http://bombsite.com/issues/29/articles/1264.

Mishra, Vijay. 2007. *The literature of the Indian diaspora: Theorising the Diasporic Imaginary*. London: Routledge.

Narayan, Uma. 2000. "Undoing the 'Package Picture' of Cultures." *Signs* 25(4)(Summer): 1083–86.

———. 1997. *Dislocating Cultures: Identities, Tradition and Third World Feminism*. London: Routledge.

———. 1995. "Eating Cultures: Incorporation, Identity and Indian Food." *Social Identities* 1(1): 63–86.

Puwar, N., and P. Raghuram. 2003. *South Asian Women in the Diaspora*. Oxford: Berg.

Rajan, S. R. 1993. *Real and Imagined Women: Gender, Culture and Postcolonialism*. London: Routledge.

Ranasinha, Ruvani. 2016. *Contemporary Diasporic South Asian Women's Fiction Gender, Narration and Globalisation*. London; Palgrave Macmillan.

———. 2015. "Redefining Britishness: British Asian women's writing." In E. Parker and M. Eagleton (eds.). *The history of British women's writing*. Basingstoke: Palgrave. 229–44.

Index

Acculturation, 10, 206
Alienness and alienation, 15, 22, 24, 26, 28, 30, 34, 35, 39, 41, 42, 47, 59, 61, 64, 91, 110, 111, 114, 115, 124, 125n5, 154, 163, 180, 182, 183, 184, 188, 195, 197, 199, 201, 202, 203, 205, 206, 207, 209, 210, 211, 212
Ali, Monica, 12, 16, 53, 56, 58, 59, 61, 66
Alvi, Moniza, 6, 22, 23, 24, 25, 26, 27, 28, 29, 30, 31, 32, 34, 37
Ambivalence, 4, 9, 26, 79
Anderson, Benedict, 3
Appadurai, Arjun, 87
Ashcroft, Bill, 131

Badami, Anita Rau, 6
Bangladeshi, 121
Belonging, vii, 3, 4, 6, 7, 10, 14, 22, 23, 26, 27, 30, 31, 37, 39, 42, 56, 66, 73, 74, 79, 80, 111, 113, 115, 167, 180, 182, 183, 185, 187, 189, 190, 192, 193, 194, 195, 196, 197, 203, 204, 205, 206
Bhabha, Homi K., 6, 7, 53, 58, 91, 148, 173
Bildungsroman, 57
Border, 1, 4, 58, 118, 135
Brah, Avtar, 1, 5, 6, 22, 23, 111, 182

Carnatic music, 14, 179, 180, 182, 185, 186, 187, 188, 190, 192, 194, 195, 196, 197

Chandran, Shankari, 6, 15, 201, 202, 203, 206, 207, 211, 212
Clifford, James, 75, 76, 78, 90, 111, 180, 182
Cohen, Robin, 4, 9
Cosmopolitan, 15, 43, 203, 204, 206
Culinary, 135, 142, 202, 203, 204, 206, 207, 208, 209, 210, 212

Decolonization, 134
Demographic, 1, 190
Desai, Anita, 6
Diaspora space, 114, 115, 203, 204, 205, 206, 207, 210, 212
Divakaruni, Chitra Bannerjee, 6
Domestic spaces, 166, 180, 207, 212
Domiciles, 1, 2, 3, 4, 5, 6, 11, 12, 13, 15, 16, 23, 31, 60, 66, 95, 99, 102, 103, 104, 111, 126, 163, 201, 206, 207, 211

Ethnic, 2, 4, 9, 10, 15, 16, 23, 25, 30, 32, 33, 34, 68, 73, 74, 75, 78, 79, 81, 86, 87, 89, 90, 91, 92, 93, 96, 98, 100, 104, 105, 111, 133, 143, 169, 173, 179, 180, 183, 186, 187, 188, 189, 190, 191, 192, 193, 201, 202, 204, 205, 208, 209, 210
Ethnography, 74, 75, 76, 84, 87, 88, 90, 91, 182
Expatriate, 14

Feminism, 14, 55, 56, 68n11, 209

Fluidity, 114, 154
Food, 15, 27, 114, 117, 118, 142, 201, 202, 203, 204, 206, 207, 208, 209, 210, 211, 212

Gender politics, 105n1
Girlhood, 12, 74

Hall, Stuart, 80, 98, 111
Heteronormative, 101, 102, 159, 162, 164, 166, 174
Homeland, 1, 4, 6, 8, 9, 10, 11, 12, 13, 14, 15, 21, 35, 36, 56, 59, 60, 66, 84, 98, 100, 102, 103, 104, 111, 118, 153, 154, 155, 169, 170, 171, 172, 180, 183, 184, 185, 187, 191, 193, 196
Hostland, 1, 2, 4, 5, 6, 8, 9, 10, 13, 15, 95, 98, 100, 104
Hybridity, 22, 110, 167, 212
Hyphenated identity, 80, 87, 167

In-between space/in-betweenness, 7, 13, 34, 80, 91, 113
Identity, 4, 5, 9, 10, 11, 12, 13, 15, 21, 24, 25, 27, 28, 31, 32, 34, 35, 37, 44, 47, 49, 56, 61, 75, 78, 79, 80, 81, 82, 84, 86, 87, 88, 89, 90, 91, 95, 98, 99, 102, 103, 104, 110, 111, 114, 125n5, 125n6, 135, 142, 148, 149, 153, 154, 155, 166, 167, 169, 170, 172, 179, 180, 183, 184, 185, 187, 188, 190, 197, 201, 202, 203, 204, 205, 206, 207, 208, 209, 210, 211, 212
Immigration, 81, 180, 184, 192

Liminal space, 58, 173, 201
Literary prize, 42
Lokugé, Chandani, 201, 207, 211

Marketability, 12, 13, 39, 44, 47, 49
Mohanty, Chandra Talpade, 111, 115
Mohsin, Hamid, 13, 107, 110, 111, 119, 120, 124n2, 126n13, 171
Mukherjee, Bharati, 6, 67n2
Multiculturalism, 81, 180

Nasta, Sushiela, 53, 55
Nationhood, 24, 174
Neo-colonialism, 108
Nostalgia, 1, 3, 6, 8, 9, 14, 15, 23, 59, 60, 153, 155, 169, 206, 208

Oral histories, 183, 184, 185, 191, 197, 198n1
Outsider, 48, 99, 108, 109, 111, 124
Orientalism, 10

Patriarchal Hegemony, 64, 80, 84
Postcolonial, 4, 12, 13, 22, 24, 28, 32, 34, 43, 44, 46, 49, 54

Qawwali, 14, 153, 154, 155, 156, 157, 158, 159, 160, 162, 163, 164, 165, 166, 167, 168, 169, 171, 172, 173, 174

Racial purity, 10, 12, 27, 32, 74, 81, 86, 109, 118, 121, 143, 149, 180, 204
Rushdie, Salman, 132, 154, 158

Safran, William, 4, 17, 180, 199
Shamsie, Kamila, 22, 38
Spivak, G. C., 55, 172
Sri Lankan, 13, 14, 95, 96, 97, 99, 100, 102, 104, 153, 179, 180, 182, 183, 184, 185, 186, 187, 188, 189, 190, 191, 192, 193, 196, 197, 201, 202, 203, 204, 207, 208, 209, 210, 211, 212
Stereotype, 39, 48, 67, 83, 121, 132, 203, 209

Third space, 7
Third world, 54, 57, 76, 77
Translation, 44, 46, 136, 145
Transnationalism, 69
Trishanku, 7

Unhomeliness, 53, 56, 59, 66
Urban space, 28

Vertovec, Steven, 59, 69, 182

Womanhood, 30, 170, 189

About the Editor

Shilpa Daithota Bhat is an assistant professor at Ahmedabad University, Gujarat, India. She was a Bodleian Fellow, Oxford University, UK (2019–2020); Visiting Fellow, McGill University, Montreal, Canada (2017); International Visitor, York University, Canada (2015). She visited Trinity College, University of Toronto, Canada (Commonwealth Fellowship, 2011–2012), University of Western Ontario (2011), Korea University (PANCS Grant, 2011) for research and conferences. She has published articles in reputed journals like *Culture and Religion* (Routledge); *Sikh Formations* (Routledge); and *Journal of Tourism and Cultural Change* (Routledge). Her book-length publications include *Indians in Victorian Children's Narratives: Animalizing the Native, 1830–1930* (Lexington Books, 2017); *Diaspora and Homing in South Asian Women's Writing: Beyond Trishanku* (Lexington Books, 2018, edited anthology); and, most recently, *Women Writers of the South Asian Diaspora: Interpreting Gender, Texts and Contexts* (Rawat Publishers, 2020, co-edited anthology).

About the Contributors

Alejandra Moreno-Álvarez holds a PhD in Women's Studies (University of Oviedo, Spain). Currently, she is a senior lecturer in the English department of the University of Oviedo. Her teaching and research are centered in Literatures in English Language and Feminist and Postcolonial Theory. She has been a research fellow at Rutgers University, Cornell University, and the University of Leeds, among others. She is the author of *Lenguajes comestibles: Anorexia, bulimia y su descodificación en la ficción de Margaret Atwood y Fay Weldon* (Edicions UIB, 2009); *El lenguaje trasgresor de las Ciborgs Literarias* (ArCiBel Editores, 2011) and *Ambai: Un movimiento, una carpeta, algunas lágrimas/A movement, a folder, some tears (*KRK, 2011).

Gurbir Singh Jolly is a Mumbai-born, Toronto-raised educator and writer who works chiefly with literature and film to explore how political economies pattern post-colonial migrations of peoples and cultures. Gurbir's publications—including three co-edited collections, *Bolo! Bolo!*, *Desilicious: Sexy. Subversive. South Asian*, and *Once Upon a Time in Bollywood*—forefront the cultural dynamics of "second-generation" South Asian youths in Canada and the United States. Gurbir teaches in the humanities department at York University, Toronto, where he won a Departmental Award for Excellence in Teaching. He is currently helping document an oral history of South Asian Canadian anti-racism in the 1970s.

Jasmine Hornabrook is a research associate in the School of Social Sciences and Humanities at Loughborough University, where she is conducting research on cultural memories of Partition within British South Asian diasporic groups. She has been researching South Indian music and the Tamil diaspora in London since 2009 and completed her PhD thesis, entitled "Becoming One Again: Music and Transnationalism in London's Sri Lankan Tamil Diaspora" in 2016 at Goldsmiths, University of London. This thesis is based on multi-sited ethnographic fieldwork in the UK, South India, and Sri Lanka. Since completing her PhD, Jasmine's research has focused on diasporic transnationalism and belonging in relation to the performance of Tamil devotional songs and musical creativity and innovation among second-generation Carnatic musicians in London.

Lara Virginia Kattekola is an associate professor of English at LaGuardia Community College of the City University of New York. She holds a PhD in English from Temple University. Her scholarly interests include British novels of empire and films and novels produced by South Asian diaspora writers and artists. In a forthcoming essay on Gurinder Chadha's *Quais de Seine*, she examines the short film's promotion of Paris as a global city space and its critique of hegemonic perceptions of Muslim women and the veil. Her current projects include an article on Tom Stoppard's *Indian Ink* as well as a pedagogical paper on teaching technical writing.

Lauren Bettridge has a PhD in Social & Cultural Studies (her thesis was titled *Contested Spaces: Performances of Marginality in Popular Hindi Cinema*) and First Class Honors in arts from The University of Western Australia. She also holds a Bachelor of Arts (journalism) from Curtin University. A specialist in post-Independence and contemporary Bollywood and parallel Hindi cinema(s), her research connects with and contributes to a body of work that considers how Bollywood interprets and is interpreted by the nation. She is also interested in the increasingly contested place of religious and ethnic minorities in modern India, especially the Indo-Muslim minority and how Sufi music forms like the *qawwali* can perform syncretic Indian cultural traditions.

Maryse Jayasuriya is a professor of English and associate dean of the College of Liberal Arts at the University of Texas at El Paso. She received her PhD from Purdue University. She is the author of *Terror and Reconciliation: Sri Lankan Anglophone Literature, 1983–2009* (Lexington Books, 2012), which explores the English language literature that has emerged from Sri Lanka's quarter-century long ethnic conflict, and editor of *The Immigrant Experience: Critical Insights* (2018) and a special issue of *South Asian Review* (2012) entitled "Sri Lankan Anglophone Literature." She has published articles on South Asian and Asian-American literature in such venues as *South Asian Review, Journeys, Margins,* and *The Journal of Postcolonial Cultures and Societies.* She is an associate editor of *South Asian Review.*

Sam Naidu is a professor in the department of English, Rhodes University, South Africa. Her main research and teaching interests are transnational literature, crime and detective fiction, and the oral-written interface in the colonial Eastern Cape. She holds a PhD in transnational feminist aesthetics in South Asian diasporic literature. Presently, she is the coordinator of a Mellon Foundation research project, "Intersecting Diasporas." Two recent publications are *Sherlock Holmes in Context* (Palgrave Macmillan, 2017) and *A Survey of South African Crime Fiction: Critical Analysis and Publishing History* (2017).

Setara Pracha is a lecturer in the department of English at the University of Buckingham. She has studied at the Universities of Buckingham and Toronto, and was awarded the first Ondaatje Scholarship to Massey College, University of Toronto, where she specialized in postcolonial literature. She is a fellow of the Higher Education Academy, and her research interests lie in the area of difference: the writing of gender; diasporic literature; and otherness and the uncanny in twentieth-century literature. Her full-length critical reassessment of Daphne du Maurier's short stories is due to be published shortly.

Shashikala Assella is a senior lecturer in the department of English, University of Kelaniya, Sri Lanka. She received her PhD from the University of Nottingham, UK, and is an alumna of Jawaharlal Nehru University, New Delhi, and Sabaragamuwa University of Sri Lanka. She was a bursary holder at the Oxford Summer School on Digital Humanities (2018), recipient of the Vice-Chancellor's Scholarship for Research Excellence (International) from the University of Nottingham, and won the Faculty Award for the best academic performance from the Sabaragamuwa University of Sri Lanka. She teaches and researches on diaspora studies, women's writing, science fiction and dystopian literature, and popular cultural texts.

Shuhita Bhattacharjee has a PhD from the University of Iowa and is assistant professor of English literature in the department of liberal arts at the Indian Institute of Technology, Hyderabad. She has forthcoming publications on diaspora and on victorian literature and culture, in journals like *English Literature in Transition* and *Victorian Popular Fictions Journal*, and with presses like Palgrave Macmillan, Lexington Books, and Edinburgh University Press. She is currently working on monographs on colonial idols (Routledge) and postsecular theory (Orient Blackswan). Alongside her academic interests, she has worked extensively in the social sector at national and international levels in areas such as violence against HIV-positive women, sex education, HIV media campaigns, and anti-sexual harassment laws in universities.

Lightning Source UK Ltd.
Milton Keynes UK
UKHW012316050320
359861UK00001B/18